Introduction to Social Psychology

Rebekah Ellis

D1523527

Proofed and edited by Highgate Publishing, Highgate Street, London N195BH. Printed and distributed by Amazon.com.

Printed in the United States of America. Copyright 2019.

ISBN-13: 9798618666831

Editor: Samantha Darrington
Author: Rebekah Ellis
Designer: Max Gorsch

Visit our website at: https://highgatepublishing.org

Table of Contents

Chapter 1: The Role of Theory and Research in Social Psychology

The Role of Theory in Social Research

What is **theory** and why is it important? For lack of a better phrase, let's accept that it is human nature for humans to want to know about others. Perhaps this goes back to early man who needed to know about others to identify threats. **Stereotyping** and **profiling** still says a lot about man's need to know about others. Man has always yearned to understand his physical world. Why do objects fall from trees or when dropped? Why does the temperature of the earth become hotter towards the center than at the surface? How were the planets formed? Where does space end? And these things have been studied down through time as science developed. But even though science has been attempting to explain physical phenomenon for centuries, it has only been in the past 150 years or so that man has used scientific principles, procedures and theories to study **human social behavior**.

Theory is simply a process whereby we attempt to understand something well enough that we can then make predictions based on that accumulated theoretical knowledge. In social psychology, theory attempts to help us understand why and how people are influenced by their social environment.

Theory needs to provide insight into three crucial ideas:

1. Theories are about abstract concepts called constructs. To say something is abstract implies it cannot be easily observed. In physical science, we might say that humans need oxygen to survive, but oxygen is not something we can easily observe, though we know it is there. Within social psychology, constructs might include concepts like intelligence, depression, self-esteem, self-esteem bias, social facilitation effect, and many, many more. We are capable of knowing about these concepts, though probably never completely since we are dealing with humans and not rocks, but using theory allows us to understand these constructs that are not easily seen or even measured.

2. Theories attempt to explain causal relationships. Remember that the primary goal of any science is to know something so well that we can make relatively accurate predictions about that phenomenon at least some of the time. The goal is to find causal relationships. This is where the terms **independent and dependent variables** first come into play. An independent variable is manipulated in some way and that manipulation produces an effect in a dependent variable—hence the term "**cause and effect**." There are so many things in our social world that we have, will, and will continue to explore to learn more about ourselves as a species. This is where social psychology comes into play. Why do some people have low **self-esteem**? Is it entirely biological—in other words, if one or both of a person's parents have or had low self-esteem is that a good enough explanation of why their son or daughter would also have low self-esteem? So, we might propose a research question that attempts to investigate that. Research has told us that yes, children raised by parents who have low self-esteem are at higher risk of developing low self-esteem themselves, but is that the end of the story? No. Many people have low self-esteem and were raised in homes where their parents had normal levels of self-esteem. So, what would cause someone to have low self-esteem and what theory might we use to help us find those causes?

      Social comparison theory (Festinger, 1954) might be a theory we could use to investigate why some people have low self-esteem. Let's identify our independent variable as someone's social environment and the dependent variable their self-esteem level. Social comparison theory states: our knowledge of other people's outcomes, performances, or opinions causes changes in how we evaluate our own outcomes, performances, or opinions. So, if we were to use social comparison theory to look for a cause for low self-esteem, we would identify a person's **social environment** as the independent variable. Imagine that for some people they have friends who, when comparing themselves to their friends, develop a feeling as if they are at least as intelligent, desirable, good-looking, and so forth, which then we could argue could cause that person to have a healthy, positive and well-developed sense of self. But on the other hand, what if someone had friends, who when they compared themselves to them, came away feeling as if they weren't as attractive, or as intelligent, or as desirable—we would then expect to see a difference in the dependent variable, which in this case would be different self-esteem levels.

3. Theories are usually general and large-scale in nature (i.e., macro-level). Generally, theories should be applicable to many situations. For instance, social comparison theory can be used to study many evaluations people make about themselves (and others). So, it has broad applicability. On the other hand, a theory like Homans' Social Exchange Theory (Homans, 1958) would have very limited applicability and could really only be used in small group interactions and therefore is considered a **micro-level theory**.

Doing Science

When we think of sciences, we think of biology, chemistry, and physics. But social sciences are just as valid and follow the same path to discovering facts as do those "hard" sciences. Science in general is a **body of knowledge** that has been collected as a result of the **scientific method**—a methodology that uses **systematic** steps to discover facts. To say something is systematic means there are precise steps and procedures that must be followed in order to establish scientific **validity**. The social sciences study humans and interaction with their environment—which consists of people and things. As previously discussed, sociology studies groups, and the way people affect the groups to which they belong, but also the groups affect their members. Sociology is not only interested in studying the interactions between people and groups, but also in studying how people's **attitudes** and **beliefs** are influenced by those interactions.

All social sciences study people, and people are much more difficult to study, studying humans is significantly different in the approach we use to study them. For instance, if I hold up a pen in the air and let go, it will fall. If I hold that same pen up one hundred times and let go, it will fall one hundred times. Even if I held up that pen in the air one million times and let go, it would still fall one million times. That's simple physics. Though I am over simplifying the hard sciences, if we found that each time we evoke a stimulus of some kind, and we get the same reaction each and every time we could state it as: if a given stimulus produces the same response each time, we have a **law**. Therefore, we could write it as: S > R. But because sociology studies humans and human interactions, it's not that simple. No single **stimulus** will produce the same reaction each and every time. For instance, let's say I walk into my introductory class one morning, and the students could see that I was irritated or angry about something. I stand behind the podium and begin lecturing. As I lecture, I notice several students in the back row are talking to each other while I am lecturing. My anger peaks. I can't control it anymore. Furious and out of control, I reach into the back of the podium and whip out my Super Soaker. As I began to waive it around angrily, students begin to react. If studying humans was as predictable as studying organisms, or rocks, or Newton's Law of Gravitation, I would know how the students would react because they would all react in the same way. Do you think that you and your classmates would all react in the same way? Of course not. Some students would run out of the room not wanting to get squirted by their crazed professor. Some students might shriek and hide under their desk. Some students would laugh, and some not wanting to get wet, would try to stare me down as if saying, "Don't you dare get me wet!"

Humans don't react in the same way to a singular stimulus and that is why there are no laws in the social sciences. Instead, we react the way we do because we are all different and have a lifetime's worth of different experiences. It is those experiences, stored in the brain, that mediate between a given stimulus and our response to that stimulus. For instance, let's say the night before you came to class you had seen a news report about a crazed professor who had thrown water balloons at his or her students. Having seen that news report it is stored in your brain as information that will influence you in some future way. Now, you come to class the next morning and experience me waiving my Super Soaker around. Do you think you would react in the same way after having seen the news report the previous night as you would if you had not seen that news report? Almost certainly you would react differently. Why? Because when we experience our social world, all those experiences are stored in the brain and serve to affect the way we react to things. Me waving my Super Soaker around is a stimulus. Your reaction to that stimulus is the response. In this case you will not simply react innately like you would when a nurse sticks a needle into your arm. Instead, even though the processing time might be measured in milliseconds, you will react to my stimulus of waiving the Super Soaker around only after accessing your memory in order to interpret the stimulus and decide your reaction.

When studying humans, the equation would be like this: S > I > R (i.e., stimulus > interpretation of the stimulus > response). With the exception of a few **innate** reactions to stimuli (e.g., pain, hunger, thirst, or the sex drive), we are social creatures and act according to who we are as a result of all those myriad things we've experienced during our lifetime. Those experiences that make us wonderfully unique make us incredibly difficult to study scientifically.

Should sociologists throw up their hands and state categorically that humans cannot be studied therefore we shouldn't study them? Of course not! Even though there are no laws in the social sciences, we can still study humankind in their social environment and discover facts. These facts benefit humans, their cultures, and their societies in some way. We need to utilize the same tools to study humans in their social environments as we use to study plants, or planets, or organisms. Those tools are called the steps of science or the **Scientific Method**.

Emile Durkheim was a French sociologist and considered the father of sociology. Durkheim wanted sociology to be completely distinct from other disciplines like philosophy and psychology and have its own methods for discovering **social facts** (Durkheim, 1895). Emile Durkheim was the first to use scientific principles in the relatively new science of sociology. He used those principles to study people and groups. Durkheim was the first to advocate that the social world affected people's behaviors. Having identified a concept, he called "**anomie**" (i.e., social estrangement, isolation, feeling lost, and alienated), he sought to study this phenomenon. In the 1800's, Durkheim studied European religions and believed that Catholics experienced less "anomie" than did Protestants. His reasoning was that Catholicism advocated that they approached God as a community and therefore were accountable to God as a community.

Protestantism on the other hand, with the Protestant work ethic widely accepted in the Protestant community, believed that they approached God as individuals and were therefore individually accountable to God. Durkheim believed that the bonds between Protestants were weaker than they were for Catholics. Based on this premise, Durkheim believed that Protestants would have higher rates of anomie than Catholics. Using scientific principles, he wanted to employ within sociology, he proposed that Protestant countries would have higher rates of anomie than would Catholic countries. To test this, Durkheim reasoned that people who suffered from the effects of anomie would be more likely to commit suicide than others. After finding that Catholic (European) countries reported almost nonexistent suicide rates and Protestant (European) countries reporting significantly higher rates, he concluded that his hypothesis had been proven correct: Protestants were more likely to suffer from the effects of anomie. While there were methodological problems with Durkheim's study, he is still credited for being the first to make sociology a science.

The Axioms of Science

Before we can use the steps of science to study humans in their social world, there are things we must accept and acknowledge before doing so. All sciences share in that there are **axioms**, taken for granted assumptions, which must pre-exist the steps of science (the scientific method). The following would be regarded as axioms for all sciences:

> 1. Axiom 1: This is a real(ist's) world. A world of "things in themselves" objectively out there whether we can perceive them or not).
> 2. Axiom 2: The world is ordered. Even a world that was chaotic. If one of the main goals of science is the ability to predict, there could be no such thing as science if the world was not ordered.
> 3. Axiom 3: We can perceive this world. Our five senses allow us to come into contact with 'things in themselves.'
> 4. Axiom 4: The world is ordered. We can discover order, logic, meaning, explanations, understanding and reason.

The axioms of science are necessary assumptions because without them science could not exist. If we could not perceive our world, there would be nothing to study. If we could not use our senses to perceive this world, there would be nothing to perceive. Finally, if the world was chaotic, and not ordered, science could not exist because the primary goal of science is to understand a phenomenon so well that we can use that knowledge to predict future outcomes of that phenomenon.

The Steps of Science

The **steps of science**, or the **scientific method**, are those steps and processes used in science to discover and collect facts about our world. Ultimately, the collection of these facts, tell us something about our world and may result in our ability to predict.

> 1. Step 1: We first perceive a phenomenon or phenomena (things we have not yet labeled or named).
> 2. Step 2: We conceptualize (we name the phenomenon or phenomena).
> 3. Step 3: We hypothesize (we construct a hypothetical cause and effect relationship between two or more concepts).
> 4. Step 4: We arrive at a fact. After testing empirically (i.e., scientifically by experiment or study) we attempt to verify our hypothesis.
> 5. Step 5: We now construct a theory. After testing and retesting our hypotheses many times, and collecting facts that support our hypothesis, we now attempt to put them together and construct a theory.
> 6. Step 6: If we empirically verify our theory, we have a scientific law.

Steps in the Social Research Process

Every science modifies the general steps of science to make them work for their specific discipline. Below are the steps of science used in the social sciences.

1. Step 1: Select a research topic.
The research topic should be timely, relevant to their field, and maybe even more so to their specialization. Once the research topic is identified, researchers need to define the problem. What is the particular problem they wish to investigate? Why? In social psychological research, there is also the concern as to whether the phenomenon to be investigated can be explained by a particular theory. The more specific a researcher is in defining their topic and the theory to be applied, the more definitive are their research results.

2. Step 2: Review the Literature.
The next step is to review the **existing literature** related to the problem the researcher wishes to study. Prior research findings will likely influence their research methodology and the theoretical orientation they have chosen to use in order to study the phenomenon.

3. Step 3: State the Hypothesis.
A **hypothesis** is a testable statement between two or more variables. Hypotheses are formulated from previous research. In other words, there must be a scientific basis for a hypothesis.

4. Step 4: Identify the Research Design.
After formalizing the hypothesis, researchers must then decide what research method would be best in order to collect the information necessary to prove the hypothesis. The most common type of research method used in social psychological research are experiments, but survey instruments also can play a role depending on the research.

Questions to be dealt with at this point include:

1. How will the **variable** or variables be measured?
2. How will the research sample be selected from the research population?
3. What type of statistical analysis will be used? (if it is a quantitative study)

5. Step 5. Obtain permission to conduct the research.
Researchers need to obtain permission to conduct their

intended research from their university's institutional review board. While there are a number of protections placed on academic research, the primary concern is that there be no harm to participants. Only after obtaining person from a researcher's institutional review board may they begin their research with human subjects.

6. Step 6: Collect the Data.

There are a number of research tools that can used to gather information. For instance, surveys, experiments, interviews, participant observation, or content analysis. As stated above, the most commonly used tools in social psychological research are experiments and surveys.

7. Step 7: Analyze the Data.

Using the appropriate **data analysis** tool, analyzing the data will tell researchers if their hypothesis is supported or not. Generally, there are two types of statistics used in social psychological research: descriptive and inferential.

Descriptive statistics summarize and describe the behavior or characteristics of a particular sample of participants in a study. **Inferential statistics** are the results of mathematical analyses that move beyond mere description of research data to make inferences about the larger **population** from which the **sample** was drawn. The advantage of using experimental research methods is that it is capable of showing cause and relationship relationships, whereas **correlational research** methods usually cannot. This is done by manipulating the **independent variable** and looking for an effect on the **dependent variable**. While much social psychological research is done under highly controlled situations in laboratory settings, they can be criticized for not being truly **representative** of real-life situations and therefore lack external validity.

8. Step 8: Report the Findings.

Researchers need to publish their findings as this potentially provides the basis for future research. This is how the body of knowledge in each scientific field is increased.

9. Step 9: State the Research Study's Conclusions and Introduce a Discussion.

Drawing conclusions involves trying to answer your specific research questions. For instance, was your research question supported? If not, why not? What limitations in the study should be considered in evaluating the results? Do your research findings suggest directions for future research on the same topic? Were there methodological issues with your research that might be important for future research?

Types of Social Research

Experiments

The most common type of research design used in social psychological studies are experiments. **Experiments** usually occur in laboratories or carefully controlled environments where the independent variable can be manipulated. The manipulation of the independent variable ideally will lead to a corresponding change in the dependent variable. If there is a change in the dependent variable, and in the predicted direction, researchers would consider the result supporting the stated hypothesis. Advantages of experiments are that they are easily controlled and repeated.

Disadvantages of experiments include that they can only collect information from small groups, subjects might not behave as they would in the real world, they take time to collect sufficient data, and they can be expensive. To help you understand the experimental research process, I have provided two famous examples.

Example 1. The following is an excerpt from Brad Bushman's article titled, "The Effects of Apparel on Compliance" (Bushman, 1988). Past research indicates that apparel influences our behavior and our impressions of others. One type of apparel that is both noticeable and symbolically significant is the uniform. Few studies, however, have examined the influence of uniforms on behavior, especially with female authority figures. In this study, a female confederate who was dressed in uniform, professional attire, or sloppy clothing told subjects to give change to a person who was parked at an expired parking meter (Bickman, 1974). The results showed that compliance was higher when the confederate was dressed in a uniform. Verbal reasons given for complying also differed across conditions. The study shows that a uniform is a certificate of legitimacy (Joseph & Alex, 1972) for females as well as males and that both sexes are influenced by a female dressed in a uniform.

In 1988, Brad Bushman decided to take the experiments on compliance to perceived authority one step further. As in previous experimental studies, he had a female research confederate stand on the street next to a parking meter pretending to search her purse for the necessary change. As she frantically searches for coins to feed the meter, another woman, either dressed in a uniform or dress, would walk by and order passers-by to give the first woman a nickel for the meter. In this research, the independent variable is manipulated. That variable was perceived authority, and the dependent variable was obedience. And, like in previous research, Bushman **operationalized** perceived authority by varying the apparel the second female wore (i.e., the one who yelled at passers-by to give the other woman a nickel).

In the first condition, passers-by would start to walk by a woman frantically searching her purse for change and beside her stood a woman dressed in something like a uniform.

In the second condition, passers-by would start to walk by a woman frantically searching her purse for change and beside her stood a woman dressed in a business suit.

In the third condition, passers-by would start to walk by a woman frantically searching her purse for change and beside her stood a woman dressed like a panhandler.

Bushman's results showed that more passers-by gave money to the woman needing money for the parking meter when they were ordered to do so by the woman wearing something that looked like a uniform. Bushman's hypothesis was supported: subjects in his study were more likely to comply with an order given by someone they perceived as having authority.

Example 2. In another classic experimental study, Solomon Asch (1951) wanted to investigate the effects of peer-pressure (i.e., social pressure) on conformity. Asch recruited fifty undergraduate male students to participate in an experiment they were told was designed to "test vision." A total of eight undergraduates were selected to participate in the study, though only one was a real subject, the other seven were actually research confederates of Asch, but of course, the real subject was unaware of this latter fact. All eight subjects were brought into a room and were seated around a large square table (so that all research subjects could see each other). Research confederates of Asch had previously been instructed on how to act and respond during the experiment. As the experiment began, subjects were seated around the table so the real research subject was the last. Asch handed two placards to the first subject (who was a research confederate). One placard had a single line on it and the other placard had three-line lengths labeled A, B, and C. Asch then asked the first subject of lines A, B, and C, which is the single line closest to in length? The first subject responded by stating that clearly the single line was closest to the line labeled A. The researcher would thank the subject who then passed the placards to the subject seated to his right. Again, Asch asked the second subject of lines A, B, and C, which is the single line closest to in length? The second subject gave the same answer. Each of the seven subjects gave the same obviously incorrect answer. The real subject showed visible signs of confusion. At the end of his research, Asch found that about 1/3 of the "real" subjects conformed to the majority opinion even though the majority opinion was clearly wrong. While some of the subjects said they really did not believe that the majority opinion was correct, but that they had went along with the group because they felt pressured to do so; in other words, they were afraid of being ridiculed or thought of as strange or deviant. Asch concluded that people conform for two reasons:

1. they wanted to fit in with the group and not stand out. Asch called this the normative influence, and
2. because they believed the majority were better informed than them. Asch called this the informational influence.

Survey Research

Another common research method employed in social psychological research, and heavily used in sociological research, are surveys. **Survey research** can be either **quantitative** or **qualitative** in nature.

Advantages of survey research include:
1. Answers are easily quantifiable as data,
2. Large groups can be studied,
3. Researchers can employ others to collect response data,

4. Survey research is quick, and
5. Inexpensive when compared to other designs.

Disadvantages of survey research include:

1. Research findings might be superficial or doubtful, and
2. Return rates may be low and therefore challenge the validity and **reliability** of the study.

In order to reduce the potential for research bias, researchers often use a pilot study to verify that their survey instrument is valid. **Validity** refers to the idea that researchers are measuring what they intend to measure. For instance, if I propose that the more time students spend studying, the higher their GPAs, I might unintentionally be measuring intelligence rather than study time. There is a positive relationship between hours spent studying and GPA. The more time students spend studying, the higher their GPA. However, we all know that some students don't have to study as many hours as others to earn good grades. In some cases, intelligence is the more important factor than is time spent studying.

Scales

A **scale** is a type of composite measure that is composed of several items that are logically related to one another and is used to extract data on a relatively complex variable or phenomenon. For instance, depression is a relatively complex phenomenon to measure. You can't ask just one question about some issue related to depression and expect to know just how depressed someone really is. You need a scale because there are a number of factors that are needed to adequately assess depression.

The most commonly used scale is the **Likert scale**, which contains response categories such as "strongly agree," "agree," "disagree," and "strongly disagree." For instance, if we are interested in measuring self-esteem, we might use the **Rosenberg Self-Esteem Scale**. For the following: SA=Strongly Agree; A=Agree; D=Disagree; and SD=Strongly Disagree.

1. On the whole I am satisfied with myself.

SA   A   D   SD

2. At times I think that I am no good at all.

SA   A   D   SD

3. I feel that I have a number of good qualities.

SA   A   D   SD

4. I am able to do things as well as most other people.

SA   A   D   SD

5. I feel I do not have much to be proud of.

SA   A   D   SD

6. I certainly feel useless at times.

SA   A   D   SD

7. I feel that I am a person of worth, at least the equal of others.

SA   A   D   SD

8. I wish I could have more respect for myself.

SA   A   D   SD

9. All in all, I am inclined to feel that I am a failure.

SA   A   D   SD

10. I take a positive attitude toward myself.

SA   A   D   SD

Coding

For the above scale, each response is coded with a number. The higher the number for each scale item, the more it is associated with high self-esteem. If we code the items towards high self-esteem, the range of possible scores for this scale is 0 (for those who always chose the response associated with low self-esteem) to 30 (for those who always chose the response associated with high self-esteem). Therefore, the higher the score, the higher the self-esteem. For instance:

1. On the whole I am satisfied with myself.
SA=3   A-2   D=1   SD=0

2. At times I think that I am no good at all.
SA=0   A-1   D=2   SD=3

3. I feel that I have a number of good qualities.
SA=3   A=2   D=1   SD=0
4. I am able to do things as well as most other people.
SA=3   A=2   D=1   SD=0

5. I feel I do not have much to be proud of.
SA=0   A-1   D=2   SD=3

6. I certainly feel useless at times.
SA=0   A-1   D=2   SD=3

7. I feel that I am a person of worth, at least the equal of others.
SA=3   A=2   D=1   SD=0

8. I wish I could have more respect for myself.
SA=0   A-1   D=2   SD=3

9. All in all, I am inclined to feel that I am a failure.
SA=0   A-1   D=2   SD=3

10. I take a positive attitude toward myself.
SA=3   A=2   D=1   SD=0

Sampling

Social research is almost always concerned about specific populations of people— for example, people in the US age 65 and older. However, if I were to attempt to survey all Americans 65 years of age and older, I would need to survey almost 50 million people. As you can imagine, that would take a great deal of money and time. Instead I would use a smaller **sample** instead. **Sampling** is the process of selecting people from a research population so that by studying the sample we may **generalize** our results back to the population from which they were chosen. The logic of **random**

sampling is that if the sample is drawn randomly from the research population (i.e., the population we wish to study), everyone in the population has an equal chance of being selected for the sample. If that's the case, the random sample we drew should mirror the characteristics of the research population being studied. The average annual income of elderly in the US is $25,000 per year. I should expect to see that same average income, or close to it, in my randomly drawn sample. Additionally, maybe I also know that the average age of Americans 65 years and older is 75.1 years and I find that the average age of my sample members is about the same. Therefore, we can legitimately say that what is true of the sample, is also true of the population. Once we have drawn our random sample, we perform our research using that sample. When we get done with our research on our sample, and reach some conclusions based on the data we have collected from them, we are ready to generalize our results from the sample to our research population. If that sample was randomly drawn from our research population, the sample should mirror the characteristics of the research population. This allows us to say that if the sample mirrors the characteristics of our research population, sample results should be true for the population as well.

Participant Observation

A research method in which the researcher observes while taking part in the activities of the social group being studied to some level of involvement is called participant observation. That involvement ranges from pure observation and therefore no involvement to the other end of the spectrum where there is pure observation and involvement. There are four roles of participant observation:

1. Complete participant. In complete participant observation, the researcher completely engages with the group being studied and their true identity is hidden from the group.
2. Participant as observer. The researcher engages with the group but makes no pretense as their true identity as researchers.
3. Observer as participant. In this type of participant observation, the researcher observes, but does not participate.

4. Complete observer. In this situation, the researcher is completely detached from the group being studied and simply records observations for future analysis. For instance, a researcher might decide to sit in a corner of a bar and record their observations of how people act when in a bar while drinking and socializing with others.

Ethnography

The study of unique cultural elements of a given culture and the lives of its individual people is called ethnography. It is a type of qualitative research (as opposed to a quantitative research) using participant observation. As a type of qualitative research, advantages of ethnography include a greater depth of information and can lead to a broader understanding of the group and social processes being studied. Disadvantages include that it can only be studied relatively small groups and it is not easily generalizable to other groups.

One example of ethnographic research might include female victimization by male partners (i.e., domestic abuse). Based on ethnographic research, we now understand why women who are being abused by their male partners remain in those abusive relationships. Historically, Americans have had little sympathy for female victims of domestic abuse because they believe all an abused woman has to do is to walk out the door. Research has found a significant number of reasons why women remain in those relationships. It takes female abuse victims on average six or seven attempts to leave.

Secondary Analysis

Making use of data that has already been collected and is accessible for public and scientific use is called secondary analysis. For instance, the University of Wisconsin has four large datasets that are available for scientific research. If data that has already been collected can be used to study a researcher's interests, secondary analysis saves researchers time and money.

Content Analysis

A research method used to describe and analyze the media in general is called content analysis. For instance, content analysis has been used to study cartoon violence. Researchers would watch children's cartoons and count acts of violence (as previously qualified before the research began). Based on that research, and similar research on other types of TV programming, researchers concluded that children's TV cartoons have the greatest amount of violence in all TV programming.

Variables

Variables are any factor, trait, or condition that can exist in differing amounts or types. Generally, there are three types of variables:

1. independent, which is manipulated,
2. dependent, which means the variable is dependent on how the independent variable is manipulated, and
3. controlled variable, which is held constant and usually only used in experiments which occur in highly controlled situations.

An example of an independent variable is age. An example of a dependent variable might be income, which would be dependent on the independent variable of number of years of education.

Operationalization

In research, **operationalization** is the process of making a variable testable. To do so, researchers need to be highly specific in how they choose to measure that variable. Operationalizing a variable reduces the potential for bias introduced when:

1. subjects might be confused by research questions, and
2. researchers are unclear what respondents have reported.

For instance, if we wanted to know about someone's income we might ask, "What is your individual, gross, annual income in US dollars?" If income is our variable, we have now fully operationalized it.

Generalizing

The goal of most research, experimental or survey research using random sampling, is to be able to apply research findings discovered on a smaller sample of the research population to the research population. In other words, if my sample was randomly selected, and I find some research finding where the independent variable caused some effect in the dependent variable in that research sample, I want to be able to say that if it's true for my sample, it should be true for my research population. This is the value of random sampling. If everyone in the research population has an equal chance of being randomly selected and placed in the sample, the sample should mirror the characteristics of the research population.

So, for example, let's say that I wanted to study all elderly (65 years and older) in the US receiving Social Security Retirement benefits. There are approximately 46 million in the US. Obviously, I cannot study all 46 million, but what I can do is to select a smaller sample of those elderly by obtaining a list from the Federal Government and then randomly selecting a small sample out of those 46 million elderly men and women. Let's say I have enough money and time to work with a sample of 2,000 elderly Americans. And, let's also say that the US Census Bureau has provided me with some demographic data about the 46 million elderly Americans drawing retirement benefits, and those demographics show that the average income of the elderly drawing Social Security Retirement benefits is $1,360/month and the average age of those receiving retirement benefits is 73.5 years. If I have randomly drawn my sample from the research population of all 46 million Americans drawing Social Security Retirement benefits, so that everyone in that population has an equal chance of being selected, I should expect to see roughly the same average income and age in my sample as is in the overall research population. That is the value of random sampling.

So, by using a random sample on which to conduct research, researchers in theory can effectively say, "If it's true of the sample, it should be true of the population." That's generalizing. In other words, **generalizing** the research results from a sample of the overall research population to that research population.

Correlation

A statistical tool used to assess the relationship between variables. For instance, as years of post-high school education increases, income increases. A **correlation** does not necessarily imply cause—simply that a relationship exists between the two variables. A perfect correlation exists when a one unit rise in the independent variable leads to a corresponding one unit rise in the dependent variable. A perfect correlation would suggest that if we could know the independent variable, one hundred percent of the time we could predict what the dependent variable would be. There are two types of correlations: those that are referred to as positive and those that are referred to as negative. A **positive correlation** is one that finds that a one unit rise in the independent variable leads to a one unit rise in the dependent variable. Whereas a **negative correlation** shows that a one unit rise in the independent variable leads to a one unit decrease in the dependent variable.

Causality

Once two variables are correlated with another, the question of **causality** needs to be addressed. Correlations by themselves cannot establish causality. To establish causality the independent variable must precede the dependent variable in time and be a necessary or sufficient cause of the dependent variable.

For instance, in biology it has been proven that smoking causes cancer. When smokers and non-smokers are compared on rates of cancer, it is obvious that smokers are at significantly higher risk of developing cancer; that is enough to allow us to say smoking is a sufficient cause of cancer. And among our sample of smokers, they started smoking before they developed cancer. Consequently, doctors today would agree with the statement that smoking causes cancer.

Research has found that as family income increases, child S.A.T. scores also increase; this is both a positive and significant relationship. However, it is not causal. It is not family income that would increase a child's S.A.T., but rather income serves as an indication of parental education. Generally, increased education leads to higher income. People with a bachelor's degree earn more than people with high school diplomas only, and people with graduate degrees tend to earn more than people with bachelor's degrees, etc. Since the amount of money people earn seems to be a result of their educational level, we would normally identify education as the independent variable and income as the dependent variable.

Spuriousness

There are two conditions where there may appear to be an association between an independent and dependent variable but in fact doesn't provide accurate data. This may be the result of spuriousness. The first is where there is an accidental association between the independent and dependent variables and would not occur if the research was repeated elsewhere. For instance, what if a researcher found an association between shoe size and GPA among college students. Clearly, if his research was repeated in other classes or with other groups, the same association would not be found because there is no logical reason the two should be associated. The other cause of spuriousness is where there is a third unknown variable involved and is the true independent variable. The classic example is where it has been proven there is an association between the number of fire trucks at the scene of a fire (i.e., the independent variable) and the amount of fire damage (i.e., the dependent variable). But in reality, the true independent variable is size of the fire and both the number of fire trucks at the scene and the amount of fire damage are dependent variables.

Research Validity and Reliability

This is the degree to which a measure really reflects what is being studied. It is largely associated with the process of operationalizing variables. Does the measure really support the theoretical basis for the research being conducted? Does the research measure what it is supposed to measure? Is the independent variable the true cause for changes in the dependent variable?

There are four types of validity: **construct validity, content validity, internal validity and external validity**. Both are crucial to research.

> **1. Construct validity.** See also, the Role of Theory in Social Research at the beginning of this chapter. Construct validity has to do with how closely the measure accurately measures the construct that it claims to measure. There are statistical tests designed to measure the accuracy of the measure. The question we are asking when dealing with construct validity is are we in fact measuring what we say we're measuring. For instance, the Rosenberg Self-Esteem Scale has 10 items measuring self-esteem. Each item is highly correlated with the other items, which demonstrates that they are all getting at the same underlying construct. But imagine seeing the following on his self-esteem scale:
>
> 1. I feel that I am a person of worth, at least on an equal plane with others.
> SA=3   A=2   D=1   SD=0
>
> 2. I feel that I have a number of good qualities.
> SA=3   A=2   D=1   SD=0
>
> 3. I feel good when I'm playing golf.
> SA   A   D   SD
>
> Can you see that the third item has absolutely nothing to do with self-esteem? It would be completely out of place and actually damage the construct validity of his scale. So, if that statement were left in his scale measuring self-esteem, his scale would not fully be measuring what he said he was measuring with the scale.
> **2. Content Validity.** See also, the Role of Theory in Social Research at the beginning of this chapter. **Content validity** refers to whether the measure is exhaustive. Does it completely measure the construct it says it's measuring? What if we developed a measure of life satisfaction and we asked questions about how happy someone was with their job, their looks, and their future, but didn't ask about how

happy they were with their marriage (assuming they were married)? Actually, that would be a major problem since life satisfaction and marital satisfaction correlate VERY highly. So, to have left out of our construct questions about happy someone was with their marriage would greatly reduce the validity of our measure.

3. Criterion Validity. See also, the Role of Theory in Social Research at the beginning of this chapter. **Criterion validity** is whether the construct measures the real-world manifestation of the behavior or phenomenon. For instance, if we were to examine the construct "religiosity," we would expect people to report attending church, praying, reading religious material, leading their life according to their religious principles, therefore these things would be evidence of criterion validity in the case of measuring the construct religiosity.

4. Internal validity. Generally, a measure is regarded as having high internal validity if it can be logically and empirically concluded that the independent variable caused a change in the dependent variable. In a non-experimental design, a researcher might compare different groups of people living in one area and their liking or disliking of people living in other areas of an urban area. The independent variable would be identified as the particular part of town where the group of people lived, and the dependent variable might be the attitudes those people have of the people living in other parts of the city. For instance, a researcher might survey primarily Hispanics or Latinos living in one part of a city on their attitudes towards African-Americans and predominantly white neighborhoods to see if there were differences in favorable attitudes towards African-Americans. If the Hispanic and Latino parts of the city held more favorable attitudes towards African-Americans than did those surveyed in the predominantly white areas of the city, it might be concluded Allport's theory of contact (Allport, 1964) applied--in that Hispanic and Latino groups were more likely to have contact with and know African-Americans when compared to white urban dwellers. But, because this is a type of non-experimental research design, it cannot be concluded that the reason for this difference is because Hispanics and Latinos had greater contact with African-Americans than did white city dwellers--therefore cause and effect (i.e., that the independent variable caused the dependent variable) could not be established. So, this represents a threat to internal validity--did the researchers really measure what they had intended to measure--that knowledge and interaction of African-Americans by Latinos and Hispanics was really the reason that they felt more positively about African-Americans when compared to white urban dwellers or were there other variables at play?

The way to increase the likelihood of internal validity is to use an experimental design. First, the sample is randomly selected from the population of study. Second, that the independent variable is manipulated in some way as to produce an effect on a dependent variable. Even when researchers are unable to use highly controlled experiments which occur in a laboratory, random sampling is the key to helping to increase the likelihood of internal validity. In experimental research, researchers randomly assign subjects or participants to different groups and then manipulate some aspect between the two groups thus theoretically producing a different effect on the dependent variable. In survey research, the independent variable is still manipulated but largely this is done by putting people into different groups based on their answers to specific questions that serve as the independent variable (e.g., male versus female) and then looking at the differences between the groups on the dependent variable (e.g., aggression, empathy, assertiveness, and so forth).

5. External validity. External validity refers to the ability to generalize research results to other groups in other places and at other times. So, if a researcher conducts research at his or her institution and finds that study time, as the independent variable, is highly associated with GPA, and then repeats that same research at other colleges and universities across the US and Canada, and gets the same results, the argument can then be made that there is external validity. However, note that this still cannot prove a causal relationship because there are other variables that affect GPA like intelligence, and situational influences (e.g., living alone or with noisy roommates).

So, How Does Validity Support Theory?

Any theory should have strong support and achieve high validity. Think of it as a chain with each link being strong and intact or weak or even missing entirely.

1. Your theory, which is attempting to explain the independent variable as the true cause of changes in the dependent variable.
2. Does the theory measure the intended constructs (i.e., what you say it's supposed to measure) and nothing else? For instance, what if we were going to measure "religiosity" by using just one item, church attendance. So, we decide based on our research results that people who don't attend church aren't very religious but people who do attend church are religious. The problem in this case is that we are not just measuring religiosity but also physical health, ability to drive, the financial resources to own a car, lack of a support network, and so forth and not really our construct of religiosity. The theory must measure the intended constructs and nothing else, so if that's the case, then the theory can be said to have construct validity.
3. Does the theory clearly demonstrate the effect of the manipulation of the independent variable on the dependent variable? Does the dependent variable change as the independent variable is manipulated? If so, the theory has internal validity.
4. Is the research conclusion generalizable beyond the research setting and to the population of study? If so, the research has external validity.

Research Reliability

Reliability is the degree a measure (e.g., an index or scale) produces consistent results as it is administered to different research groups over an extended period of time. The measure gets repeatable results. One way to enhance reliability is to replicate the study with a different sample and possibly in a different setting done over time. It is essential that research results are considered reliable.

Statistical Terms

Mean - When a total sum is calculated and then divided by the number of cases, we have a mean. The mean is what most Americans think of as "average."

Median - The median is the midpoint of a score distribution; half of all scores fall on side of the median and half fall on the other side.

Mode - The most common score in a distribution.

Human Subjects Committees (Institutional Review Boards)

Between 1933 and 1945, Nazis murdered 11 million Jews and people from other "undesirable" groups. Fascinated by one of the most notorious Nazis responsible for the Holocaust, a social psychologist by the name of Stanley Milgram wanted to know if people in general would be more likely to commit horrendous acts because they would obey authority. To test his theory, Milgram conducted his research on obedience in the early 1960's at Yale University (Milgram, 1963). Milgram found that approximately 2/3s of his male research subjects were willing to administer 450 volt shocks to a victim, despite the fact that the victim wanted to stop participating after receiving a 150-volt shock, simply because they were told to do so by a perceived authority figure (i.e., a male researcher dressed in a white lab coat). Unbeknownst to those administering the shocks, the victim wasn't really being shocked— the victim simply acted the part, using protests and screams of pain. No one was really hurt. Milgram's research has been repeated at different locations throughout the US and around the world, and the results have always been found to be the same.

Milgram was criticized for his work because some of his subjects who administered the pretend shocks complained later of having psychological issues as a consequence of having participated in the research. While Milgram felt the criticism was overblown, his research led to the creation of Institutional Review Boards designed to protect the rights of research participants.

Ethics in Social Research

In the 1960s and 1970s, social psychological experiments were conducted that raised the question of whether subjects could be justifiably exposed to potential physical and emotional harm. This has largely been dealt with by the imposition of institutional review boards that were in place at colleges and universities to deal with research issues related to using human subjects in that research. Committees must adhere to government guidelines that serve to protect human participants in research. Specifically, committees are concerned that there be no harm to participants, that participation is voluntary, that participants are not deceived, and that participants are informed if the information provided by them will remain confidential or anonymous. In cases where there may be a need to violate one of the aforementioned principles, primarily in medical research, committees will evaluate whether the potential for good outweighs the risk of harm.

Terms and Concepts to Know

Theory
Stereotyping
Profiling
Human social behavior
Constructs
Causal relationships
Independent variable
Dependent variable
Cause and effect
Social Comparison Theory
Social environment
Macro-level theory
Micro-level theory
Body of knowledge
Scientific method
Systematic
Beliefs

Law
Stimulus
Innate
Social facts
Anomie
Axioms of science
Steps of science
Existing literature
Hypothesis
Variable
Data analysis
Descriptive statistics
Inferential statistics
Population
Sample
Sampling
Random sampling
Correlation
Correlational research
Representative
Experiments
Operationalize
Survey research
Quantitative research
Qualitative research
Reliability
Scale
Likert scale
Rosenberg Self-Esteem Scale
Coding
Generalize
Participant observation
Ethnography
Secondary analysis
Content analysis
Positive correlation
Negative or inverse correlation
Spuriousness
Validity
Construct validity

Content validity
Criterion validity
Reliability
Mean
Median
Mode
Institutional Review Board

References

Allport, G. (1954). *The nature of prejudice.* New York, NY: Addison-Wesley.

Asch, S. E. (1951). Effects of group pressure upon the modification and distortion of judgment. In H. Guetzkow (ed.*) Groups, leadership and men*, 177-190. Pittsburgh, PA: Carnegie Press.

Bickman, L. (1974). The social power of a uniform. *Journal of Applied Social Psychology*, 4(1), 47-61.

Bushman, B. (1988). The effects of apparel on compliance: A field experiment with a female authority figure. *Personality and Social Psychology Bulletin*, 14(3), 459-467.

Durkehim, E. (1982). *The rules of sociological method.* The Free Press. Introduction by Steven Lukes. First published 1895.

Festinger, L. (1954). A theory of social comparison processes. *Human Relations*, 7(2), 117-140.

Homans, G. (1958). Social behavior as exchange. *American Journal of Sociology*, 63(6), 597-606.

Joseph, N. & Alex, N. (1972). The uniform: A sociological perspective. *American Journal of Sociology*, 77(4), 719-730.

Milgram, S. (1963). Behavioral study of obedience. *Journal of Abnormal and Social Psychology*, 67, 371-378.

Chapter 2: Major Theorists in Social Psychology

Gordon Allport (1897-1967). Gordon Allport was one of the earlier contributors to social psychology as a discipline. Primarily he is known for his research on **attitudes**, especially as they relate to the development of **prejudice**, which is one of the major themes of this book and that we will discuss later. Allport also did significant work on **religion**, and the construction and dissemination of rumors, which is fascinating in itself.

Allport was born in Indiana in 1897. He was the youngest of four brothers and was shy and reserved. His mother was a teacher and his father a doctor. Interestingly enough Allport had his own printing business when he was a teenager but eventually was accepted to Harvard and graduated there with a Ph.D. in psychology. Allport is known to have personally met with Sigmund Freud in 1922 when Allport would've only been about 25 years of age. Based on his interaction with Freud, Allport later rejected **Freud's theory of psychoanalysis** (Sigmund Freud, left) because he thought it was too myopic and that people were largely unaffected by the situation. On the other hand, **behaviorism**, was a new theory on the scene of social psychology, according to Allport was not specific enough, and so therefore he rejected both psychoanalysis and behaviorism for those reasons. This was a significant movement on the part of Allport because behaviorism was a dominant force in psychology and the developing field of social psychology at the time. Most of Allport's career was spent studying the development of the human personality. In fact, while at Harvard one of his first classes that he took as a graduate student was on personality psychology. His work has had significant influence on further psychological and sociological theorists like Stanley Milgram and Anthony Greenwald.

Allport is probably best known for his **theory of personality,** which had a large influence on his work regarding the development of prejudice in his later years. Allport developed a catalog of 4500 different **personality traits** and organized them into three general categories. Those categories were:

1. **Cardinal traits**, which he defined as traits that dominated in a person's entire personality. He found this trait to be rare because it was uniquely dominant and very few people that he studied had such a commanding and domineering trait as part of their personality.
2. **Common traits**. Allport identified common traits as those that make up the greater part of the individual's personality. Those traits consisted of such things as honesty, friendliness, sincerity, and kindness.
3. **Secondary traits**. Secondary traits he believed, are those traits present only in specific situations. This is perhaps one of his most important traits because it became the connection for him between psychology and social psychology. For instance, Allport would identify as a secondary trait people who acted differently in a social environment, or perhaps someone who was nervous when delivering a speech, though that was not something that was characteristic of them when speaking in normal conversation with a smaller audience.

In 1954, and then later revised in 1988, Allport went on to describe what he felt were the social and biological determinants of prejudice and how they were acquired. He also spent a significant amount of time talking about **intergroup contact**. Bringing together people of different ethnic and racial groups can reduce prejudice at Intergroup persistent and resistant to change prejudicial attitudes were. In 1954, his work on the development of prejudice was not only novel but controversial. It should be remembered that in 1954 segregation was still the legal norm in the South and prejudice still not uncommon in the northern states. He was one of the first to discuss from a scientific perspective the idea of stereotypes and their involvement in the development of prejudice. He believed that **stereotyping** as a source of prejudice was a special case of what he considered to be ordinary **cognitive functioning**. Today, the cognitive approach is recognized as one of the dominant theoretical perspectives in research on the development of prejudice and discrimination. Unfortunately, Allport was pessimistic about the future of stereotypes and the reduction of prejudice throughout the whole of the United States. While developing his work on stereotypes and the development of prejudice, Allport recognized the value of two social constructs-**social stratification** and **social equality**. Allport argued that when two different racial groups could be brought together on an equal playing field, in other words where their position and the hierarchy of social stratification was similar and therefore they be viewed as socially equal on that playing field or in that hierarchy, he believed that prejudice could be reduced. This was radical at the time of the development of his theories on prejudice and discrimination and is still controversial today.

So when looking at the issues of social stratification and social equality, Allport developed what he called the **contact hypothesis**. Allport believed that there could be positive effects to Intergroup contact. Research using his intergroup contact hypothesis has largely focused on three groups:

1. intergroup contact and prejudice towards African Americans,
2. intergroup contact and prejudice towards homosexuality, and
3. intergroup contact and prejudice towards Muslims in Europe. Of late, this work has been used to study intergroup contact and prejudice towards Muslims here in the United States.

Allport's contact hypothesis suggests that by bringing people together who would otherwise not have opportunities to interact with members of other **out-groups**, has the potential to reduce the fear and anxiety that people have towards groups they know little about. Allport believed that by bringing these different groups together on an equal playing field dispelled any false information or false beliefs held by one group towards another outgroup, and in its fullest expression not only to better understand the outgroup but also to show **empathy** towards members of that outgroup. Further, Allport went on to propose that extended contact with members of an outgroup, such as developing a close relationship with the members of another outgroup, could lead towards more positive attitudes towards members of the outgroup and greater acceptance of their differences. Research has largely found support for this particular component Allport's theory. Further research has found that simply watching members of an **in-group** interacting with members of an out-group, for instance in the media, can have the effect of reducing prejudice. In fact, research by Richard Chris and Rhiannon Turner (2009) found that simply imagining a positive encounter between members of an in-group and members of an out-group can increase positive feelings towards the out-group.

Solomon Asch (1907 - 1996). Solomon Asch was born in Poland in 1907 and emigrated to the United States where he earned his Ph.D. at Columbia University. While he began his career at Brooklyn College, he spent most of his career at University of Pennsylvania until his retirement in 1979.

Within the field of psychology much of this work was done on **impression formation**. Asch (1946) believed that there were four components necessary for a person to form in impression of another. Those are:

1. it is an organized process;
2. the characteristics are perceived differently in relation to other characteristics;
3. central qualities are discovered, causing a distinction between them and peripheral qualities; and
4. relations of harmony and contradiction are observed.

Asch is one of the most well-known figures in the social psychology. In fact, it was his early work on prestige suggestion that many academics say made his transition into social psychology. During World War II, Asch did a lot of work on **propaganda** specifically why people believed what they were told to believe. While we think of Nazi Germany as having used a prolific amount of propaganda to keep their citizens in check during the war, propaganda was used by all sides during the war. And in fact, for the most part propaganda in those days did not have a negative connotation as it does today. So, when Asch studied propaganda, he investigated the role of **prestige** of the author or the speaker had on the likelihood the listeners and readers of that propaganda would in fact accept and believe it. Muzafer Sherif tested Asch's work on a sample of college students looking at a set of literary prose. Sherif found that the passages that were identified with highly recognized and acclaimed authors received higher ratings than did those with lesser known or unknown authors. Asch went on to say about this that when all information is the same with the exception of one piece of information, in this case the author of the prose, many subjects would likely use that as they're primary basis for highly rating that prose. In other words, Asch saw this as confirming his research that in the end the perceived prestige of the author or speaker had significant effect on how the listener, or the reader gave credit to the propaganda.

Asch also did a significant amount of work looking at **conformity** and **obedience** to **authority**. Asch showed in specific situations a significant number of his research subjects would conform to a majority opinion even if that opinion was obviously incorrect. This was especially apparent in his research on line length. In his study online-length, Asch found that at least 75% of his subjects gave an answer that was obviously wrong and they did so to conform to the answers given by others in the experiment. Asch said that these subjects conformed simply because of **social pressure** from the **majority group**. It should be noted that there were no negative consequences should a subject fail to agree with the majority of the group. And the subjects we're not likely to ever interact with each other again after the experiment was over. After conducting all the various experiments that he ran looking at line length in 12 critical trials, 75 percent of participants conformed to the majority group at least once, and on average about one third of all his subjects conformed to the majority group even though the majority group's answer was clearly incorrect.

Asch's work was criticized because he had a non-representative sample and that the experiment took place in a highly controlled situation. Newer research by Perrin and Spencer (1980) suggests that people are less likely to conform in similar situations as they did in Asch's experiments in the 1950s. The explanation for this is that conformity was more valued and expected in the 1950s than it is today. Even in the 1980s research by Perrin and Spencer found that the vast majority of their subjects did not join the majority group's false conclusion. It is suggested that today conformity is seen as a less desirable value, independence and individualism are in fact more valued today, and there is a greater appreciation for people who express nonconformist attitudes.

George Horton Cooley (1864-1929). Cooley graduated from the University of Michigan with a Ph.D. in economics. In fact, one of Cooley's first books was titled "The Theory of Transportation (1893)" in which he found that towns and cities often intended to be found near transportation routes. He also was affected by Sigmund Freud and mentioned him in the first few chapters of his book titled "Social Organization."

Cooley was very impressed by the work of Adam Smith and Smith's notion that for the marketplace to be effective, persons must put themselves into the positions of others to demonstrate empathy. So Adam Smith referred to this as "**sympathetic imagination**," and this was later developed by Cooley into one of his first works titled "Human Nature and the Social Order (1902)". Later, Cooley took this idea and incorporated it into his conception of **role-taking**. It should be noted that Dewey, Mead, and Cooley were together at the University of Michigan while working on their doctorate degrees and so it should not be surprising that they shared a common orientation, which in this case was towards this developing field of social psychology. Later, this common orientation became known as "**symbolic interactionism**."

Cooley began working on the notion that other people's views of us contribute to the development of the **self** or also known as the **self-concept**. In 1902, Cooley developed what he called "**the**

looking glass self." Basically, Cooley said the society in which we existed became like a mirror from which we were able to see our true self as others saw it. Similar in some respects to the concept of self-fulfilling prophecy, the looking glass self is used by everyone to formulate their own opinion of their **true self**, and based on that perceived true self people may work to enhance that image given off by others and thus become even more of the person that others see. As research has demonstrated in regards of the **self-fulfilling prophecy**, children are more likely to be affected by the perception of their true self and thus more likely to become more in line with the self-fulfilling prophecy. For instance, if people see a child as smart, they will let it be known to the developing child, but they have certain expectations of that child because of the label they have applied to him, in other words that he is a smart child. The self-fulfilling prophecy comes into play because the child will most likely accept the label and will perform as if that label is true, in other words they will work to make it true.

Cooley's concept of the looking glass self is key to the sociological process of **socialization**. Cooley believed that the looking glass self was composed of three processes or steps.

1. First, we must imagine how others see us. It is not necessarily an accurate perception of us so there can be errors made because people internalize these perceived views of themselves.
2. Second, based upon our perceived notions of how others see us we also imagine what kind of attributions or judgments others have made of us.
3. Third, taken together, which is the perception that we have of ourselves by perceiving what others see in us, and thinking about the judgments that others have made of us because of their images of us, we then make a determination of how others feel about us. So, in short, we are aware of how others see us, what kind of judgments they have made up about us, and we imagine how they feel about us.

Leon Festinger (1919-1989). Leon Festinger graduated from the University of Iowa with a PhD in psychology. It was there at the University of Iowa that Festinger worked with Kurt Lewin. Festinger conducted a great deal of research looking at attitudes--how they were formed and how they were changed. In fact, he developed what is termed **communication theory** in which he suggested that people will more likely to give into social pressure as far as attitudes go when the group is attractive to them. If the group was seen as attractive, people would strive to fit in, in other words to conform.

One of the most important social psychological theories is called **cognitive dissonance theory**--a theory developed by Festinger. The idea is that when we have inconsistent beliefs or inconsistent beliefs and behaviors that a state of discomfort is created within us. As humans, we do not like to be in a state of discomfort and so we seek ways to reduce or eliminate that state of cognitive dissonance. Cognitive dissonance is also an attitude change theory in that it can get people to change their behaviors or attitudes by introducing elements that create cognitive dissonance within someone.

The story behind how Festinger came up with his cognitive dissonance theory is very interesting. At one time Festinger was studying a **cult** that believed the earth was going to be destroyed by a second flood. But when the appointed the day arrived and there was no flood, it produced different mental reactions in cult members. Some of the members understood the cult's prediction was simply wrong and they left the cult. However, the remaining cult members rather than admitting the cult's prediction of the flood was wrong, came to the conclusion that the cult's faithfulness and willingness to believe in the flood prediction in itself prevented the flood. In other words, their belief in the cult and its message of doom saved them from the flood. Therefore, Festinger concluded that the non-occurrence of the flood produced a state of cognitive

41

dissonance in cult members, and cult members had to find a way to reduce the dissonance--because if you'll remember cognitive dissonance is a state of discomfort. So, some members were able to reduce that dissonance by simply saying the cult had been wrong and left the cult altogether, while other members of the cult reduced the dissonance by reinterpreting the evidence in a way that suggested their strong belief in the cult's dogma prevented the flood.

So, while all of Festinger's work was important, his social comparison theory and later his theory of cognitive dissonance represent some of his more major contributions to the field of social psychology.

Fritz Heider (1896-1988). Heider was an Austrian psychologist whose work was in the field of **social cognition**. He is most widely known within the field of social psychology for his development of what is called **attribution theory**. "Attribution theory deals with how the social perceiver uses information to arrive at causal explanation for events. It examines what information is gathered and how it is combined to form a casual judgment (Fiske & Taylor, 1991). Heider basically had two overriding principles when it came to his theory of attribution. The first he called **internal attribution**, which is basically where people almost automatically want to say the cause of some behavior is due to an internal characteristic within that person. So, for instance if we were trying to explain the behavior of someone else, Heider would suggest we attempted to find internal attributions in that other person that would explain the behavior. As an example, if another person that did well on an exam Heider would suggest it was because of some internal mechanism within them such as their personality, their work ethic, which would represent their beliefs, or any punishments or rewards that could serve as motivations for their doing well on the exam.

Finally, Heider is also known for his **balance theory**, which stresses that there is harmony in our relationships with others when we agree on the value or lack of value on some other element. As a very simple example, imagine that John likes Mary, and Mary likes John, and both Mary and John like pizza. Heider would say that the relationship is harmonious and balanced. But what if John liked Mary, Mary liked John, Mary liked pizza, but John did not like pizza? Heider would say of this that the relationship is not harmonious and balanced. Does this necessarily mean that John and Mary will stop being friends? No, but it does mean that they will look for something to restore the balance in their relationship. It could be as simple as John saying, "It's no big deal that Mary likes pizza and I don't because when we go out she can order pizza and I will order something else." But what if that element that they could agree or disagree on was something more serious? What if John liked Mary, Mary liked John, Mary was pro-choice but John did not believe in abortion? Again, Heider would say that the relationship was not harmonious and balanced and therefore in this case, because the element they disagree on is relatively serious, it could end the friendship. But again, there are usually ways to make a relationship balanced if it is valued enough. So, in this case it might be simply that both John and Mary agree to disagree and maybe they agree never to talk about the issue because they know that they both feel differently about it and consider the friendship more important than their different opinions about a women's right to choose. In other words, the element is minimized as a divisive element.

George Homans (1910-1989). George Homans earned his undergraduate degree in English and then went on to serve as a newspaper editor in Emporia, Kansas. When World War II broke out he joined the Naval reserve where he spent the rest of the war. Homans had a keen interest in the lives of people and of the American character. Homans eventually became interested in sociology and he described that as a matter of chance. Homans developed many important associations the first was with a group at Harvard called the Pareto Circle, which basically met to discuss the work of Vilfredo Pareto who was a very famous Italian economist. This led to a book written by Homans called "An Introduction to Pareto." It was during this time that Homans also took an interest in psychology and history which further broadened his perspective on people and American characteristics. Further Homans became friends with Pitirium Sorokin who was the founder of Harvard University's sociology program and it was Sorokin brought Homans into that program. While Homans' contributions to social psychology are lengthy and important, he is primarily known for two: the first was the **Human Group** (Trevino 2006 and 2009) and the second his **Exchange Theory**. In the Human Group Homan's proposed that when looking at social reality there were three levels:

1. for social events,
2. customs, and
3. hypotheses that attempted to describe how customs become cultural characteristics and are both maintained and changed by circumstance and the situation.

Homans is also known for his social exchange theory. The source for Homans' social exchange theory and its subsequent propositions came from several places:

1. the economic model that was in place to explain exchanges between people, and
2. from B.F. Skinner's behaviorism. So, the basis of what became known as Holman's social exchange theory can be found both in economic and psychological principles.

Homans' social exchange theory had a number of propositions, but the chief premise was that man is rational and that man does nothing irrational. The economic model of exchange would suggest that when two people enter into an exchange they are concerned about the rewards, costs, and final profit. So that if two people enter into an economic model of exchange, at the end of that exchange though largely subconscious, the actors we'll subtract their costs from the rewards and if their rewards exceed their costs they will feel as if they have profited by that economic exchange. So, the most obvious proposition for the exchange model is that when people feel as if they have profited from that economic exchange, they will be more likely to repeat that exchange and usually with the same actor. On the other hand, if after concluding an economic exchange one person feels as if their costs outweighed their rewards, and thereby they did not profit from the exchange, the economic model of exchange would predict that that exchange would not be repeated. So Homans took this economic model of exchange, and when including behavioral work from psychology, he developed what he called social exchange theory (Ritzer, 2008).

Homans' model of social exchange works on the same essential principles as does the economic model only the social exchange model is directed at non-tangible outcomes when looking at exchanges between people. For instance, let's say that two friends get together, and because many things are exchanged between friends, those two friends enter into a social exchange with expectations of profiting from that exchange. Things exchanged for instance between friends would include affective support, information, goodwill, stress reduction through various means of support, humor, and trust. So, when two friends get together there is the expectation that when they part both will walk away feeling having been profited by that exchange. If the latter occurs, and they both feel profited after their social exchange, Homans would suggest that they would repeat that same exchange again--the logic being if they profited from the first exchange they will profit again. But conversely, what if two friends get together with their expectations that each will walk away from that exchange having been profited, but the exchange does not go as predicted and one of the actors walks away feeling that they have not profited from that exchange? Now while Homans would never argue that one single social exchange between friends that didn't lead to profit would be enough to end the friendship, in theory it could. In which case, if one of the two friends decided they had not profited by the exchange, Homans would predict that the exchange would not be repeated, though as I say Homans would never suggest that one single unprofitable exchange would lead to the end of a friendship, but depending upon what was being exchanged it is not impossible. So, when two friends enter into an exchange, for instance meeting for lunch, they expect at the end of that lunch to have profited in some intangible way by the exchange. Consequently, Homans would expect them to repeat that same exchange in the future, but on the other hand, if one of the friends walks away feeling is if they have not profited by the exchange, in theory Homans would predict they would not repeat that exchange. He called this particular type of exchange outcome the success proposition. He had a number of propositions, but this is probably what he is most known for. We shall revisit Homans in one of the future chapters of this book.

Kurt Lewin (1890-1947). Kurt Lewin emigrated to the US from Germany in 1933 before the Nazis began to instigate their anti-Semitic policies and eventual murder of Jews. Many of his family were not so lucky and remained in Germany where they were later murdered in the one of the extermination camps-- Lewin's mother and sister included. Kurt Lewin is regarded to be the founder of what we would call modern social psychology. He is considered to be the father of modern social psychology because he was the first to employ scientific methods in the study of social behavior and was one of the first to recognize that human behavior is largely the interaction of the person with their environment. In fact, he was one of the first to actually propose the argument of **nature versus nurture**--a very important argument within the social sciences.

Though primarily conducting research with children, Lewin advocated that human behavior should be seen as along a continuum of norms. He felt that the variations between people on the continuum were largely resolved of their self-perceptions and of the situation or the environment in which they found themselves. Lewin believed that in order to understand human behavior you had to take their entire "the life space" into consideration--a very difficult task. He called this **field theory**. So only by looking at a

Figure 1. Nature versus nurture.

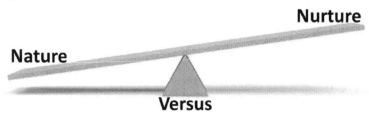

person's entire life experiences, or field, would you be able to make predictions about the reactions to changes in the environment or their situation. While the theory may seem simple it is far from that. When talking about any hard science, such as physics, chemistry, or geology there are certainly laws, but when dealing with people there are no laws, and Lewin recognized this in his theory. So, as you would look at two people standing side-by-side, maybe even appearing to be similar in some superficial way, you would not be able to see how their life experiences varied greatly. But only by understanding each of their life experiences as individuals would you be able to understand and therefore make predictions about their behaviors. Consequently, Lewin was one of the first to recognize how our environment shapes our behavior. "Kurt Lewin permanently widened the lens of psychology, demonstrating that human behavior is the product not simply of personal characteristics, instincts and other forces within us, but also of the complex dynamic environment we inhabit" (Psychology Today, March 1, 2001).

George Mead (1863-1931). George Herbert Mead died in in 1931 without ever having published a book or many monographs. But after his death, George Herbert Mead's theories were published by former students from their notes in the book "Mind, Self and Society." In those notes, and subsequently in the book created by his former students, Mead described how the **self**

47

is the result of an ongoing social process. Mead was a strong advocate for both sociology and social psychology and believed that psychology by itself as a discipline could not explain human behavior because he believed the individual can only develop as a result of the combination of biology with one's social environment.

Mead is largely credited with the theory of **symbolic interactionism**. Mead believed that human behavior is largely the result of social experiences. And these experiences result in individual and unique behaviors that essentially make up the social conditions in a society that then creates communication. Mead defined communication as simply the ability to comprehend another person's **symbolic gestures**. Mead clearly stated that he considered communication to be a social act because it could not be done w2ithout the presence of another person--in other words, two people interacting with each other using symbols to communicate.

The concept of the "**I**" and the "**me**" is central to Mead's theory. There is still controversy about the relationship of the "I" and the "me," and in particular why Mead believed that the self was social yet unfinished. According to Mead, a person's adopting some particular attitude introduces the "me" within that person and then reacts to it as an "I." And the "I" is generally how we identify ourselves. As noted, this is still a controversial theory and theorists even today argue about the reciprocal and ongoing relationship between the "I" and the "me."

We shall take another look at Mead's theory later in this book and we will also examine his concept of the "self" and the three stages he believed that humans pass through as they develop their sense of "self."

Stanley Milgram (1933-1984). Stanley Milgram was born in New York City the son of Jews who had emigrated from Central Europe during World War I. Milgram still had many extended family members living in Central Europe during the rise of

Nazism and World War II. Many of those family members died during the Holocaust. Milgram's roots and identity as a Jew, along with the suffering of extended family members at the hands of the Nazis, had a huge influence on his research. Milgram received his Ph.D. from Harvard University, though initially working at Harvard after graduating, he was later denied tenure probably because of his controversial research on obedience. From 1967 until his early death in 1984, Milgram served as a tenured professor at the City University of New York. Milgram's research on obedience to **perceived authority** had a huge influence on the work of Solomon Asch and Gordon Allport.

Within the field of social psychology Stanley Milgram's experiments with obedience to perceived authority stands out as perhaps one of the most well-known areas in social psychology. His experiment looking at subjects obeying a perceived authority figure in the delivery of what could have been deadly levels of electric shock to strangers revealed that a significant number, maybe as much as two thirds, of all people when given a command by a perceived authority figure might be capable of killing others simply because of their obedience to that perceived authority figure.

Milgram's research played out in a real-life situation where an unknown caller used his perceived authority as a police officer to get managers of fast-food restaurants to commit personal acts of crime and sexual violence against unsuspecting innocent employees. The most famous occurring at a McDonalds in Mount Washington, Kentucky in 2004. A man identifying himself as a police officer told the manager of the McDonalds over the phone that he was on his way to her restaurant to arrest an employee of hers that had been accused of stealing a purse. Based on a general description of the employee, so general that it could fit many young women, the manager brought the employee, a 17-year-old high school student, to her office where the police officer instructed the manager over the phone what to do. Ordered to make the girl take off all her clothes, the manager searched her clothing but found no evidence of the stolen purse. After telling the police office over the phone that she needed to get back to the front of the store in order to perform her duty as manager, the police officer, still on his way to the McDonalds, asked her if she knew of anyone who could watch the girl while the manager went back up to the front of her restaurant to attend to her business. The manager then called her boyfriend and asked him to watch the girl. After the manager's boyfriend arrived, the police officer, still on the phone and making his way to the restaurant, ordered the man to have the girl jump up and down in the nude in front of him, sit on his lap nude, and then to sodomize him. While this was not the only fast-food store to be targeted by this "police officer," it made national news because all of the events were captured on a camera installed in the manager's office. It was later used to prosecute the manager's boyfriend who was found guilty and sentenced to prison for his actions. By the time the hoaxes ended, the pretend police officer had pulled the same stunt in at least 68 fast-food restaurants in 32 states. The "police officer" was never caught.

While the events at these fast-food restaurants were tragic and should never have happened, they unfortunately served as evidence that Milgram's belief that even good people were capable of doing bad things if they perceived the person telling them what to do were perceived to have legitimate authority over them to do so.

Stanley Schacter (1922-1997). Stanley Schachter is known for his research on **emotions** specifically in that he proposed our emotional experiences were the result of our physiological state in interaction with our cognitive interpretation of that state. Schacter believed the interaction of social and physiological factors largely determined behavior. In his research with Singer (1962), Schacter demonstrated the interaction between physical arousal how people cognitively labeled that arousal. The major premise of their work was that simply feeling aroused was not enough to produce a behavior, they believed that people must also identify the arousal and interpret it in order to feel the emotion of the arousal and act accordingly. A good analogy of their theory begins with the application of a stimulus, followed by physical arousal, but then the addition of a cognitive label or interpretation of that arousal that then leads to the conscious experience of fear. So, for instance, imagine the following sequence of factors (Cherry, 2017):

1. I see a strange man walking towards me.
2. My heart is racing and I am trembling.
3. My rapid heart rate and trembling are caused by fear.
4. I am frightened!
5. I physically react to the emotion.

Schacter and Singer (1962) said that the situation would modify the emotional interpretation and reaction. For instance, they suggested that the same emotional interpretation and response would be different if someone were to encounter a stranger sitting on a park bench on a bright sunny day or an elderly stranger approaching them on that same bright sunny day. So that it was the combination of the stimulus and the interpretation, which itself is affected by the situation, that in fact leads to an emotional response.

"In a 1962 experiment, Schachter and Singer put their theory to the test. A group of 184 male participants was injected with epinephrine, a hormone that produces arousal including increased heartbeat, trembling, and rapid breathing. All of the participants were told that they were being injected with a new drug to test their eyesight. However, one group of participants was informed the possible side-effects that the injection might cause while the other group of participants was not.

Participants were then placed in a room with another participant who was actually a confederate in the experiment. The confederate either acted in one of two ways: euphoric or angry. Participants who had not been informed about the effects of the injection were more likely to feel either happier or angrier than those who had been informed. Those who were in a room with the euphoric confederate were more likely to interpret the side effects of the drug as happiness, while those exposed to the angry confederate were more likely to interpret their feelings as anger.

Schacter and Singer had hypothesized that if people experienced an emotion for which they had no explanation, they would then label these feelings using their feelings at the moment.

The results of the experiment suggested that participants who had no explanation for their feelings were more likely to be susceptible to the emotional influences of the **confederate**" (Cherry, 2017).

Carolyn Sherif (1922-1982). Carolyn Sherif (*see* Wood) obtained her Ph.D. in social psychology at the University of Iowa in 1944. She married Muzafer Sherif the following year and the two published numerous articles and books together. Their early collaborations led to studies on attitudes, **attitude change**, and **persuasion**. Further their work on attitudes and attitude change led to the publishing of their seminal work, "Attitude and Attitude Change:" The Social Judgement-Involvement Approach" (Sherif et al., 1965).

Along with her husband and fellow researcher Muzafer Sherif, they performed what is considered one of the classic studies in social psychology, the **Robbers Cave experiments** (see Muzafer Sherif, below). Carolyn Sherif helped develop the realistic conflict theory, social judgment theory, and was heavily involved in research on gender identity and the psychology of women.

Sherif served as president for the American Psychological Association's division on Psychology of Women, received the Association for Women in Psychology's distinguished publication award in 1981, and also received a general award for her contributions to the discipline of Psychology of Education in 1982.

Muzafer Sherif (1906-1988). Sherif was born in Turkey and during his childhood witnessed atrocities committed by Greek soldiers on Turkish civilians. This had a dramatic effect on Sherif's future research. Sherif earned his Ph.D. in psychology from Columbia University in 1935. Though Sherif was recognized primarily as a psychologist, he was the first to be awarded the Cooley Mead award for contributions to social psychology from the American Sociological Association. Sherif is most closely associated with his experiments on the **autokinetic effect, realistic conflict theory** and the Robbers Cave experiment.

"The field experiment involved two groups of twelve-year-old boys at Robbers Cave State Park, Oklahoma, America.

The twenty-two boys in the study were unknown to each other and all from white middle-class backgrounds. They all shared a Protestant, two-parent background. The boys were randomly assigned to one of two groups, although neither was aware of the other's existence. They were then, as individual groups, picked up by bus on successive days in the summer of 1954 and transported to a 200-acre Boy Scouts of America camp in the Robbers Cave State Park in Oklahoma.

At the camp, the groups were kept separate from each other and were encouraged to bond as two individual groups through the pursuit of common goals that required co-operative discussion, planning and execution. During this first phase, the groups did not know of the other group's existence. The boys developed an attachment to their groups throughout the first week of the camp, quickly establishing their own cultures and group norms, by doing various activities together like hiking, swimming, etc. The boys chose names for their groups, The Eagles and The

Rattlers, and stenciled them onto shirts and flags.

Sherif now arranged the 'competition stage' where friction between the groups was to occur over the next 4-6 days. In this phase, it was intended to bring the two groups into competition with each other in conditions that would create frustration between them. A series of competitive activities (e.g. baseball, tug-of-war etc.) were arranged with a trophy being awarded on the basis of accumulated team score. There were also individual prizes for the winning group such as a medal and a multi-bladed pocket knife with no consolation prizes being given to the "losers."

The Rattlers' reaction to the informal announcement of a series of contests was absolute confidence in their victory! They spent the day talking about the contests and making improvements on the ball field, which they took over as their own to such an extent that they spoke of putting a "Keep Off" sign there! They ended up putting their Rattler flag on the pitch. At this time, several Rattlers made threatening remarks about what they would do if anybody from The Eagles bothered their flag.

Situations were also devised whereby one group gained at the expense of the other. For example, one group was delayed getting to a picnic and when they arrived the other group had eaten their food.

At first, this prejudice was only verbally expressed, such as taunting or name-calling. As the competition wore on, this expression took a more direct route. The Eagles burned the Rattler's flag. Then the next day, the Rattler's ransacked The Eagle's cabin, overturned beds, and stole private property. The groups became so aggressive with each other that the researchers had to physically separate them.

During the subsequent two-day cooling off period, the boys listed features of the two groups. The boys tended to characterize their own in-group in very favorable terms, and the other out-group in very unfavorable terms. Keep in mind that the participants in this study were well-adjusted boys, not street gang members.

This study clearly shows that conflict between groups can trigger prejudice attitudes and discriminatory behavior. This experiment confirmed Sherif's realistic conflict theory" (McCloud, 2008).

In addition to the robbers Cave experiment, Muzifer Sherif is also known for his classic study done on the autokinetic effect and conformity in 1936. Using undergraduate college students, Sherif put his subjects in a dark room and told them to watch a small pinpoint of light on the screen in front of them. They were then told to report how far the light moved during the experiment. When placed in a room by themselves, they found that most subjects reported the light to have moved anywhere from 2 to 6 inches during the experiment, but in fact this was the autokinetic effect and the light did not move at all during the experiment. In the next phase of this experiment he placed subjects together in the same room and had them watch the same light and then working in a group decide how far the light moved during the experiment. Sherif found that the subjects tended to compromise on how far they felt the light moved during the experiment. All in all, subjects either increased the distance they felt that the light moved or decreased their perception of how far the light moved so that they agreed on a group norm for the distance the light had moved, even though the light had not moved at all during the experiment. Sherif then had participants repeat the experiment individually and report on how far they thought the light moved. What he found was that the majority of subjects reported the light having moved to the same degree as was the group norm. Therefore, Sherif concluded that most participants denied having been influenced by the group norm even though clearly, they were. In the end, Sherif realized that in task groups group consensus was usually the result of compromise but that did not necessarily mean that the group decision was accurate.

Terms and Concepts to Know

Attitudes
Prejudice
Religion
Freud's Theory of Psychoanalysis
Allport's Theory of Personality
Personality traits

Stereotyping
Cognitive functioning
Social stratification
Social equality
Allport's Contact Hypothesis
Outgroups
Ingroups
Empathy
Impression formation
Propaganda
Conformity
Obedience
Authority
Perceived authority
Social pressure
Majority group
Sympathetic imagination
Role-taking
Symbolic Interactionism
Self
Self-concept
Looking glass self
True self
Self-fulfilling prophecy
Socialization
Social Communication Theory
Cognitive Dissonance Theory
Cults
Social cognition
Attribution Theory
Internal attributions
External attributions
Fundamental attribution error
Balance Theory
Human group
Social Exchange Theory
Nature versus nurture
Field Theory
Symbolic gestures
I

Me
Emotions
Confederate
Attitude change
Persuasion
Robber's cave experiments
Autokinetic effect
Realistic Conflict Theory

References

Asch, Solomon E. "Forming impressions of personality", *The Journal of Abnormal and Social Psychology* 41.3 (1946): 258.

Cherry, C. (2019). The Schachter-Singer two-factor theory of emotion. *Very Well Mind*. Retrieved November 2019 from: https://www.verywellmind.com/the-two-factor-theory-of-emotion-2795718

Crisp, R. J.; Turner, R. N. (2009). "Can imagined interactions produce positive perceptions? Reducing prejudice through simulated social contact." *American Psychologist*. 64 (4): 231–240.

Fiske, S. T., & Taylor, S. E. (1991). *Social cognition* (2nd ed.). New York: McGraw-Hill.

McCloud, S. (2008). Robbers Cave. *Simply Psychology*. Retrieved February 26, 2018 from: https://www.simplypsychology.org/robbers-cave.html

Perrin, S., & Spencer, C. (1980)." The Asch effect: a child of its time? *Bulletin of the British Psychological Society*," 32, 405-406.

Psychology Today. Kurt Lewin. *How our environment shapes our behavior*. Published on March 1, 2001. https://www.psychologytoday.com/articles/200103/kurt-lewin

Ritzer, George. (2008) *Sociological Theory*. Ch. 12. "The Exchange Theory of George Homans" New York, NY: McGraw-Hill Companies.

Schachter and Singer's Theory of Emotion. Retrieved February 26, 2018 from: https://www.verywellmind.com/the-two-factor-theory-of-emotion-2795718

Schachter, S. and Singer, J. E. Cognitive, social and physiological determinants of emotional states. *Psychological Review.* 1962; 69: 379-399.

Sherif, C., Sherif, M., & Nebergall, R. (1965). *Attitude and attitude change: The social judgement-involvement approach.* Greenwood Press.

Treviño, A. Javier. (2009). *George C. Homans, the human group and elementary social behavior.* Retrieved May 2018 from: www.infed.org/thinkers/george_homans.htm.

Treviño, A. Javier. (2006) *George C. Homans: History, theory, and method.* Boulder, CO: Paradigm.

Chapter 3: Introduction to Social Psychology

Before we begin discussing **social psychology** as a discipline in-depth, there are some concepts that we need to understand from the beginning. By doing so we could have a better understanding of how groups impact our lives, and in particular our choices and actions. Also, the understanding of these important sociological themes gives us a better view of how our perceptions of others affect our interactions with those same others. So, we need to look at five basic issues concerning social behavior that play a large part in the study of social psychology period

First, we need to understand that our social behavior is **goal oriented**. Essentially, for everything we do that involves **interacting** with others we have unmet needs or goals that we want to fill. For instance, we want to understand not only others but ourselves as well, because of ego needs we wish to gain **status** in some particular social arena and therefore we worked to maintain that status. To do so, we look for others who share the same goals and status aspirations.

Second, we also need to understand that outcomes are largely determined as a result of the interaction between the individual and the social situation he or she finds him or herself in. In order to understand ourselves, and people in general, we need to look at individual characteristics, the particular situation and the context in which it occurs, and then we examine the interaction between those two variables. People are difficult to study. We are not rocks. We are not things falling from a great height. We are social creatures. Therefore, it is important to understand that we behave very differently depending on the social context of the situation in which we find ourselves. As the situation changes, it's very likely we change as well. So, for instance someone who's normally shy and meek might be very different when they find themselves in a situation where they feel threatened. As we will see as we progress through this book, we behave differently in those social situations such as when we're in groups. We may be more likely to do things we normally would not do because if the group is large enough, we feel anonymous. In group work we develop our identity by seeing ourselves through the eyes of others, hence the term looking glass self. So, we imagine how other people see us and

Figure 1. Charles Cooley and the Looking Glass Self.

"I am not what I think I am, I am not what you think I am, but I am what I think you think I am."

that then affects the way that we assume leadership roles because others won't or because we feel that our views sure the paramount in achieving the groups tasks. In task groups, we may become **social loafers** and sit back and let others do the work.

Third, as individuals, we spend a great deal of time thinking about social situations. In fact, our sense of self, in other words who we think we are, comes from our social interactions with others and our perception of how others see us.

Cooley's the Looking Glass Self is based on the premise that we form our self-see ourselves. Also, there is a process of social comparison where we

Figure 2. Cooley's Looking Glass Self. How do I know who I am?

Who am I, really? How do I know who I am?

compare ourselves to others who belong to the same groups as do we. When we make these comparisons, we may do so to enhance our self-image. For instance, if a person has low self-esteem, they will likely compare themselves to somebody they think is significantly below them in some characteristic they share so that their self-evaluation is enhanced. We generally compare ourselves to those in our in-group and this is a concept that you will hear again when we get to the material on prejudice.

Fourth, as the social creatures we are, we find ourselves wanting to predict the behavior of others and in order to do that we have to be able to explain and analyze the behavior of those others. This is also the basis for any science, which is the ability to know and understand some phenomenon so well that it allows us to make predictions. For instance, one issue that we will discuss in this book is **self-confirmation theory** which suggests that when we look at our social world, we look for those things that serve as evidence for confirmation of our pre-existing ideas or attitudes. This is why people tend watch cable news networks that are consistent with their political views. People look for information that confirms their pre-existing attitudes or ideas and tend to resist information that discounts or disconfirms their pre-existing attitudes or ideas. Of course, this is a significant bias in humans and something that needs to be resisted on the part of any reasonably intelligent person.

Fifth, as humans, we often assume that the way a person acts is a good indicator of their true self and of their personality. There is a **theory of correspondent inferences** which suggests that we assume the actions and behaviors of others represent something deeper in terms of their inner core or personality. So, if you were to see someone holding a door open for and elderly person to enter a building, we might infer the person holding the door open is a good spirited, honest, friendly, well-mannered person. But the reality of that situation is that we simply cannot know that much about a person based on such limited observations. This can be a serious flaw in humans because such inferences can be very misleading even to the point of being dangerous. Most serial killers are often described as nice neighbors, friendly, and polite. Unfortunately, often times victims of serial killers haven't heard these things which can result in their death.

While social psychology can be a very interesting academic discipline, it has far more potential than that. Knowledge about why people do the things they do relevant to social situations and the social world in which they live, can help us learn about ourselves, our culture, our society, and about the world itself. Social psychology helps us to understand ourselves through the lens of our social world. How we behave and why we behave the way that we do as part of a social group and are influenced by our social world. This is how we get a greater understanding of how social relationships are developed.

What is Social Psychology?

Social psychology is the study of people's attitudes and behaviors in a systematic way. It's the same way that any science studies the phenomenon of its discipline. To say something is systematic implies that there are standardized methods for discovery. So, if there was such a thing as "pure" sociology unaffected by biology, it would attempt to explain everything about human behavior as a result of the environment. Likewise, if there was such a thing as pure psychology unaffected by the environment, it would attempt to explain everything about human behavior as a result of biology. In fact, both disciplines recognize the contributions of each discipline to human behavior. Social psychology it Is often considered the point of intersection between those two disciplines. Generally sociological social psychology focuses on larger social forces that affect our daily lives, while psychological social psychology tends to focus on individual's mental processes that are both explained by biology and the environment. So, both psychology and sociology employ the scientific method to study people and society within the discipline of social psychology. Therefore, social psychology is interdisciplinary.

Simply put, social psychology is the scientific investigation of how individuals are influenced by the thoughts, feelings, and behavior of others—whether those thoughts, feelings and behaviors of others are perceived or real.

It differs from psychology and sociology in is that the focus is on real or imagined presence of others. For instance, while people may be influenced by their friends and family, they are also influenced by social forces—seen or unseen. So, while social psychologists focus on the individual, and groups of people are made up of individuals, there is successful, productive and overlapping interaction between psychological social psychologists and sociological social psychologists.

In May 2016, Greg Subiszak was seen not moving at the bottom of a hotel pool in Cape May, New Jersey. People who tried to get in the water were met with an electric shock—one of the pools lights had shorted. A crowd gathered around helplessly watching Greg Subiszak at the bottom of the pool obviously

Figure 1. Ivan Martinez.

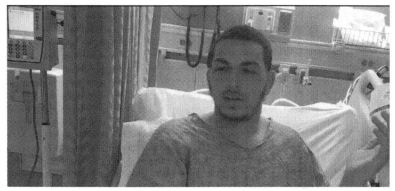

unconscious. Seventeen-year old Ivan Martinez couldn't just stand by, so he dove into the water. Martinez later said, when I first got in the water "my body tensed up. I couldn't stop shaking." Martinez said the man was obviously having convulsions as he was being electrocuted by a short-circuit in a pool lamp. Martinez managed to drag the unconscious Subiszak from the bottom of the pool where other rescuers waited to pull him out of the water. Subiszak survived the accident. Martinez is quoted as later saying, "I wish I had jumped in sooner to save him." How do we make sense of Martinez's behavior? Why did he wait before jumping in the pool? Why didn't others jump in? Why did he jump into the pool and risk his own life?

We all try to explain the behavior of others, but since most people aren't scientists, it is more speculation than science. Two things separate science from speculation: the first is that scientists use the **scientific method** to test **theories**, and the second is that social scientists do not form theories about individual people but rather about groups of people. Instead, social scientists develop theories about why different people act in similar ways in similar situations. Types of research used by social scientists include **surveys**, **experiments**, and **participant observation**—all research tools you will be exposed to in the module on research methods.

In summary, social psychology has been described as the study of social interactions. Gordon Allport, a major contributor to the field of social psychology, defined social psychology as an attempt to understand and explain how the thoughts, feelings and behaviors of individuals are influenced by the actual, imagined, or

Figure 2. The reciprocal relationship between the individual and the group.

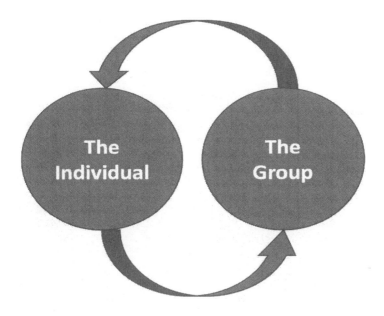

implied presence of others. In fact, Allport went so far as to suggest that our social world influences us even when it appears to be unseen; in other words, people do not have to be present for us to be affected by them and the larger culture which we and they are part of. Second, social psychology investigates and attempt to describe how the individual's perceptions of others' behaviors have on the group itself. Likewise, it understands and investigates the reciprocal relationship between individuals and groups. In other words, social psychology investigates how the individual affects the group and how the group affects the individual. Third, social

Figure 3. William McDougal's Introduction to Social Psychology (1908)

psychology examines the relationships between groups as ongoing and constantly changing.

Historical Development of the Discipline

Before we begin our study of social psychology, we need to take a brief look at the historical development of the discipline. between 1885 in 1934, saw the birth of the discipline and is therefore called the *early years* of social psychology as a discipline.

Generally, there are three periods that represent dramatic changes in the study of social psychology. The first, Triplett (1895) is credited for the first scientific study of social psychology. In 1908, William McDougall published the first social psychological text from an evolutionary psychological perspective and focused on instincts. Later that same year, Ross (1908) published a psychological text that focused on interpersonal processes--the first work to examine interpersonal relationships. The in 1924, Floyd Allport wrote a social psychological text that emphasized experimental methods that should be employed within the new discipline of social psychology.

The next significant development of social psychology as a discipline occurred between 1935 and 1945 and is considered the *coming of age* for the discipline. It was in 1936, The Society for the Psychological Study of Social Issues was formed perhaps formally launching the new discipline. The first person to present the issue of interactionism was Kurt Lewin. Interactionism suggests that people are in a constant state of interaction with their social environment whether there are other people physically present or not. His work on interactionism continues to be important theoretical orientation within the discipline of social psychology. It was from Kurt Lewin's work that **symbolic interaction** was developed--perhaps one of the most important theories used in social psychology. Symbolic interaction deals with how people attempt to find shared meaning and their overlapping social lives and interactions with others as well as with institutions. For instance, the concept of deviance is **socially constructed**. It only has meaning when people in their interactions with each other are able to essentially come to some agreement as to what the concept means. So once people accept a shared understanding of some concept, that concept then becomes a social reality.

We can also look at issues of social structure and the personality. While there is a reciprocal relationship between the two, social psychology investigates how social structure affects the individual's personality. From an interactionist point of view social structure is simply common and repetitive interactions and behaviors between people in a given culture. Therefore, it is interactionist in that the social structure only has meaning when people agree on that meaning. For instance, the educational system is a type of **social structure**. It's nothing that I can hold in my hand or see in its entirety, but it exists and it does so because people have come to have a shared meaning and understanding of what the educational system is in the United States. So, while the interactionist perspective suggests that people can be influenced and change because of societal influence, it also suggests the people as social actors and participants in particular culture and society have the ability to change any particular social structure. It is important to note that this theoretical viewpoint allows for the fact that man will continue to change as a result of the ongoing process of redefining the social structure of their culture.

It should be noted that during World War II, social psychological theories were employed in the war effort. Psychological and social psychological researchers spent

Figure 4. Walter Langer's The Mind of Adolf Hitler (1943).

a great deal of time and effort developing profiles of high-ranking enemy politicians and military figures. A great deal of work was done when developing a profile of Adolf Hitler and was used in an effort to understand the infamous leader with the intent of being able to project his future actions. Walter Langer (1899-1981), working for the Office of Strategic Services during World War II, was probably the most famous social psychologist and psychoanalyst to analyze Hitler, and much of his characterization of Hitler is still today considered to be relatively accurate today.

The following is the preface Walter Langer wrote about his analysis of Adolf Hitler in 1943 (Nizkor Project, 2012):

> "This study is not propagandistic in any sense of the term. It represents an attempt to screen the wealth of contradictory, conflicting and unreliable material concerning Hitler into strata which will be helpful to the policy-makers and those who wish to frame a counter-propaganda. For this reason, the first three parts are purely descriptive and deal with the man (1) as he appears to himself, (2) as he has been pictured to the German people, and (3) how he is known to his associates. These sections contain the basic material for the psychological analysis in sections IV and V in which an attempt is made to understand Hitler as a person and the motivations underlying his actions.
>
> The material available for such an analysis is extremely scant and spotty. Fortunately, we have at our disposal a number of informants who knew Hitler well and who have been willing to cooperate to the best of their abilities. The study would have been entirely impossible were it not for the fact that there is a relatively high degree of agreement in the descriptions of Hitler's behavior, sentiments and attitudes given by these several informants. With this as a basis it seemed worthwhile to proceed with the study filling in the lacunae with knowledge gained from clinical experience in dealing with individuals of a similar type. This is not an entirely satisfactory procedure, from a scientific point of view, but it is the only feasible method at the present time. Throughout the study we have tried to be as objective as possible in evaluating his strengths as well as his weaknesses.

All plain numbers in parentheses refer to the page of The Hitler Source Book, a companion volume in which the original material is to be found together with the complete reference. Numbers in parentheses preceded by M.K. or M.N.O. refer to pages in Mein Kampf and My New Order, respectively. A detailed Index to the original material is to be found at the beginning of the Source-Book. A complete bibliography is appended to this study.

It is hoped that the study may be helpful in gaining a deeper insight into Adolf Hitler and the German people and that it may serve as a guide for our propaganda activities as well as our future dealings with them."

Perhaps one of the most profound conclusions that Langer reached about Hitler was the following:

"Hitler might commit suicide. This is the most plausible outcome. Not only has he frequently threatened to commit suicide, but from what we know of his psychology it is the most likely possibility. It is probably true that he has an inordinate fear of death, but being an hysteric he could undoubtedly screw himself up into the super-man character and perform the deed. In all probability, however, it would not be a simple suicide. He has too much of the dramatic for that and since immortality is one of his dominant motives, we can imagine that he would stage the most dramatic and effective death scene he could possibly think of. He knows how to bind the people to him and if he cannot have the bond in life he will certainly do his utmost to achieve it in death. He might even engage some other fanatic to do the final killing at his orders."

The above excepts from Langer's book are important because this was the first-time social psychology had been put into practical use. In this case, it was used to predict the behaviors and intentions of one a war time enemy like Adolf Hitler. The use of such analysis has grown to where it is commonly used by military forces to study and understand enemy leaders.

Finally, in the **maturing of the discipline**, there was a rapid expansion of the discipline between 1946 and 1969. Adorno's work on the **authoritarian personality**, which will be discussed in the chapter on **prejudice**, Milgram's and Zimbardo's research on **obedience to authority**, which will be discussed in the chapter on obedience, Festinger's work on **cognitive dissonance**, which will be discussed in the chapter on attitudes and behavior, and Hatfield and Berscheid's work on romantic and **interpersonal** (i.e., non-romantic) **attraction** were major research works during this period. Also, during this time more women and minorities entered the field of social psychology, which countered criticism that most social psychological research was focused on white males.

One of the chief challenges in the social sciences is to dispel the myth that the social sciences are nothing more than common sense. Unfortunately, as the social sciences, through rigorous scientific procedures, discover facts and then publish those facts, over time those facts are so well accepted by the population that they do not understand that those facts were the result of scientific investigation. Hence, the belief the social sciences, including social psychology, is really nothing more than reporting common sense. Social psychology is so much more than common sense. Because it is a science and uses the scientific method to discover facts pertaining to the individual and his or her cultural environment, social psychologists are able to shed light on how people think and behave in social interactions while in an all-encompassing social environment. Finally, and I've stated this already, remember that social psychology is interdisciplinary and seeks to discover and report scientific facts found by both psychology and sociology.

Now that we know a little about social psychology as a discipline, let's move onto the next chapter which focuses on the historical development of social psychology.

Terms and Concepts to Know

Social psychology
Goal oriented
Interacting/interaction
Status
Cooley's the Looking Glass Self
Self-confirmation theory
Theory of correspondent inferences

Scientific method
Theories
Surveys
Experiments
Participant observation
Early years of social psychology as a discipline
Coming of age of social psychology as a discipline
Maturing of social psychology as a discipline
Symbolic interaction
Socially constructed
Authoritarian personality
Prejudice
Obedience to authority
Cognitive dissonance
Interpersonal (i.e., non-romantic) attraction
Social structure

References

Nizkor Project. (2012). Retrieved March 23, 2017 from
http://www.nizkor.org

Chapter 4: The Self

Our **self-concept** is basically, "Who are we?" If I was in the classroom and I asked you to write five statements about yourself, you would get a lot of very different statements. Some people might say I'm honest, others might say I'm a mother, I'm a good student, and many more. Our self-concept is basically just how we answer the question, "Who are we?" for ourselves. All of those self-statements refer to a number of different roles that we occupy at any one time.

Figure 1. Self-concept example.

Roles of the Self

The first role of the **self** is that of **self-awareness**. The self is an observer, the receiver of the attention of others in our social environment. It is also a participant because the self may change as a result of feedback from that social environment. Research has found that self-awareness begins to develop roughly around the age of 18 months (Rochat, 2003). Evolutionary kin like gorillas and chimpanzees have been shown to also have self-awareness, so it is not unique to humans.

The self goes through two temporary states: that of being **privately self-aware** and that of being **publicly self-aware**. Being privately self-aware means that the self while developing wants to hide or keep secret certain aspects of a person's developing self-concept until after taking in more feedback from the social environment so that it becomes clearer about those particular aspects, but then leads greater adherence to newly created standards of conduct. Once these new standards of conduct are adopted and made a more permanent part of the self-concept, the feelings toward that particular aspect of the self-concept is reinforced and intensified. Whereas public self-awareness, while still a temporary state, is simply being aware of our public image and those specific aspects of the self.

The second role of the self is **self-consciousness**, which is a personality trait and something we will look at more closely later in this chapter. Like self-awareness, there are two states associated with self-consciousness: the private and the public. Also, like private self-awareness, **private self-consciousness** is where specific aspects of the self-conscious are hidden from public view until such time they become more of a permanent aspect of the self. Public self-consciousness is the awareness of how he or she is presenting themselves in their social arena. People who are judged to be high in **public self-consciousness** generally have a more objective and realistic perception of how they appear to others in their social environment than do people who score low in public self-consciousness. Further, people who are judged to be high in public self-consciousness have higher **self-esteem** (Fenigstein et al., 1975) and care more for their physical appearance (Turner et al., 1981).

Another function of the self-concept is self-regulation. Self-regulation refers to the manner in which people control and direct their own behaviors relative to their social environment. Being self-aware then allows us to measure how well we are doing in meeting our behavioral goals. If there are discrepancies between how we want to be perceived by others consistent with our self-concept result in either reinforcing those aspects of our self-concept, or if we fail at having those self-statements reinforced by our social environment, the result may be an emotional response—like depression or low self-esteem.

The self-concept is composed of many **self-schemas**. Schemas are collections of beliefs about themselves and specific objects—including groups and situations. The development of schemas are the result of life course experiences and interactions and then are stored in memory as organized collections of beliefs. Schemas are then used in future encounters as the foundation or short

Figure 2. Self-schema as a friend.

cut for understanding any new experience or interaction. They also serve as filters when the mind processes new information relevant to any particular schema. Schemas, like schematics, serve to explain how components of the overall structure are linked and work together.

There are many examples we could look at when investigating schemas. For instance, someone who lives in the country could have a schema about cities. Components might include:

1. they have a lot of cars with frequent traffic jams,
2. crime rates are high and so cities are dangerous,

3. they are dirty, pollution fills the air, and
4. they are expensive.

Or we can have schemas about ourselves. For instance, a female might have a schema about being female that includes components like:

1. I am quiet,
2. I am studious,
3. I am supportive, and
4. I am emotional at times.

In fact, gender identity schemas are important aspects of the self-concept. We have expectations concerning how we should act in specific situations. For instance, someone may have a schema on how to act when in a college classroom. As a student that might include components like:

1. I should take notes about what the professor is saying.
2. I should listen to what the professor is saying and not talking to the student beside me.
3. I should raise my hand if I have a question.
4. I should raise my hand if I have a comment to make during a discussion.
5. I should study before exams.
6. I should do my best on exams.

Self-schemas are a little more complex and are the result of subjectively seeing ourselves through the lens of our social environment. For instance, someone might have a self-schema of themselves as intelligent, fair, objective, attractive, overweight, tall, a good person and many more components. These images of our self become processing tools. They become filters of how we interpret things around us and interact with our social environment.

Role schemas refer to associated beliefs an individual has about the particular roles they occupy. These schemas typically adjust as the particular situations change. For instance, if Mary is a banker, she has beliefs about what it means to her to be a banker and acts out those beliefs in her daily behavior as a banker but will act differently when at home and she uses her schema as "wife" or "mother." Likewise, as we interact with Mary in her different roles, we would use our different schemas associated with our expectations of "banker," "wife" or "mother."

We also have schemas associated with certain events. Sometimes these are referred to as **scripts**. These kinds of schemas set the stage for what we should expect and/or how to act in specific situations. For instance, most people have a schema or script for riding in an elevator. Generally, eyes are forward or directed at the lights indicating the floor. The "script" would dictate that:

>   1. We be a certain distance from the other occupants of the elevator.

Figure 3. A violation of the "script" for riding an elevator with strangers.

>   2. We should only exchange eye contact when we first enter the elevator or if someone gets on and we are already in.
>   3. Our eyes should be directed straight in front of us or at the lights indicating which floor the elevator is passing.

These kinds of schemas are very important and often powerful and may evoke sanctions if violated.

Finally, consistent with Piaget's theory of cognitive development, children learn about who they are and develop self-schemas by adaptation, accommodation and equilibration, which then provides them with the basic tools necessary to navigate the life course.

Self-Confirming Bias

Confirmation bias is seeing and believing what we want to see and believe from our social environment. When we want something to be true, we seek out information from our social environment that supports our desire for it to be true. The problem with this kind of thinking, other than it is obviously flawed thinking and biased, is that once we find support for something we want to be true, we stop looking and thus disregard opportunities for more information that may suggest contrary to what we want to be true. We lose our ability to be objective.

People who hold strong beliefs about something often fall into the self-confirmation trap. Take **prejudice** for instance. People who are prejudice towards people of an outgroup look for evidence to support or justify their prejudice and fail to objectively take in other evidence that fails to support their prejudicial beliefs. The self-confirmation bias is often seen in people with low self-esteem as they comb their social world seeking evidence that they are not liked, people harbor grudges against them, speak badly about them behind their back, and crosses over into the realm of paranoia.

In the end, to seek out the truth of a situation, one must be open and objective. In fact, the goal of science is actually to do the opposite of what self-confirming bias would suggest: deliberately seek out information that disconfirms our already held beliefs or hopes. It is only be seeking out information that might be in opposition to what we already believe do we have a greater chance of arriving at the truth.

Self-reference

Self-reference is basically the idea that we are center stage and the world revolves around us. So, when we are engaged in conversations with others, we are more likely to attend to those statements made about us that confirm our view of our self. If something said fits our self-concept and our self-schema we are more likely to remember the statement and enhance or strengthen that particular component of our self, but if a statement doesn't fit our self-concept, we tend to ignore the statement or turn the statement against the person making the statement--"they don't know what they're talking about," or "they're just jealous."

Self-Esteem

Self-esteem is an important component of the self-concept. We maintain our self-esteem by making comparisons with others in our social environment. By comparing ourselves to others we obtain information that allows us to reflect on the results of our social comparisons. Like other aspects of the self-concept, we generally like to be around others who validate our self-esteem and avoid others in our social environment who might threaten our self-esteem.

When others in our social environment do well in some behavior and that behavior is a central component of our self-concept, we may reflect on our abilities in comparison to that other person. If we are not confident in our ability to excel in that particular behavior, we are more likely to be threatened by that other person's superior behavior.

If our self-esteem is threatened, a normal human reaction is to find a way to reduce or eradicate the self-esteem threat. We may distance ourselves from that person, devalue that other person's performance, or change the importance of the particular component as part of our self-concept.

We may also seek out others in our social environment who we judge to be less good at performing that particular behavior so that by default we are able to more easily judge our performance as superior and thus reduce or eliminate the self-esteem threat. Both people with low or high self-esteem have been found to change their peer network in order to reduce the self-esteem threat, but only people with low self-esteem seem to benefit from it. However, people high in self-esteem are more likely to react to the threat by rationalizing the superior performance of another or by trying harder in the future (Van Dellen et al., 2011).

Generally, high self-esteem is a protective factor, though there is such a thing as having excessive, unrealistic and damaging levels of high self-esteem. High self-esteem has been found to be linked to **narcissism** in some cases, which can then be associated with a lack of caring for others, empathy, and aggressive counter-attacks (Campbell et al., 2007; Bushman and Baumeister, 1998). Research has found that people with low self-esteem tend not to fair as well through the life course. People with low self-esteem are more likely to make less money at their jobs, be depressed, and abuse drugs (Orth & Robins, 2013; Salmela-Aro & Nurmi, 2007).

One question that is addressed in the research is what leads to someone having low self-esteem? There has been a great deal of research investigating the causes of low self-esteem, but there does seem to be some definitive results. Research has found that people who were abused as children, came from impoverished families, or whose parents had drug or alcohol problems were more likely to have low self-esteem in adulthood (Boden et al., 2008).

One myth the research has dispelled is that people with narcissism are covering for low self-esteem, but the research says that's not true. It is common for narcissists to truly believe they are superior to and better than others in their social environment (Campbell et al., 2007).

Self-Efficacy

According to the famous psychologist and researcher Albert Bandura (1977), **self-efficacy** is "the belief in one's capabilities to organize and execute the courses of action required to manage prospective situations." Self-efficacy simply refers to a person's belief that they can control the events around them--that they can succeed in those tasks they choose to master. It is important to note that the development of self-efficacy occurs over the entire life course and not just in childhood.

Bandura went on to describe the sources of self-efficacy. There are four. They are:

> **1. Mastery experiences.** Our self-efficacy is strengthened when we perform a task successfully. On the flipside however, if we perform a task at a level less than that of which we judge to be successful, our self-efficacy takes a hit and can weaken.

2. Social modeling. Seeing others perform a similar task successfully can increase our belief that we too can master that task. Even seeing struggle to perform that task but ultimately succeed is an important learning tool when it comes to someone developing the belief that they too can accomplish and master that specific task.

3. Social persuasion. Being cheered on by others can lead to the belief that someone can in fact perform the task successfully. We need cheerleaders in our social environment to persuade us that by perseverance we too can accomplish the task successfully.

4. Psychological responses. Essentially, Bandura stressed that our own psychological and emotional states, stress levels, physical reactions, and overall mood can play an important role in whether or not we feel we can perform a particular task successfully. It would be important for someone to minimize their stress levels, enhance their mood, and have control over their fears and anxieties about performing the particular task in order to successfully perform that task.

Characteristics of people who have a strong sense of self-efficacy:

1. Tend to have a strong sense of dedication or motivation to achieve a particular task.
2. Recover from their failures more quickly than do people with weak levels of self-efficacy.
3. Enjoy or welcome the challenge of mastering a particular task.

On the other hand, people who have a weak sense of self-efficacy tend to:

1. Focus on their shortcomings.
2. Avoid challenging tasks.
3. Rapidly lose confidence in their own abilities to master that particular task and others as well.
4. Tend to believe in general that they are incapable of performing tasks.

Basic Assumptions About the Self

In order to better understand the self, who we think we are, we need to accept some basic fundamental ideas about the self. The first is that the self is learned. Those beliefs that we have about ourselves make up the self-concept is learned. It is learned over time as we experience new and novel situations, interaction with others, and generally learn from others about our identity.

It is important to note that we are not born with a self-concept. Imagine that right after birth, an infant was left on a desert island. The infant grew to become a child and the child into an adult. One day a ship drops anchor offshore of the island. The people aboard the ship descend onto the island where they find the marooned man or woman. Even though our stranded adult is human, he or she would not be capable of recognizing that they were human like the ship's passengers. Now take our analogy even further. Imagine that the marooned person was able to speak English without being socialized in it. One of the ship's passengers asked the marooned person, "Who are you?" The marooned person would be incapable of answering that question. It is only through social interaction that the self can emerge and develop. There is nothing to indicate the self is a product of instinct or pure biology.

Second, because our self-concept is learned through interaction with others in our social environment, self-concepts develop through unique personal experiences. Through these unique personal experiences, no two people will have the same self-concept. Our self-concepts are developed within a social and cultural arena and therefore change as we progress through life. A person's self-concept may not necessarily reflect the way other people see him or her. Also, people "see" what they want to "see." As we travel through life, our self-concept changes as well. We often seek out information from our social environment that confirms beliefs that are already part of our self-concept. We disregard statements that are not part of our self-concept. More on this when we discuss self-confirmation bias.

Third, the self-concept is stable, but not unchanging, in the way that it is organized. The self-concept is generally orderly and structured to maintain relative stability. Change to the self-concept may change over the life course, but it is resistant to sudden and dramatic change as this would lead to a fluid personality rather than a relatively stable personality. The more important a self-statement is to the overall self-concept, the more resistant to change it is and the more it seeks out confirming rather than disconfirming information about that particular self-statement. For instance, if an important component of a person's self-concept was that they were vegetarian, the more important that would be in defining themselves and therefore more resistant to change.

Fourth, the self-concept provides stability and direction to the personality. The relative stability of the personality is largely the result of a self-concept that is not easily influenced or changed. Further, the social world is understood through the "lens" of the self-concept. The self-concept is unique to us all, we all experience that social world differently and obtain different information or experience from it. Also, the self-concept, though resistant to sudden change especially when dealing with core beliefs or self-statements, it does change over time as it traverses the life course. As we age, some of our beliefs are discarded for new ones, while other more central beliefs may be strengthened. Rarely does the personality change dramatically over the life course short of someone experiencing a life-altering or traumatic event. People tend to exhibit behaviors that are consistent with their self-concept. They try to protect their self-concept by maintaining a healthy sense of self-esteem. They are open to small changes over time, which is healthy and normal for the continuously developing and evolving self-concept.

Who am I?

The self-concept is made up of many beliefs and **self-statements**—each the result of interaction with the social and cultural environment. Some self-statements represent more core beliefs than do others. One question that social psychologists like to ask others is, "Who are you?" The "Twenty Statements Test" (Kuhn, 1960) is a simple measure designed to get people to think about core components of their self-concept by asking them to write down self-statements. Sometimes people are resistant to writing particular self-statements because they fear showing a weakness. If the exercise only serves to enlighten an individual about aspects of their true self and is kept private or only used by clinicians for diagnosing psychological issues, it can be a useful tool for self-discovery. The goal is to have respondents simply write down on paper 20 statements about who they are. Generally, those self-statements fall into one of four categories: (a) the physical, (b) the social, (c) personality traits, and (d) abstract concepts.

Physical descriptions are always the result of social interaction and are generally objective. For example, "I am short," "I am young," "I have brown eyes," or "I have flat feet," are objective self-statements that come from a general knowledge of the social and cultural arena in which a person exists. Statements about the physical self change slightly over the life course because of the changes that commonly occur as we get older. For instance, "I am middle-aged," "I am in shape" (which can often be a change in middle-age as people encounter unwanted general declines brought about by the aging process), "I weigh more than I should," or "I am a grandparent."

We also define ourselves by the **social roles** we play. For instance, "I am a father," "I am an employee," "I am a waitress," and so forth. So, the roles that we perform also find their way to the self-concept as individual self-statements about who we are. These too change as we progress through the life course as a result of starting a family or changing jobs or careers.

Personality traits are the most resistant to change as we travel through the life course, but some change does occur and can often be a good thing because it may mean personal growth or maturity. For instance, someone might write "I am smart," "I am a good parent," or "I am attractive." While these latter statements make up part of someone's self-concept, they are more subjective because they require more feedback and comparison with others in their social environment in order to develop that particular concept of themselves. So, how does someone "know" they are smart? "Attractive?" "A good parent?" The answer is by comparing themselves to others in their social environment. However, remember that self-statements made by observation and comparison with others in our social environment are highly subjective and that just because someone may think of themselves as being "attractive" or "a good parent," doesn't necessarily make it so. If you'll remember, the self often resists or ignores feedback from the environment that doesn't support that self-concept and the individual self-statements that make up the self-concept, so just because someone has developed a self-concept that includes beliefs about being a good parent doesn't mean others would see he or she in that same way. A healthy mind is more willing to change their self-concept and the individual self-statements that make up that self-concept. By being open to feedback from their social environment that may allow them the opportunity to reformulate their self-concept and grow as a result.

Finally, we can also describe ourselves in more abstract ways. For instance, "I'm religious," "I'm a leader and not a follower," or "I am empowered."

Self-awareness and the Potential for Growth

As previously discussed, we tend to seek out situations and information that reinforce those components that already are part of our self-concept and try to avoid situations where those components might be challenged. Both people with low and high self-esteem do this. However, people with low self-esteem respond by immersing themselves in a new social arena in which they believe those components of their self are stronger and better than are others that make up the new social environment. People with high self-esteem, while they still may enter into a new social environment (e.g., make new friends), they are more likely to respond to the self-esteem threat by trying to improve that particular skill or component of the self-concept. Generally, people tend to engage in self-awareness in order to understand themselves better after some tenant negative experience with their environment that has the potential to damage someone's self-esteem and alter the overall self-concept. However, and especially in low self-esteem people, if the negative event is severe enough, and causes them to doubt their performance or that component of the self-concept, they may become depressed. Depressed people may involve themselves in self-destructive acts because of the negative experience thus reducing their self-awareness--at least temporarily. However, it should be noted that in order to stop self-destructive behaviors it is necessary to be self-aware. In the emotionally healthy individual, dealing rather than avoiding the self-awareness is associated with growth and development.

**Theoretical Understandings of Socialization
and the Development of the Self**

As a sociological concept worthy of study, **socialization** is relatively new. The study of socialization first became popular as a sociological research subject as a result of the work by C. Wright Mills (1916 – 1962). Prior to his work,
socialization was simply part of work that theorized the development of the social self. Because of this, the understandings of socialization have varied through the years. Each associated with particular theoretical approaches.

Role Theory

Role theory suggests that socialization is the response by humans to their social world in which everyone has a role or roles to play. It is during the socialization process that people begin to adapt the **norms**, **values**, **attitudes**, and **behaviors** associated with the specific roles they are expected to hold. Role theory, with George Herbert Mead's development of the self and the "generalized other," is also a key component of another topic we will discuss later, social reproduction (Faris, 1937).

Internalization Theory

Largely formulated by Talcott Parsons (1902-1979) internalization theory suggests that people internalize a system of rules to be used in their association with others. Internalization theory is associated with theories of **cognitive development**. People construct a cognitive framework in stages and with which they use to guide their interactions at the various levels of social organization (e.g., the family, school, the community). For instance, internalization theory would suggest that children learn "**expressive symbolism**." That includes norms and role behaviors that are used in their interactions with others. Parsons believed that it is during this period that children learn moral codes and develop a conscience.

Symbolic Interactionism

Two major tenets are:

1. We use symbols in our daily interactions with others.
2. Those symbols have shared meanings.

Without shared meaning or understanding the symbol has no agreed upon meaning. While many theories associated with socialization are more concerned with socialization during childhood, symbolic interactionism does not limit itself to that framework. It socialization as a lifelong process. The key process here is that the individual situations people find themselves in are interpreted in order to define their meaning. Socialization is the process by which they learn appropriate norms or ways to act within those situations.

Reinforcement Theory

Borrowing a little from psychology and Homans' Social Exchange Theory, reinforcement theory suggests that as we begin to assume new roles, we seek to negotiate that role to our advantage. In approaching new roles, we evaluate our costs and benefits in order to enhance our position as the one being socialized.

We are unique from one another in a number of ways, and those differences influence the process of socialization as it applies to us. This uniqueness can be referred to as our self; our unique identity. Before we begin looking at the overall process of socialization, let's begin with some ideas about how the "self" is formed.

Mead and the Self

The "self" is what George Herbert Mead (1863 – 1931) referred to as self-awareness. Mead was a sociologist credited for being the main contributor to the development of social interactionism. He believed that we developed our self-identity through interactions with other people. Further, Mead proposed that we develop our self as we progress through three stages of development. Those stages are:

1. Preparatory Stage. This stage occurs during the first several years of life. This is when the child begins to mimic the actions of others in his social world. Children in this stage are unable to understand what the actions mean, but by mimicking the actions of others, they begin to develop as actors in a social world.

2. Play Stage. In the play stage, occurring between the years of two and six, children begin to model the roles of others who are close to them (e.g., parents, siblings, grandparents). It's at this point that they begin role-play; which allows them to see themselves as others might see them.

3. Game Stage. In the final stage, the game stage, occurring in children aged seven years and older, children have mastered the ability to mimic the behaviors of others for given roles and the ability to act out those roles with an understanding of what those roles mean. Also, in this final stage, children learn their roles while continuing to act out the roles of others much as someone would when playing a game. During this stage the child takes on the role of the generalized other and thus learn the "rules of the game" when that game refers to the values, beliefs, and rules of their culture.

Cooley and the Looking-Glass Self

Charles Cooley proposed another prominent theory that explains the development of our social self. He outlined his theory in his book "Human Nature and the Social Order (1902)". That theory is called the looking-glass self. Cooley was a prominent philosopher and social psychologist who believed that our sense of self develops from interactions with others in our social world. Cooley emphasizes the importance of **feedback** from those interactions. Using that information or feedback, humans begin to modify their self-perceptions. Cooley identified three stages that are involved in the development of the self. Those are:

1. Stage 1: We imagine how others see us. In this first stage, humans imagine how they appear to others.

2. Stage 2: We imagine how others are judging us. In this second stage, humans evaluate the feedback they get from others about who they are and compare that feedback with how they view themselves.

3. Stage 3: We react accordingly. In the third stage, if humans accept the imagination that others have of them, they will react positively or negatively and act accordingly. In other words, if people imagine others in their social world look at them positively in regard to some aspect of their self, that component of the self will be reinforced and internalized; on the other hand, if he/she imagines people think about them negatively in regard some component of their self, they might feel ashamed that others feel about them in that way and that might change that part of their self in order to avoid negative feelings.

Klaus Hurrelmann and the Self and Personality

Klaus Hurrelmann. In his book titled, "Social Structure and Personality Development", Hurrelmann proposes that socialization is entirely tied to a person's personality development. The theory suggests there are two "realities" to the self: (1) the inner reality, which is composed of mental traits, and (2) external reality, which refers to the social and physical environment. In his theory, Hurrelmann proposes that the developing self wrestles with the developmental tasks particular to the groups to which he or she belong. Whether a person is successful in self-development is dependent on the social, physical, and personal resources that are available to him or her. Within all the developmental tasks the self is expected to perform, is the need to work out a personal fit between personal individuation and social integration. If successful, the individual has developed what Hurrelmann called the "I-Identity" (Hurrelmann, 2009).

Erikson and his Psycho-Social Stages of Development

Erik Erikson (Erikson, 1950) developed his psycho-social stages of development and noted that these changes occurred throughout the life course. They are:

1. Stage 1: In infancy children learn to trust.
2. Stage 2: Children struggle with autonomy versus doubt (i.e., of their abilities).
3. Stage 3: Preschool children attempt to work out the difference between initiative and guilt (i.e., was I wrong to have done what I did?).
4. Stage 4: In pre-adolescence, children must work out the difference between industriousness and inferiority (i.e., can I master what I set out to do?).
5. Stage 5: In adolescence, teenagers must work out the conflict of identity versus confusion (i.e., who am I? Do I know who I am?).
6. Stage 6: In young adulthood struggle to work out the relationship between intimacy versus isolation.
7. Stage 7: In middle adulthood people work to make their mark—to make a difference in some way.
8. Stage 8: In later life people must work out the challenge of integrity versus despair.

Kohlberg's Stages of Moral Development

Lawrence Kohlberg's Stages of Moral Development (Snarey et al., 1985). Kohlberg developed a theory of moral development that consisted of three stages. They are:

1. Stage 1: Pre-conventional stage. In this stage children see the world in terms of pain and pleasure; moral decisions are largely worked out as children wrestle with their experiences.
2. Stage 2: Conventional stage. Adolescents and adults work to accept society's definitions of right versus wrong. It is during this stage they begin to explore the consequences for obedience or disobedience.
3. Stage 3: Post-Conventional stage. The highest stage of development and not everyone reaches it. This is when a person is able to think more abstractly and make judgments about right or wrong regardless of how society has done so. Abstract ethical principles are used when making decisions involving morality

William James and the Self as a Process of Identification

James believed that we develop emotional ties with objects and thus identify with them. When we emotionally identify with those objects, they become integrated into the "me." Consequently, the self is in a constant state of flux as these emotional components themselves change. Those things with which we identify eventually will come to represent the basis for making statements about our self. And from that comes the idea that we are constantly evaluating our self-worth.

Self-serving Bias

Two weeks ago, you made a D on an exam in your chemistry class. You would have made a better grade if you'd gotten more sleep the previous weekend or if you hadn't helped a friend move. It was just out of your hands. Your D wasn't your fault—it was because of things that just happened to you and you had no control over. Fortunately, today you were just handed back the exam you took last week. You made an A. Outstanding work! As the old saying goes, hard work pays off. And you did just that. You spent hours studying for the exam. Are these really accurate explanations for why you did well on one exam and poorly on another? The answer is probably not. They are more likely to be examples of self-serving bias.

So, what is a self-serving bias? To talk about self-serving bias we first need to talk about something called locus of control. Locus of control refers to where people attribute the cause of events. There are two polar opposites on a continuum representing causal events: external, where people believe the cause is in the environment and beyond their control, and internal, where they feel the cause or outcome is in their control. When people favor an internal locus of control, they believe their successes are found in their own efforts—e.g., hard work, persistence and perseverance. On the other hand, if they have an external locus of control, they would likely believe their successes or failures are due to luck or external factors beyond their control. On the other hand, people with an internal locus of control they might be more likely to have a self-serving bias.

Self-serving bias is where someone takes credit for the positive outcomes that take place in their life but believe that the negative events in their life are the result of outside influences like luck, chance or deliberate prejudicial acts by others.

Research has shown that generally there are two reasons people use a self-serving bias: one, they want to enhance their self-image to boost their self-esteem, and two, to enhance the perception others have of them (i.e., their self-presentation).

Enhancement of someone's self-image is necessary to preserve their ego. By attributing positive outcomes to their abilities and negative outcomes to outside influences like luck, chance or prejudicial treatment by others, allows someone to maintain a positive self-image, which is important for their overall presentation of themselves thus maintaining their self-worth and ego maintenance. So, if someone were to receive a bad grade on an exam, they might blame the professor for giving a bad exam or deliberately giving them a bad grade because the professor doesn't like them, allows someone to still consider themselves a good student and protects them from harm to their ego, self-image, and their presentation of self.

Irving Goffman wrote about the presentation of self in everyday life. The idea is that we work, using symbols, to maintain the image others have of us based on the image we have of ourselves. In other words, we work so that others see us as we see ourselves. So, using the previous example, if someone thinks of themselves as being a good student, it is important that others see signs that you are a good student—good study habits, good exam scores, seem to know course material and being able to help others with understanding course concepts. So, if someone who sees themselves as a good student, and works to get others to see them in the same way, would need to dismiss a bad exam score in order to maintain their self-image and the image others have of them as a good student. They might do this by saying the exam contained bad questions, their roommate played loud music all night when they were trying to study, or the professor doesn't like them and deliberately gave them a bad exam score. In these ways their self-image is maintained as well as their image in the eyes of others. Interestingly enough, someone who might have a poor impression of themselves—low self-esteem, poor self-image, might do just the opposite—they may believe that good things that happen to them are the result of luck or chance but believe that the negative events that occur in their life are the result of their poor performance or inability.

Gender and age are associated with self-serving bias, but the research is difficult to interpret. Many studies have attempted to answer the question whether males or females are more likely to exhibit self-serving bias, but the research is mixed (Mezulis, 2004). Age seems to be more clearly associated with self-serving bias in that older people tend to be less prone to having a self-serving bias. It is thought that older people are less likely to have a self-serving bias because of experiential and emotional factors that are associated with older adults. Also, it's possible that seniors are more likely to have a more objective and accurate view of themselves when evaluating traits that are associated with self-serving bias.

As we interact with our social environment, we seek out information that enhances or preserves our self-esteem. As social creatures, we have a tendency to perceive ourselves favorably. In a study by Gentile et al., 2010) researchers found college students were more likely to rate their self-esteem as the highest possible on that scale. As we act in our social environment, we tend to evaluate our successes as indications that our positive thoughts about our self are correct and well-founded. That means our successes are thought to be the result of abilities and efforts (Campbell & Sedikides, 1999). We are successful because we are good at this or that, our self-esteem is protected and even furthered, and this leads to positive self-esteem. On the other hand, we explain our failures or shortcomings on the environment or external factors beyond our control. Imagine someone mentally trying to explain why they did well on a test. They would likely have self-statements like, "This proves that I am smart, a good student, and take my studies seriously." Now imagine that same person trying to explain a poor test grade: "This proves that the professor doesn't like me." or "I wasn't able to study well because my roommate kept disturbing me," or "It was a bad test."

The danger of self-serving bias is that it is just that, a biased view of themselves and events and behaviors in their social environment. Are we truly better than the average person? No. Research has found that when husbands and wives were asked who provided most of the childcare, half of all married men said they did about half of the childcare, but their wives reported that their husbands only averaged around one-third of the childcare (Galinksy et al., 2009). Research also has found that most people think they are more intelligent, better looking and less prejudice than the average person (Public Opinion, 1984; Watt & Larkin, 2010; Wylie, 1979).

Research has shown that culture has a part to play in self-serving bias. Here in the West, we tend to practice individualism which lends itself to self-serving tendencies. This means that people in the West place a greater value on competition and therefore individual abilities, so we are more prone to protecting our egos and self-image from damage by having a self-serving bias. On the other hand, in Asian cultures, which are more collectivist, people are less prone to self-serving bias and see successes and failures as a result of communal forces. Therefore, in Asian cultures people are more likely to blame failures on the lack of particular skills and successes on luck or chance.

Does self-serving bias have any benefits? The answer is yes. If one believes that their failures are due to external influences and not their own traits, they are more likely to persevere to achieve a specific goal. Whereas if someone feels that they failed because they see their failure as their own fault, they are more likely to give up and not pursue a particular goal.

Conclusion

The self-concept is constructed over the life course. It is not stagnant and therefore changes as we travel through life. The self is formed in much the same way as we form opinions about others in our social environment. We often infer our characteristics from thinking about our observed behaviors but are more likely to attend to those situations that confirm to strong components of our self-concept. In that sense, the development of the self-concept is heavily biased and can often be one-sided, which is often the case in people with low self-esteem.

In developing and maintain our self-concept, we look for coherence as this potentially adds stability to the self-concept. But when attempting to find evidence of coherence in our self-concept, we often limit the information about particular aspects of the self by selectively remembering those situations and behaviors that reinforce the self-concept. This is done by completely disregarding the importance of situations or behaviors that do not allow for a coherent self-concept, and by focusing on components or traits of the self that are subjectively considered positive representations of the self-concept.

Self-esteem, an important part of the self-concept, is largely motivated by our need to evaluate ourselves in positive terms. As we make comparisons with others, we subconsciously try to remember more situations that allow for positive esteem and remember fewer situations that might reduce or damage our self-esteem. Further, we often engage in activities in which we think we would perform well to bolster and solidify our level of self-esteem. Having an accurate view of ourselves is important, but that doesn't necessarily mean we strive for it objectively--though people with high self-esteem are more likely to work harder when they fail some activity or behavior so that they may perform better in the future. This confirms their self-esteem or even enhances it. In fact, people with high self-esteem are far more likely to see challenges as ways to grow and improve. Further, high self-esteem can protect us against stress and threats to the self.

We will revisit the self when we investigate attribution theory later in this book.

Terms and Concepts to Know

Self
Self-awareness
Self-concept
Self-serving bias
Privately self-aware
Publicly self-aware
Self-consciousness
Private self-consciousness
Public self-consciousness
Self-schemas
Scripts
Confirmation bias
Narcissism
Self-efficacy
Social modeling

Social persuasion
Self-statements
Social roles
Personality traits
Socialization
Norms
Role behaviors
Values
Attitudes
Cognitive development
Expressive symbolism
Preparatory stage
Play stage
Game stage
Feedback
Erikson's Psycho-Social Stages of Development

References

Bandura, A. (1977). *Social learning theory.* Englewood Cliffs, NJ: Prentice Hall.

Boden, J., Fergusson, D., & Horwood L. (2008). Does adolescent self-esteem predict later life outcomes? A test of the causal role of self-esteem. *Development and Psychopathology*, 20(1), 319-339.

Bushman, B., & Baumeister, R. (1998). Threatened egotism, narcissism, self-esteem, and direct and displaced aggression: Does self-love or self-hate lead to violence? *Journal of Personality and Social Psychology*, 75(1), 219-229.

Campbell, W., Bosson, J., Goheen, T., & Kernis, M. (2007). Do narcissists dislike themselves "Deep Down Inside?" *Psychological Science*, 18(3), 227-229.

Campbell, W. & Sedikides, C. (1999). Self-threat magnifies the self-serving bias: A meta-analytic integration. *Review of General Psychology*, 3(1), 23-43.

Cooley, C. (2009). *Human nature and the social order.* Cornell University Library. First published in 1902.

Erikson, E. H. (1950). *Childhood and society.* New York: Norton.

Faris, E. (1937). The social psychology of G.H. Mead. *American Journal of Sociology,* 43(8), 391-403.

Fenigstein, A., Scheier, M. F., & Buss, A. H. (1975). Public and private self-consciousness: Assessment and theory. *Journal of Consulting and Clinical Psychology,* 43(4), 522-527.

Galinsky, A., Fast, N., Gruenfeld, D., & Sivananthan, N. (2009). Illusory control: A generative force behind power's far-reaching effects. *Psychological Science,* 20(4), 502-508.

Hurrelmann, K. (1988). *Social structure and personality development: The individual as a productive processor of reality.* Cambridge University Press.

Kuhn, M. (1960). Self-attitudes by age, sex and professional training. *Sociological Quarterly,* 1, 39-56.

Mezulis, A., Abramson, L., Hyde, J. & Jankin, B. (2004). Is There a Universal Positivity Bias in Attributions? *Psychological Bulletin,* 130(5), 711-747.

Mills, C. (1959). *The Sociological Imagination.* Oxford University Press, London.
Orth, U. & Robins, R. (2014). The Development of Self-Esteem. Current Directions in Psychological Science, 23(5), 381-387.

Rochat, P. (2003). Five levels of self-awareness as they unfold early in life. *Consciousness and Cogniti*on, 12, 717-731.

Rosenberg, M., Schooler, C., Schoenbach, C., & Rosenberg, F. (1995). Global self-esteem and specific self-ssteem: Different concepts, different outcomes. *American Sociological Review*, 60(1), 141-156.

Salmela-Aro, K., Aunola, K., & and Nurmi, J. (2007). Personal goals during emerging adulthood: A 10-year follow up. *Journal of Adolescent Research*, 22(6), 690-715.

Turner, J., Hogg, M., Oakes, P., Reicher, S., & Wetherell, M. (1981). *Rediscovering the social group: A self-categorization theory.* Oxford/New York: Blackwell.

Twenty Statements Test (TST) and Guidelines. Retrieved April 23, 2018 from http://www.angelfire.com/or3/tss2/tst.html

VanDellen, M., Campbell, W., Hoyle, R., & Bradfield, E. (2011). Compensating, resisting, and breaking: A meta-analytic examination of reactions to self-esteem threat. *Personality and Social Psychology Review*, 15, 51-74.

Watt, S. & Larkin, C. (2010). Prejudiced people perceive more community support for their views: The role of own, media, and peer attitudes in perceived consensus. *Journal of Applied Social Psychology*, 40(3), 710-731.

Chapter 5: Attitudes and Behaviors

Attitudes are positive or negative evaluations of another person, an idea, or object. Normally attitudes are either positive or negative and depending on the theory, involve different components. Social psychologists believe that there are attitudes that are deliberately formed, and these are called **explicit attitudes**, and some attitudes are subconsciously formed, and these are called **implicit attitudes**. It is more common than not that people are often unaware of their subconscious implicit attitudes.

Further, attitudes can also be defined as learned habits. **Habits** are learned as a response to stimuli we experience in our social environment. So, attitudes are more than just positive or negative **conscious or subconscious beliefs**, they have other characteristics and those include: (1) the importance of the attitude relative to the individual, (2) the certainty of the attitude, (3) how excessive build the attitude is to memory, and (4) the knowledge that attitude is associated with.

Attitudes serve variety of different functions, sometimes they are **utilitarian** and they serve as a means to an end, sometimes they are the result of knowing something about other people, an object, or their social environment, and they also tend to be ego-defensive. **Attitude formation** is influenced by many things including learning about some new phenomenon, a personal experience, and they are also formed by simple observation. Once formed, attitudes guide our actions and responses to our social world. As it fits into the theory of symbolic interactionism, attitudes help us define social reality.

While everyone has attitudes about objects, other people or their environment, people do differ in their need to develop and form attitudes. The majority of people are able to evaluate and thereby form attitudes about things that exists in their social environment, even though they may have limited knowledge about that thing or object. So, it should be noted that even though many people have attitudes about things, objects or other people in their social environment, that does not mean they have extensive or even accurate knowledge about those things, objects or people.

Generally, once formed by values, which are relatively fixed beliefs about many things, attitudes are then formed and are then referred to as symbolic attitudes. **Symbolic attitudes** tend to be resistant to change while **instrumental attitudes** are relatively simple in nature because they are simply about costs and rewards associated with a particular attitude.

Attitude Formation

There are a number of ways that attitudes can be formed. First, simple exposure to some neutral object could lead to a positive attitude. For instance, imagine when you've tried your first cup of coffee. For most people, their reaction is neither positive or negative. But now imagine if in your workplace you took a morning and afternoon break where coffee was freely available. And many of your co-workers drink coffee on those breaks. Overtime as you begin to drink coffee because they are drinking coffee, you might come to have a positive attitude about coffee. So, repeated exposure to some kind of object can lead to a positive attitude about that object.

Attitudes can also be the result of **classical conditioning**. For instance, associating some kind of neutral stimulus with an object and that object provokes a negative attitude, over time that same neutral experience provokes the same negative attitude. This is often associated with the development of prejudice. In other words, if John has a negative experience with a person of his **outgroup**, the neutral stimulus which may be skin color, facial appearance or color of hair, could then in itself provoke a negative attitude which is associated with a prejudice.

Other theories that address attitude formation include **self-perception theory**, which suggests that behaviors can create attitudes over time. Up until this point, we have looked at the idea that the development of an attitude could lead to the performance of a behavior, but with self-perception theory a person performs some behavior that then creates either a positive or negative attitude. Self-perception theory advocates that most people do not spend a great amount of time thinking about their attitudes. They are not very **introspective**, and so for many attitudes, we are unaware of them. In time as we perform specific behaviors, we begin to realize what our attitude towards that specific behavior is. Of course, you find this theory most applicable to far more neutral attitudes than to more important or more salient attitudes. For instance, "I guess I must like coffee because I routinely drink it when I'm on break with my coworkers." So, in the end, an attitude can evoke a behavior, but a behavior can also evoke an attitude (see Figure 1).

The functional approach to attitudes maintains that we develop attitudes to address or satisfy a specific need. Consequently, we develop positive attitudes towards objects for which we are often rewarded, and negative attitudes towards objects for which we are often punished. Further, we develop attitudes towards

Figure 1. Attitudes lead to action and action leads to attitudes.

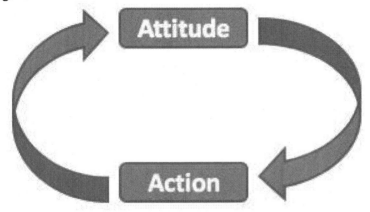

things that help us understand the world around us and make sense of it all. This last feature allows us to develop a sense of stability. On the other hand, sometimes we develop positive attitudes towards things or events that keep us from realizing some unpleasant truth about ourselves or something we do: "Yes, I smoke, and I realize that smoking is associated with cancer, but I'm different from most people and while they may develop cancer, I won't." We also develop attitudes about things that are related to our self-concept in some way. "I'm a good American. I hang the American flag outside on July 4th, which proves that I'm a good American."

Attitudes and Behaviors

Behavior can also affect attitudes. **Reinforcement** or punishment that is associated with that behavior will likely result in a positive or negative attitude. For instance, behavior that is rewarded is far more likely to be repeated then behavior that is punished. In such cases where the behavior was rewarded, it is likely to result in a positive attitude towards that behavior. Conversely, behavior that is punished likely results in a negative attitude towards the behavior and decreases the likelihood of that behavior being repeated. Likewise, attitudes about certain behaviors can be learned through simple observation and not necessarily the result of someone performing the behavior. In other words, through simple observation people know what kinds of behaviors are rewarded in our social environment and what kinds of behaviors typically are punished.

Unfortunately, knowing someone's attitude is not a good predictor of their behavior of something relevant to the attitude. There are many reasons that attitudes do not **correlate** well with behavior, and we will cover several theories that attempt to explain that discrepancy. The simplest explanation is that the reason our expressed attitudes don't predict

Figure 2. The way the attitude behavior link should work.

Figure 3. The way the attitude behavior link really works.

behavior well is because both the attitude and the behavior are subject to other influences. For instance, if someone proudly proclaims to be a member of a particular political party, we would naturally assume that he or she would vote. But what if his or her spouse, or other family members took the opposing political side of the fence? Could that lead to him or her not voting? Yes. Also, when speaking of the actual behavior, voting, might something keep them from voting? Might they say to themselves, "Ah, my one vote won't make a difference anyway," in which case they don't vote. So, even though the attitude would suggest they would perform the specific behavior, there are both intrinsic and extrinsic reasons why their attitude might not predict their behavior.

There are other factors that influence whether the attitude is correlated with behavior including the strength of the behavior has been shown to be correlated with behavior but only when the attitude is very strong. The strength of an attitude would include components of the amount of knowledge someone has about the object of the attitude, the degree to which someone is personally involved with the object, and whether or not the specific attitude is the result of an interaction with the object of the attitude--i.e., first-hand experience. Also, attitudes that someone thinks about routinely are more likely to influence behavior than attitudes that are rarely thought about and thus not that important.

Ajzen and Fisbein's Theory of Reasoned Action

Ajzen and Fishbein (1967) developed a **theory of reasoned action**. The theory attempts to explain behavior while investigating the three factors they postulated determined voluntary behavior.

1. A person's intention to perform a specific behavior was enough to actually predict whether someone would perform a specific behavior. The model offered a specific condition under which knowing a person's intent to perform a behavior required that both the intention and behavior be highly specific with no room for ambiguity.
2. They also maintained that the time from the expressed intent to behave an action and the actual performance of that specific behavior be highly controlled in order to achieve "stability."
3. Finally, the third requirement for the model was that the performance of the behavior was voluntary and within the person's control.

Ajzen (1991) went on to modify the theory of reasoned action to a new model that included the addition of another requirement, that the person feels as if they have control over the behavior. Ajzen's model included three components involved in attitude formation (see Figure 4): behavioral processes, affective

Figure 4. Ajzen and Fishbein's theory of reasoned action.

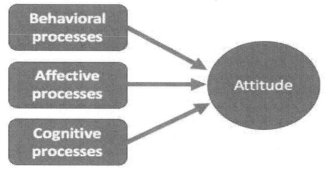

processes, and cognitive processes. The behavioral component would be to simply look at someone's behavior in a given situation or with some object about which they would be expected to have an attitude. Affective processes would involve emotional components, which could be any number of things. For instance, how does the object or situation make me feel? What do my significant others and friends think about the object or situation? Cognitive processes are aimed at thinking about the object or situation more logically and with the idea of whether the object or situation was good or bad in some relevant way.

Theory of planned behavior asserts that attitudes influence behavior by shaping intentions. The idea is that the immediate cause of behavior is **behavioral intention**, which is in turn influenced by (a) attitude, (b) subjective norms, and (c) perceived behavioral control. The main premise of this theory is that a person's intention is the main predictor and influencer of the attitude. If a person intends to do something, then they will more than likely do it. If they do not intend to do a behavior, then they will more than likely not do it (Ajzen & Fishbein, 1970). The three components explained are:

> **1. Attitude toward the behavior.** Determinants of attitudes refers to a person's belief about the consequences of performing a particular behavior. In other words, people evaluate the possible consequences of performing the behavior. The more conscious someone is of their attitude towards the specific behavior, the more likely they are to

perform that behavior.

2. Subjective norms about the behavior. What are the determinants of subjective norms? A subjective norm is a person's judgment about whether other people will approve of a particular behavior they are thinking about performing. Subjective norms about the behavior are determined by the perceived expectations of significant others (e.g., friends and family) and one's motivation to conform to those expectations. Normative beliefs are a person's perception of the pressures put on them by conventional social norms about the performance of the particular behavior.

3. Perceived behavioral control. Does someone believe that they are capable of successfully performing the behavior? It is important to note that people must believe they are capable of performing the behavior, which means they must imagine the ease or difficulty of the specific behavior. If after assessment about the difficulty of performing the task they believe they can perform the behavior successfully, have a strong sense of self-efficacy and are
more likely to perform the behavior.

Figure 5. Ajzen and Fishbein's elaborated theory of reasoned action (1974).

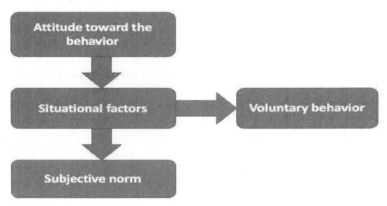

Criticisms of Ajzen and Fishbein's models include:

1. Is the person capable of accurately assessing their ability to successfully perform the specific behavior? If someone is not capable of accurately
2. Imagining whether they can perform the behavior successfully, the component of perceived behavioral control is greatly weakened.

Figure 6. Theory of planned behavior (1980).

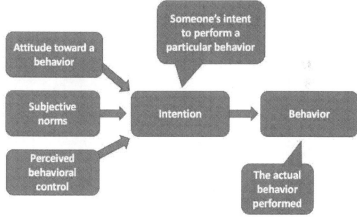

3. Are there adequate and sufficient resources for the person to carry out the planned behavior?
4. Ajzen and Fishbein's model cannot explain unintentional, spontaneous or irrational behavior.

Exchange Theory

George Homans (1961) based his model of **social exchange theory** in part on the previous works of Thibault and Kelly (1959) and Kelley and Thibault (1978). Homans defined social exchange as any action where the exchange of information, affect, or any activity was either rewarding or non-rewarding. Homans posited that people entered into dyadic relationships where tangible or intangible things could be exchanged between them. In deciding whether to enter into the exchange relationship, Homans argued that people looked at three components: (a) their potential for reward, (b) the potential cost of the exchange, and (c) whether they were likely to profit from the exchange (calculated simply by subtracting potential cost from potential reward and if the latter exceeded the potential cost, a prediction of profit would be made).

Therefore, Homans believed his social exchange model could be used to predict whether someone would perform a specific action based on the person's estimate or whether they

Figure 7. Example of the theory of planned behavior.

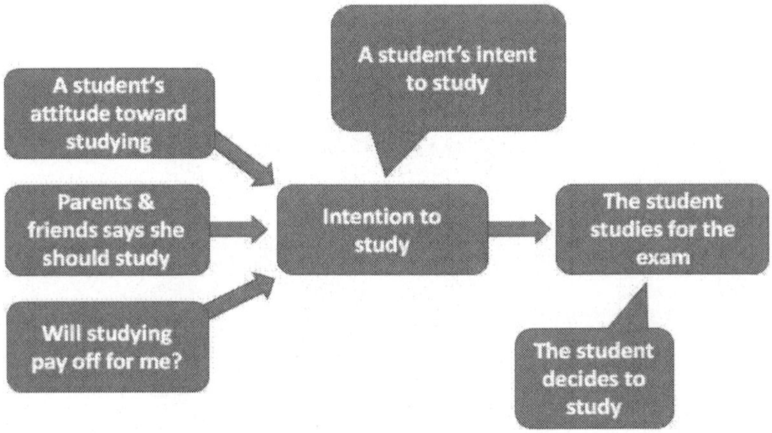

A student's intent to study

A student's attitude toward studying

Parents & friends says she should study → Intention to study → The student studies for the exam

Will studying pay off for me?

The student decides to study

would profit by performing the exchange or behavior. While his model has 13 propositions, the most prominent of them, the success proposition, suggests that if people perform an activity and come away feeling profited, they are more likely to repeat the exchange. Homans' model suggests that we can rationally predict whether someone will perform a specific action (i.e., exchange) if: (a) they have predicted the initial exchange will profit them, and (b) they will repeat the action if they were rewarded for the first action/exchange.

Peter Blau (1964) in his exchange theory to explain the attitude behavior link, came up with a model that incorporated both Homans' social aspects of exchange and combined them with economic aspects of exchange. Blau suggests that rewards are the key to knowing whether someone will perform a specific behavior. When specifically looking at an enjoyable activity, and one that someone has the capability to perform, in other words the behavior is within their control, **Blau's exchange theory** predicts that people are more likely to perform some activity they enjoy if two primary conditions are known: (a) will there be intrinsic and (2) extrinsic

Figure 8. Homans' social exchange theory.

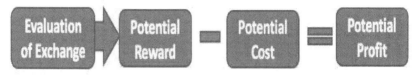

Figure 9. Homan's success proposition: having profited leads to another exchange.

Figure 10. Homan's success proposition: not having profited doesn't lead to another exchange.

rewards for the performance of the behavior. In this case, intrinsic rewards might be "I would enjoy doing it," "it allows me to feel good about myself," and other intangible benefits. **Extrinsic rewards** are tangible--like being paid. Figure 12 below illustrates the model. Exchange theory suggests that if someone believes they will be intrinsically rewarded, and extrinsically rewarded, they will likely perform the activity.

Figure 13 shows an example of exchange theory put into action. Someone is considering driving for Uber. So, they consider their potential intrinsic and extrinsic rewards. Even though there might not be an external reward, because they enjoy meeting new people, we could make the argument that meeting new people serves as an **intrinsic reward**, and therefore they are intrinsically motivated to perform the action or behavior. Then they think about the extra money they could earn by driving part-time for Uber. So, that obviously serves as an extrinsic reward, which then provides extrinsic motivation for the behavior. According to Blau's exchange theory, we would then predict this person would, assuming he met Uber's criteria for being a contractor for them, become a driver for Uber.

Figure 11. Using Homans' model to predict behavior.

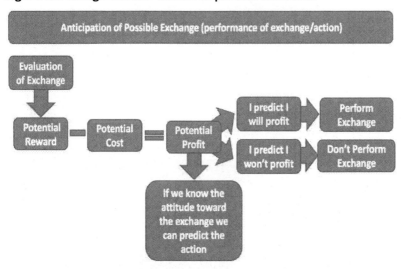

Figure 12. Intention to behave enjoyable activities within a person's control based on Blau's model to predict behavior.

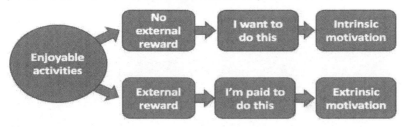

Now, let's take this one-step further. So, if someone thinks they would enjoy delivering Meals on Wheels, they would think about their intrinsic and extrinsic rewards for the action. Obviously, the intrinsic reward would be that delivering Meals on Wheels would support their self-concept in that they are selfless and a

108

charitable person. But what about the extrinsic reward? People aren't paid for delivering Meals on Wheels--it is voluntary.

Figure 13. Example of Blau's exchange model to predict behavior.

Remembering Homans (1961) social exchange theory might be helpful here. Does an extrinsic reward necessarily have to be money, gifts, or tangible goods? No. In this case, we could make the argument that the extrinsic reward might be that others, significant others and friends, would know he or she was delivering Meals on Wheels and knowing that enhances their opinion about their self as a good person.

Cognitive Dissonance

Have you ever bought something and then experience **"buyer's remorse"**? In other words, regretted the purchase? If so, you experienced cognitive dissonance. **Cognitive dissonance** is a state of mental discomfort. Imagine your brain like two people squaring off to fight about who gets the last flat screen TV at Walmart on Christmas Eve. Now imagine your brain preparing to duke it out. One will lose and one will win. For the most part, your brain doesn't really care who wins, it just wants the fight to be over so that the stress or discomfort it is feeling goes away. That's cognitive dissonance from a non-clinical perspective.

Cognitive dissonance theory suggests that people are motivated to keep their cognitions organized in such a way so that they are organized and consistent. When cognitions are consistent, the brain is in a tension-free state, which is the desired normative state. Sometimes however we develop behaviors that are not consistent with our attitudes and sometimes we develop attitudes that are not consistent with other attitudes. This leads to a state of tension and distress--in other words, a state of cognitive dissonance exists. The theory suggests that when the discrepancy between conflicting attitudes

Figure 14. Cognitive dissonance theory. Dissonance between attitudes.

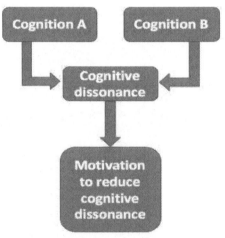

or attitudes that are not consistent with behaviors are significant or strong, the brain, as it tries to reduce the tension, explores different ways to bring things back to their normally consistent and balanced state.

The problem with the theory is that while theories relating to instrumental conditioning should apply, they don't. Those theories suggest that we would have greater motivation to rebalance our cognitions the greater the reward, but cognitive dissonance research has found just the opposite. In one classic study, students in a social psychology class were given an assignment. The class was divided into two groups. Both groups were given a message that they were required to pass on to as many people as they encountered and was judged not to be

Figure 15. Example of cognitive inconsistency that leads to behavioral change.

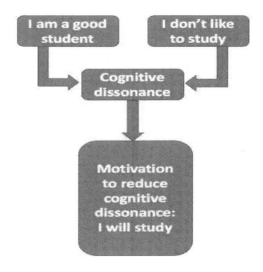

accurate or objective. In other words, it was a lie. The lie itself was not overly strong, but nevertheless it was still a lie.

One group was given $20 to pass along their message to others, while members of the other group were only paid $1 to do the same thing. At the end of the week, the instructor asked students of both groups what they thought about their message. The group that was paid $20 to tell their lie to others, laughed it off and experienced no discomfort or cognitive dissonance as a result having passed along an obvious lie. No doubt every member of the group considered themselves to be honest, so having to go around telling others an obvious lie should have created a state of tension or cognitive dissonance, but very few students in the first group said they were uncomfortable about having told a lie.

Students in the group that were paid $1 to spread their message surprisingly reported little discomfort or cognitive dissonance. When the instructor began to ask those students how they felt about spreading their message, in other words spreading a lie, they became defensive. A majority of the members of the second group made statements that indicated they believed that their message was in fact not a lie. They believed what they had told others during that week was in fact the truth.

Evaluating the different attitudes between the two groups as to how they felt about having told what was an obvious lie led researchers to conclude that cognitive dissonance had occurred in the second group, but not the first. Researchers explained it by writing that all students in both groups identified themselves as honest people in a survey given to them before the research had begun. However, they believed for the first group, the group that was paid $20 to spread their lie, experienced no cognitive dissonance because the reward of $20 outweighed their self-concept of being an honest person. On the other hand, the group that had been paid $1 to tell a lie, and considered themselves as honest people, developed cognitive dissonance because $1 was not enough to justify them telling an obvious lie. So, to reduce the dissonance, they reorganized their cognitions and came to the belief that the lie was in fact not a lie. This allowed them to maintain their self-concept of being an honest person. In other words, as far as one's psyche goes, $1 was not enough to go around telling a lie, but $20 was.

The aforementioned dissonance was between attitudes and behavior, but sometimes attitudes can be in conflict with one another. The way I began this discussion is a good example. If you bought something and then developed buyer's remorse, which is cognitive dissonance between attitudes or attitudes and behavior depending on the elements of the purchase, you were in a state of discomfort. Chances are excellent that you found a way to reduce your dissonance. What kinds of things could you have done to reduce your discomfort with the purchase? Maybe you were able to return the purchase. Maybe upon re-evaluation of the purchase you decided that you got a better deal than you originally thought. Maybe you upgraded the quality of the item your purchased so that again, you convinced yourself you got a good deal. Or maybe you decided that you could make more use of the item than you had originally thought, so there again, you made a good purchase. If it was a large purchase, such as a car, you might reduce your dissonance by comparing prices that you would have paid at other dealerships and hopefully finding out that you would have paid more elsewhere. Also, imagine a friend says to you one day they need to look for a new car and asks if you have any recommendations. There's better than a decent chance you

Figure 16. Revised model of cognitive dissonance.

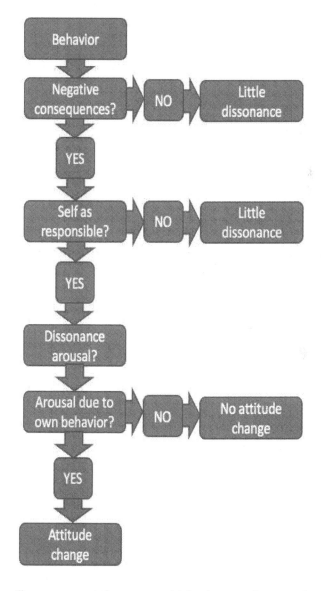

will recommend the same vehicle that you just purchased. It's called validation--feeling better about a decision we've made by trying to get others we know to make the same decision. It reinforces our belief that we made the correct decision. One way or

Figure 17. Example of cognitive dissonance caused by dissonant attitude and behaviors and that leads to attitudinal change.

another, you will almost certainly find a way to justify the purchase because you need to reduce your cognitive dissonance.

Cognitive dissonance theory states that being forced into a belief or action does not produce cognitive dissonance in people whose attitudes don't support what they're being forced to accept. Cognitive dissonance can only exist when the action was voluntary. People who freely accept an attitude that is counter to their existing attitude or behavior will almost certainly experience more cognitive dissonance than those who feel they're having a belief or behavior forced on them. Because of this, people who freely adopt a dissonant attitude or behavior will develop greater cognitive dissonance, and the greater the cognitive dissonance a person experiences the more likely there will be attitudinal or behavior change to reduce the dissonance.

Figure 18 would be another example of attitude change resulting from cognitive dissonance. Imagine a new husband and father's self-concept that includes the self-statement, "I am a conservationist and believe in global warming." His wife wants him to buy a new Chevy Suburban, and while he has some attitudes that are in favor of buying a new Suburban, pros, he has some attitudes as a conservationist against buying the new Suburban, cons. He is experiencing a state of cognitive dissonance. He is in a state of discomfort and wants to reduce it because it is causing him distress. He must make a decision that restores balance.

In the above case, the new husband and father finds more, or more heavily weighted, reasons to buy the Suburban thus reducing the cognitive dissonance he feels because he is an environmentalist buying a big gas-guzzling and polluting vehicle.

Heider's Balance Theory

Fritz **Heider's balance theory** (1958), like cognitive dissonance theory, is another example of a scientific model that attempts to explain attitude change. Also, like dissonance theory, balance theory suggests that humans seek cognitive consistency between attitudes and between attitudes and behavior. We seek to maintain that balance, which usually is to maintain the attitudes we have already developed, over time.

The model investigates the relationship between three components: the person whose viewpoint we wish to analyze (identified as "P"), another person (identified as "O"), and some "thing," which can be an object, an act, idea, or event. Heider's model says there should be balanced relationships between the three components. The unique aspect of his model is that it is essentially mathematical. Between each of the three components is either a positive sign to indicate a pro, liking, or positive evaluation, or a negative sign to indicate a con, disliking, or negative evaluation.

Figure 18. Cognitive dissonance in action--attitudinal discrepancy.

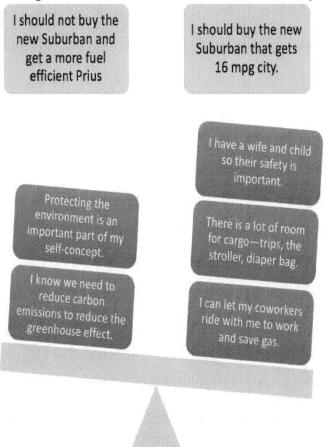

When the elements multiply out to a positive, Heider would say the elements are balanced and attitude consistency is maintained. However, when elements multiply out to a negative, Heider would say that relationships are imbalanced and that to restore balance attitude change would likely result. See Figures 19 and 21 for examples of balanced states and Figures 20 and 22 for examples of imbalanced states.

Heider attempted to explain the four-possible positive balanced outcomes in a quasi-mathematical or logical formula:

My friend's friend is my friend.
My friend's enemy is my enemy.
My enemy's friend is my enemy.
My enemy's enemy is my friend.

Figure 19. Heider's balance theory: balanced states.

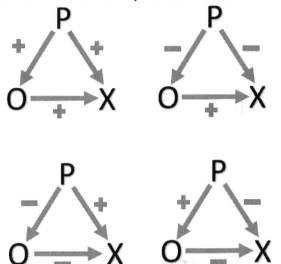

Note: Plus signs represent positive relations and negative signs represent negative relations.

In looking at Figure 21, let's say that Jim (P) likes Jane (X). Jim doesn't like to smoke (P - O). Jane doesn't like to smoke (X - O). Assuming the issue of smoking is important to Jim, this would represent a balanced relationship between Jim and Jane.

Marketers are well aware of social psychological models dealing with attitudes and behaviors like Heider's balance theory. Next time you see an actor or actress that you admire in a commercial endorsing a product, ask yourself if your opinion of the product has changed. You may not be aware that it has changed, but research has found that it probably has (Mowen & Brown, 1981).

Figure 20. Heider's balance theory: imbalanced states.

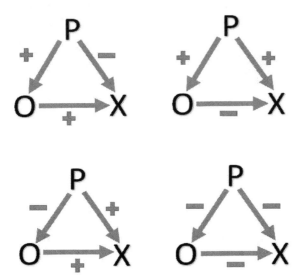

Figure 21. Example of a balanced state for Heider's balance theory.

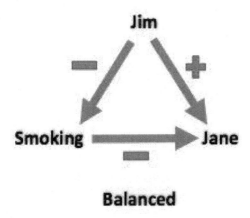

Balanced

Heider's balance theory has its critics. For instance, include that of his use of quasi-mathematical model to predict attitude change (Flament, 1963). Anderson (1979) wrote of Heider's model: "We cannot routinely identify the positive and negative lines in the formal theory with the positive and negative "sentiment relations," and identify the formal balance notion with the psychological idea of balance or structural tension."

Figure 22, by contrast, suggests say that Jim (P) likes Jane (X). Jim doesn't like to smoke (P - O), but Jane likes to smoke (X + O). Assuming the issue of smoking is important to Jim, something has to change. He can change his mind and decide to smoke, to tolerate

Figure 22. Example of an imbalanced state for Heider's balance theory.

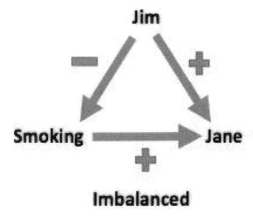

Jane's smoking, or he can decide that Jane is not right for him.

Like many aspects of social psychology, studying humans is a complex and less than a perfect science. However, while there are no laws in the social sciences, social psychology included, simply because no model or theory has yet to completely allow us to predict the attitudes or behaviors of others does not in any way deter our efforts. Research on attitudinal consistency and on the attitude behavior link has been one of the largest areas of study within the discipline of social psychology. While marketers may benefit from this particular area of social psychological research, society can benefit as well. Knowledge, even if not complete, that allows us to understand why people develop the attitudes and behaviors they do and helps us to understand ourselves better. And with that understanding, we have the potential to change social problems like prejudice, discrimination, obedience to immoral laws, and the fear that engenders conformity.

Heider also believed that there were **external attributions** made when looking at someone else's behavior. And this involves the individual saying of that other person's behavior that it was due to the situation or external events that surrounded that person but not to any internal characteristics as we've already discussed. So Heider suggested that when we attempted to explain our own behaviors, we tended to use external attributions that took into account situational factors, but that we do not do the same when looking at others and instead use internal factors to explain their behavior. These two attributions eventually lead to Heider's theory of the **fundamental attribution error**. The idea here would be if person a did well on an exam they would explain that by suggesting it was because of their work ethic, studying hard, or maybe even innate intelligence, but if someone else were to receive an A on exam they would be more likely to explain the other persons doing well on that exam by suggesting the external factors played more of a role in they're doing well, such as they are Asian and everyone knows that Asians value education and are smart-- in other words, Asians cannot help but to do well on a test because they are Asian. Nowhere in that explanation is the possibility that the Asian student who did well on the exam did so because he or she studied hard for the exam. On the other hand, if an individual did poorly on the exam, they would most likely blame it on the situation. For instance, "I did not do well on the exam because my roommate kept playing loud music and I was not able to study," or "I had to help my parents and simply did not have time to study as much as I would have liked." In other words, they are blaming the situation for their not doing well on the exam. But if that same person was asked why someone else did well on the exam they would most likely say it was because of some aspect of their personality that prevented them from doing well on the exam-- such as they're lazy, or they don't value education as much as they should. But nowhere in their explanation of someone doing poorly on the exam like themselves is the possibility that situational factors caused them to do poorly on that exam. To put this in naïve terms, it is unseen hypocrisy.

Two Routes to Persuasion

The **central route** to persuasion is most effective when the audience is intelligent, thoughtful, and thinks about the facts of the argument. They are usually unaffected by the emotional content of the message. The central route is driven by critical, relevant and logical review of the message by a review of the facts. Those who are more prone to using the central route to persuasion focus on the quality of the message and are unaffected by the **peripheral** route to persuasion in that emotional influences are irrelevant. For instance, Volvo has always emphasized the safety features of their vehicles and thus delivered the facts related to those safety feature. This is a great example of the central route to persuasion. However, for the central route to persuasion produce the intended results, which is changing someone's attitude, the peripheral route to persuasion, in other words the message, must be strong, based on facts rather than emotional cues, and appeal to the intelligent and logical tendencies of the audience.

The peripheral route to persuasion uses emotional cues to appeal to audiences prone to such appeals (Petty & Cacioppo, 1986). The peripheral route depends on the audience's preference for positive or negative emotions. For instance, while Volvo may appeal to viewers by vocalizing the safety features of its vehicles, another car company may appeal to audiences by showing a sporty vehicle with all the creature comforts available for "creature comfort." Likewise, a car company may appeal to viewers desire to have a safe car but not by listing accident statistics and survival rates of people in crashes in their vehicles, but rather show video of car crash tests that clearly show "dummies" seemingly surviving a crash. Also, celebrity endorsements are appealing to audiences that are prone to make decisions based on the peripheral route. The peripheral routes don't require audiences to think or process the message as does the central route. The route to change for the peripheral route simply requires a person's emotional reaction to the message. While the peripheral routes may promote positive emotions to the message, the research finds that such messages are less likely than the central route to result in permanent change to an attitude or behavior change.

Is a message effective? Well, it depends on the credibility of the person delivering the message, (Hovland & Weiss, 1951)and the attractiveness of the person delivering the message (Eagly & Chaiken, 1975; Petty, Wegener, & Fabrigar, 1997). People who are perceived as credible and knowledgeable about the message content, are more likely to be perceived as trustworthy and therefore more persuasive. For instance, if your instructor wanted to inform you of the fire safety issues, who would persuade your more--the local city fire chief or the president of your university?

Likewise, research has found the more attractive speakers are more likely to persuade people using the peripheral route to persuasion. This is the case when you have celebrities giving a message. For instance, television commercials for Lincoln automobiles use a very famous and attractive male celebrity in their commercials. And while this likely has increased sales of Linncoln automobiles, it is still a case the that the longterm effect of messages using the peripheral route or the central route is dependent on the credibility of the messenger (Kumkale & Albarracín, 2004).

Also, messages that are one-sided have been found to be less effective in the long run than messages that seem to present both sides of the argument. For instance, a politician who says that they agree with many of the issues of an opponent, are more effective in their message than politicians who denigrate the issues and views of their competitors (Crowley & Hoyer, 1994; Igou & Bless, 2003; Lumsdaine & Janis, 1953);

Features of the audience that affect persuasion are attention (Albarracín & Wyer, 2001) and intelligence (Festinger & Maccoby, 1964). Also, research has found that for a message to be accepted, and therefore the audience persuaded to accept a new attitude or behavior, they must be paying attention and concentrating on the message and this is obviously more true of those persuaded by the central route to persuasion. Not surprisingly, audiences with lower intelligence are more easily persuaded by peripheral route messages whereas people with higher intelligence are more likely persuaded by the central route message (Rhodes & Wood, 1992).

Elaboration Likelihood Model

A model that looks at the components of persuasion is called the Elaboration Likelihood Model of Persuasion which was designed by Petty & Cacioppo in 1986. The **elaboration likelihood model** investigates the source of the message, the message contents, and the intended audience. This then leads to a somewhat successful prediction of the success of a message and which route to persuasion the audience will employ. Again, the point of this model is to predict attitude and behavioral change.

Figure 23. Elaboration Likelihood Model of Persuasion.

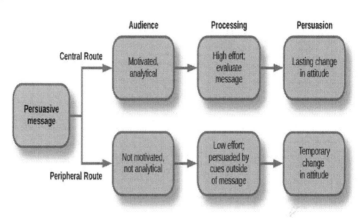

Terms and Concepts to Know

Attitudes
Explicit attitudes
Implicit attitudes
Habits
Conscious beliefs
Subconscious beliefs
Utilitarian
Attitude formation
Symbolic attitudes
Instrumental attitudes
Classical conditioning
Outgroup
Ingroup
Self-perception theory
Introspective
Reinforcement
Correlate
Affective processes
Behavioral processes
Cognitive processes
Ajzen and Fishbein's theory of reasoned action

Ajzen and Fishbein's elaborated theory of reasoned action
Ajzen and Fishbein's theory of planned behavior
Social exchange theory
Reward
Cost
Profit
Blau's exchange theory
Intrinsic rewards
Extrinsic rewards
Buyer's remorse
Cognitive dissonance
Heider's balance theory
P-O-X

References

Ajzen, I. (1971). Attitudinal vs. normative messages: An investigation of the differential effects of persuasive communications on behavior. Sociometry, 34, 263-280.

Ajzen I. (1991). The theory of planned behavior. *Organizational Behavior and Human Decision Processes Volume,* 50(2), 179-211.

Ajzen, I., Darroch, R., Fishbein, M., & Hornik, J. (1970). Looking Backward Revisited: A reply to Deutscher. *The American Sociologist,* 1970, 5, 267- 273.

Ajzen, I., & Fishbein, M. (1970). The prediction of behavior from attitudinal and normative variables. *Journal of Experimental Social Psychology*, 6, 466- 487.

Ajzen, I., & Fishbein, M. (1973). Attitudinal and normative variables as predictors of specific behaviors. *Journal of Personality and Social Psychology*, 27, 41-57.

Ajzen, I., & Fishbein, M. (1974). Factors Influencing Intentions and the intention-behavior relation. *Human Relations*, 27, 1-15.

Ajzen, I., & Fishbein, M. (1977). Attitude-behavior relations: A theoretical analysis and review of empirical research. *Psychological Bulletin*, 1977, Vol. 84, No. 5, 8-918

Ajzen, I., & Fishbein, M. (1980). *Understanding attitudes and predicting social behavior*. Prentice-Hall.

Albarracin, D., & Wyer, R. S. (2001). Elaborative and nonelaborative processing of a behavior-related communication. *Personality and Social Psychology Bulletin, 27*(6), 691–705.

Ames, D. L., & Fiske, S. T. (2010). Cultural neuroscience. *Asian Journal of Social Psychology, 13*(2), 72-82.

Blau, P. (1964). Justice in social exchange. *Sociological Inquiry*, 34(2), 193-206.

Crowley, A., Hoyer, D. (1994). An Integrative framework for understanding two-sided persuasion, *Journal of Consumer Research*, Volume 20, Issue 4, March 1994, Pages 561–574.

Draganski B, Gaser C, Busch V, Schuierer G, Bogdahn U, May A. (2004). Neuroplasticity: Changes in grey matter induced by training. *Nature, 427*:311–312.

Eagly, A. H., & Chaiken, S. (1975). An attribution analysis of the effect of communicator characteristics on opinion change: The case of communicator attractiveness. *Journal of Personality and Social Psychology, 32*(1), 136–144.

Festinger, L., & Maccoby, N. (1964). On resistance to persuasive communications. *The Journal of Abnormal and Social Psychology, 68*(4), 359–366.

Flament, C. (1963). Applications of graph theory to group structure. Prentice-Hall Series in *Mathematical Analysis of Social Behavior*, Englewood Cliffs, N. J.

Gardner, W. L., Gabriel, S., & Lee, A. Y. (1999). "I" value freedom, but "we" value relationships: Self-construal priming mirrors cultural differences in judgment. *Psychological Science, 10*(4), 321-326.

Gutchess, A. H., Welsh, R. C., Boduroĝlu, A., & Park, D. C. (2006). Cultural differences in neural function associated with object processing. *Cognitive, Affective, & Behavioral Neuroscience, 6*(2), 102-109.

Han, S., & Humphreys, G. (2016). Self-construal: a cultural framework for brain function. *Current Opinion in Psychology, 8*, 10-14.

Han, S., & Northoff, G. (2008). Culture-sensitive neural substrates of human cognition: A transcultural neuroimaging approach. *Nature Reviews Neuroscience, 9*(8), 646-654.

Hedden, T., Ketay, S., Aron, A., Markus, H. R., & Gabrieli, J. D. (2008). Cultural influences on neural substrates of attentional control. *Psychological Science, 19*(1), 12-17.

Heider, Fritz (1958). *The Psychology of Interpersonal Relations*. John Wiley & Sons.

Homans, G. (1961). *Social behavior: Its elementary forms*. New York: Harcourt, Brace & World.

Hovland, C. I., & Weiss, W. (1951). The influence of source credibility on communication effectiveness. *Public Opinion Quarterly, 15,* 635–650.

Igou, E., & Bless, H. (2003). Inferring the importance of arguments: Order effects and conversational rules. *Journal of Experimental Social Psychology*, 39:91-99.

Jiang, C., Varnum, M. E., Hou, Y., & Han, S. (2014). Distinct effects of self-construal priming on empathic neural responses in Chinese and Westerners. *Social Neuroscience, 9*(2), 130-138.

Kelley, H. H., & Thibault, J. W. 1978. *Interpersonal relationships: A theory of interdependence*. New York: John Wiley.

Kitayama, S., & Uskul, A. K. (2011). Culture, mind, and the brain: Current evidence and future directions. *Annual Review of Psychology, 62*, 419-449.

Kitayama, S., & Park, J. (2010). Cultural neuroscience of the self: understanding the social grounding of the brain. *Social Cognitive and Affective Neuroscience, 5*(2-3), 111-129.

Lumsdaine, A. A., & Janis, I. L. (1953). Resistance to "counterpropaganda" produced by one-sided and two-sided "propaganda" presentations. *Public Opinion Quarterly, 17*, 311–318.

Maguire E., Gadian D., Johnsrude I., Good, C., Ashburner J., & Frackowiak R. (2000). Navigation-related structural change in the hippocampi of taxi drivers. *Proceedings of the National Academy of Sciences*, USA. 97:4398–4403.

Markus, H. R., & Kitayama, S. (1991). Culture and the self: Implications for cognition, emotion, and motivation. *Psychological Review, 98*(2), 224.

Mezulis, A., Abramson, L., Hyde, J., & Hankin, B. (2004). Is there a universal positivity bias in attributions? A meta-analytic review of individual, developmental, and cultural differences in the self-serving Aatributional bias. *Psychological Bulletin*, 130(5), 711-747.

Mowen, J., & Brown, S. (1981). On explaining and predicting the effectiveness of celebrity endorsements. *Advances in Consumer Research*, 8, 437-441.

Obhi, S. S., Hogeveen, J., & Pascual-Leone, A. (2011). Resonating with others: the effects of self-construal type on motor cortical output. *Journal of Neuroscience, 31*(41), 14531-14535.

Park, D. C., & Huang, C. M. (2010). Culture wires the brain: A cognitive neuroscience perspective. *Perspectives on Psychological Science, 5*(4), 391-400.

Petty, R., Wegener, D., & Fabrigar, L. (1997). Attitudes and attitude change. *Annual Review of Psychology*, 48:609-47.

Petty, R. & Cacioppo, J. (1986). The elaboration likelihood model of persuasion. *Advances in Experimental Social Psychology*, 19:123-205.

Rhodes, N., & Wood, W. (1992). Self-esteem and intelligence affect influenceability: The mediating role of message reception. *Psychological Bulletin, 111*(1), 156–171.

Tang, Y., Zhang, W., Chen, K., Feng, S., Ji, Y., Shen, J., & Liu, Y. Arithmetic processing in the brain shaped by cultures. *Proceedings of the National Academy of Sciences, 103*(28), 10775-10780.

Thibaut, J. W., and Kelley, H. H. (1959). *The social psychology of groups*. New York: John Wiley & Sons.

Varnum, M. E., Shi, Z., Chen, A., Qiu, J., & Han, S. (2014). When "Your" reward is the same as "My" reward: Self-construal priming shifts neural responses to own vs. friends' rewards. *NeuroImage, 87*, 164-169.

Zhu, Y., Zhang, L., Fan, J., & Han, S. (2007). Neural basis of cultural influence on self-representation. *Neuroimage, 34*(3), 1310-1316.

Chapter 6: Socialization and Social Interaction

Socialization and Interaction

Many people think that socialization is a process that only applies to children, but that's not true. **Socialization** is a lifelong process. Through socialization we learn about the **social roles** that we are expected to follow. Consequently, we develop a sense of **self** and a sense of **self-knowledge** that is shaped over our lifespan and in turn shapes how we see and interact with the world.

One of the most famous studies that investigated the relationship of socialization and **social interaction**, was done by the husband-and-wife team of Harry and Margaret Harlow. The Harlow's took baby monkeys and divided them into two groups, one group was left with their biological mothers the other group was given to a surrogate mother constructed out of wire. The latter group of monkeys was given all the necessities that they needed to survive, such as food, water and warmth. When the experiment concluded, the research was indisputable: the monkeys that have been raised by wire mothers developed a significant range of abnormal behaviors.

Another example on the long-term consequences of **social isolation** is research done by René Spitz (Spitz, 1945). René Spitz looked at children who have been removed from the biological families for one reason or another. Some children were placed in foster care, but because of a lack of room, some children had to be placed in nursing homes. You can imagine the very unhealthy environment in which those children were raised. Care was provided by nurses whose primary job was to take care of elderly patients and not to provide care to infants. Approximately one-third of the children raised in nursing homes died and another one-third lived in mental institutions for most of their lives, as they were incapable of functioning physically and mentally on their own. The research concluded that a lack of social interaction has significant and long-term consequences on the infants.

A very famous case of poor or absent socialization happened in 1797 when Victor, a so-called "**feral child**" was captured in France. He was incapable of speaking, had numerous scars on his body, and lacked any social graces. A medical student by the name of Jean Marc Gaspard Itard took an interest in Victor and began to work with him and even allowed him to live in his house. Gaspard believed that there were two characteristics that separated animals from humans: **empathy** and language, neither of which Victor demonstrated. After working with him for quite some time Victor was able to learn one word. It was the word for milk. Itard was disappointed with this outcome. However, one day Itard had come home to find Victor attempting to comfort his housekeeper who had recently lost her husband. Itard saw this as an example of empathy. In the end, Itard was not able to demonstrate that Victor was in fact human as opposed to a feral animal. Victor died in 1828 in Paris. Controversy still exists about the case. Some researchers believe that Victor was not a feral child, but rather he was the victim of an abusive father and had run away. The existence of a feral child, raised by animals, has never been proven.

Severe social isolation that makes interaction impossible, contributes to poor **social development**. Depending on the severity and duration of the isolation, long-term consequences can be severe and even lead to death. For example, in 1970 an elderly woman walked into a social services agency with a 13-year-old

Figure 1. "Genie" the feral child.

girl. The girl was emaciated, pale, walked in a strange manner, and was unable to speak. Workers got suspicious and began asking questions. What they found out astonished them. At the age of four, Genie's father was so convinced she was mentally retarded that he confined her to her room. During the day, she was chained to a potty chair, and at night she was put into a crib with a chicken wire top that kept her from climbing out. Genie remained in that

130

state of isolation for nine years—from the age of four until the age of thirteen.

Social workers began working with her intensely to repair the emotional and intellectual damage done by the years of isolation. They named the girl "Genie" in order to keep her real identity confidential. At first clinicians were successful when working with Genie and she learned a few words she could speak, and her walking greatly improved. However, after several years Genie stopped learning and in fact regressed to an earlier stage. As of this writing, Genie is still alive, but because she is incapable of living independently, she has lived in a nursing home since shortly after she was rescued.

In another similar case that occurred in 1999, a man grew suspicious and called the police because he had not seen his neighbor's young daughter for several years. When the police investigated, they found the girl, who was age six at the time, chained to her bed and confined to her bedroom, which she had been since the age of two. The girl used the corner of her bedroom as a latrine. Conditions were appalling. Once removed from the home, clinicians began working with the girl in an effort to repair the emotional and intellectual damage that had been done by the social isolation. Unlike with Genie, results were much better, and while the girl is capable of living independently, some emotional and cognitive damage remain. Psychologists believe the reason they were successful in the latter case, but not in Genie's, is because of the age difference when rescued. Significant brain changes occur in children around the age of 10, and those changes affect the way we learn. Genie had gone past that developmental window, whereas the other girl had not.

Social interaction involves the shared experiences through which we relate to other people. How we relate to other people to a large degree is shaped by a **perception** of who they are in relation to us. It is also affected by the meanings that we attach to other people's actions. Social interaction is affected by **status**, the **normative actions** we expect from others, and even our **cultural values**.

Types of Social Interactions

There are different types of social interactions. They are:

131

1. Exchange. When two or more people exchange something–for example, material goods, advice, and affect, it is a type of social interaction. Of all the reasons for social interactions, exchange is by far the most common. People interact with each other because they have things to exchange, tangible or intangible.

2. Cooperation. An example of cooperation is when two or more people work together to reach some shared goal. In other words, people feel that they must cooperate to achieve their mutual ends, but by so doing they are interacting.

3. Conflict. When two or more people compete for the same goal, or reward, or scarce resources, that type of interaction is called conflict.

4. Coercion. Finally, coercion is using illegitimate authority to get something from others. If I were to demand that a student get me coffee, and threatened to fail them if they didn't, that would be an example of coercion because I have no legitimate authority to demand a student get my coffee.

Goffman's Dramaturgical Model

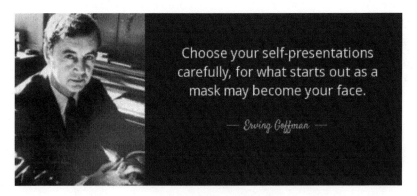

Choose your self-presentations carefully, for what starts out as a mask may become your face.

— Erving Goffman —

Erving Goffman (1922-1982) believed that humans work to manage the impressions others have of them through to interactions in their social environment in an effort to preserve and protect their self-concept. He proposed what is referred to as the dramaturgical model. It is called the dramaturgical model because like the actor who performs a role on stage but then returns to his or her home where he or she can relax in preparation for the next show, humans manage the impression others have of them when they are "**on stage**" or "**front stage**" and let their guard down and don't work as hard or even at all to manage the impressions others have of them when they are "**off stage**" or "**back stage**." It is in this way that Goffman believed that we humans were like actors on stage playing a part, but that once we were off stage, we no longer had to work to play that part (Goffman, 1958).

Goffman believed that our **self-presentations**, in other words when we're on stage, are carefully constructed and monitored. These self-presentations when we're on stage are represent conscious and manipulative attempts to manage others' impression of ourselves in order to enhance or protect the image we have of our self. The tools we use to manage the impression others have of us when we're on stage include **false modesty**, **self-promotion**, demonstrations of **competence**, **ingratiation**, and other actions or behaviors that promote the image of the self the person wants others to see and accept.

In working to manage the impression others have of us, Goffman said we **interpret symbols** to do so. Let's say that you think of yourself as a courteous person. Because you want others to think of you as you think of yourself, a courteous person, you work to manage your impression by saying, "Please," "Thank-you," "You're welcome," or "After you." Here's another example. Let's say a friend of yours named Jake gets a job interview for an assistant manager position at the local bank. Jake asks you what he should wear. Knowing that banks are conservative institutions, you tell Jake he should wear a dark suit, a crisp shirt, a light-colored tie, and dress shoes. You're a little concerned about his pony-tail and nose ring, so you suggest that he might want to have his hair cut and lose the nose ring. Knowing what you do about banks, you have helped Jake "dress the part," in other words, to help him give off the impression that he is professional and conservative. Jake calls you later and thanks you because he got the job. Pat yourself on the back, you have just helped Jake manage his impression.

Symbols

Next, we need to talk about symbols. There are three primary things we need to mention about symbols. First, *a symbol is anything that conveys meaning*. For instance, let's say I was sitting at my desk. If I were to pound on my desk, my hand would hurt. The desk is real, it is made of wood and wood is real. But my use of the words "desk" and "wood" are symbolic. A tree is real but the word "tree" is symbolic. Words are great examples of symbols, but certainly not the only ones.

Figure 2. Why is she crying?

Second, *symbols are interpreted contextually*. Because symbols always represent something else, they are contextual. In other words, they are interpreted with the situational context in mind. For instance, let's use tears as our symbol we need to interpret. Tears are real but the act of crying is symbolic.

For instance, imagine going to the wedding of a good friend of yours. As you sit in the pew waiting for the wedding to start, you notice a woman several rows up who is obviously crying because she is dabbing her eyes with her handkerchief.

While her tears are real, they are symbolic because now we have to ask the question why is she crying? In that situation or context, which in this case is a wedding, we would likely interpret her tears to be tears of joy. She is excited for her friend who is getting married. So, *we interpret symbols*, but because we interpret

Figure 3: Why is she crying?

symbols interpretations can sometimes be wrong. What if the reason this young woman is crying isn't because she's happy about her friend getting married but rather unhappy that her former boyfriend is the one getting married?

So, the tears again are real but the act of crying is symbolic and therefore up for interpretation. To take this example one step further what if after the wedding you were walking across the park to get to your car. As you walked across the park you noticed a young woman sitting on a park bench who was crying. Just like the woman at the wedding, she is shedding tears. Would you interpret her tears in the same way that you interpreted the tears of the woman at the wedding? Of course not, because the context has changed. Now, in the latter case, you would be far more likely to interpret the young woman's tears as an indication she was sad or unhappy, but certainly not as tears of joy. So, symbols are interpreted contextually. Third, *symbols define the situation*. A symbol can be anything that conveys meaning, and that meaning is derived from the context, symbols may define a situation.

Encounters

Erving Goffman called focused interactions an encounter. **Encounters** are separated by what Goffman called **brackets** (Goffman, 1961). Brackets help us understand when a **focused**

interaction begins and ends. For instance, can you think of ways that you would acknowledge the beginning of an interaction with a friend? One of the most common ways is to simply say, "Hello." Likewise, one of the most common ways to end the interaction is to say, "Bye." These are examples of brackets. There could be many examples of brackets. However, not everyone says hello and goodbye, but usually people have something symbolic in either their words or actions that signal to the other party that the interaction is over. Along with this are the subtle nonverbal cues that we may give people we are interacting with that we wish to end the interaction. A good example might be, "I've got to go study for an exam." It would be expected that the person with whom you are engaged in conversation understands that you need to end the interaction, which then would leave it up to them in most situations to say something to the effect of, "Okay, I'll talk to you later." But sometimes that doesn't happen. Sometimes you could be engaged in interaction with a friend that doesn't pick up on those subtle cues that you want to end the interaction. Have you ever been in that kind of situation? How have you handled it? Another good example would be that of telemarketers. When a telemarketer calls, and because we don't know who it is when we answer the phone, we say "Hello," and by doing this we have signaled that the interaction (i.e., a bracket) has begun. After they begin their scripted speech, and you realize he or she is a telemarketer, you look for a way to end the interaction. Unfortunately, you realize they have a script so they can counter anything you say to end the interaction. You want to end the interaction, but you have been taught that it is rude to just hang up the phone. So, you keep repeating, "I'm sorry, but I'm just not interested." At some point one of two things will happen: either they finally accept your desire to end the conversation, or you simply press the button on your phone and end the call.

So, this latter situation would be a good example of differences in brackets—saying "hello" was a bracket indicating the beginning of the interaction but hanging up the phone while the telemarketer was still talking served as a bracket saying that the interaction was over.

Focused Versus Unfocused Interactions

As we move further into talking about interactions, we need to talk about two specific types that have to do with our **situational awareness**. **Unfocused interaction** refers to that mutual awareness that people have of one another in large gatherings even though they may not directly be involved in conversation. For instance, let's say you walk into a party, there are many people at the party, and most are talking to other people. The room is filled with conversation, but you are not directly involved in any of those conversations—you simply know that they are occurring. That would be an example of an unfocused interaction. On the other hand, a **focused interaction** is when two or more people are directly attending to what another person is saying. So, let's say that you are now at that same party and you see a friend. You walk up to the friend and begin to talk to them—you are now engaged in a focused interaction because your attention is now on the conversation occurring between you and your friend.

Channels of Communication: Verbal and Non-Verbal

Verbal Communication

Social interaction involves **nonverbal communication** as well as **verbal communication**. Verbal communication requires both language and para-language, whereas nonverbal communication involves such things as body language, eye contact, and facial expression. When we speak of nonverbal communication, the first thing we need to identify is called channels of communication. Channels of communication has to do with the way that symbols are communicated or interpreted to define the situation.

Let's start with **verbal symbols**. There are two types: **Language**, words and spoken language represent language, and **para-language**, which is the way that words are spoken.

Language

The words coming out of your mouth as you speak to others obviously fall under the category of language. But all language is symbolic in that those individual words you are speaking have no real meaning in themselves--words are entirely symbolic in that they always represent something else. So, while you may be speaking about the construction of a new building, the words spoken to describe the construction process, the purpose the building, where the funds to build it are coming from, and how it will add to the mission of the larger company or entity, the words are symbolic for those components. Words are just words. Maybe the old expression summarizes this best: actions speak louder than words--the actions may be concrete, real and measurable in some way, but the words used to describe those actions are just words-- symbols to represent those actions.

Para-language

Now that we understand that words are just symbolic, we need to move and discuss how words are interpreted. Because words are symbolic, they are always interpreted because they represent something else. For instance, are the words spoken quickly or slowly? Are the words spoken with a shaking or quivering voice? What about if someone speaks with a thick accent? If you wanted to work as a news anchor at the national level, you would learn very quickly that a deep southern accent or a thick New York/New Jersey accent has to go. Why? Because our society does not interpret those accents positively. On the other hand, Americans love the British accent (Kitching, 2014). Also, people who speak quickly often do so because they are stressed (Siegman et al., 1990), and that stress is something others can pick up on, and when combined with a loud voice, can produce anger or fear in a listener. On the other hand, someone who speaks slowly projects a calming effect on others who are feeling anxious. If you were a car salesman, would you rather speak softly and slowly or loudly and quickly? So, while pace of speech, accent, or whether someone stammers and shakes as they deliver a sentence may not necessarily tell us anything by themselves, when combined with spoken words, they may be used to define the situation, whether that situation is defined correctly or not.

Non-Verbal Communication

Nonverbal symbols include two categories the first is body language, which in itself includes body movement, facial expression, eye contact, civil inattention, marking our territory, and interpersonal distance, and the second is physical characteristics.

Figure 4. Both of these men have their arms crossed, but would we interpret this to mean the same thing in both cases?

Body Movement

Body movement is often interpreted in our society. The way someone stands, folds their arms, crosses their legs, or even slouches, all represent actions that are interpreted. As an example, in our culture, how would we interpret someone talking to us with his or her arms crossed? Generally, we would regard that action as indicating the person is defensive or resistant to questioning.

Facial Expression

When we interpret what someone is verbally saying, we usually scrutinize their face. Again, we need to know whether they are telling us the truth. The **survival value hypothesis** states: "attending to facial expressions allows people to predict behavioral intentions and understand how others are interpreting the world. This hypothesis predicts people will be most attentive to facial expressions that signal potential danger" (Pinker & Bloom, 1990).

Figure 5. Culture can also influence on how body language is interpreted.

Figure 6. Susan Smith pleading with the kidnapper of her two young boys for their safe return.

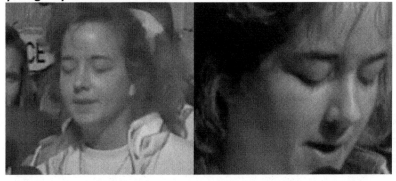

Eye Contact

Eye contact is also very important in our culture. We expect others to maintain eye contact with us when we are engaged in focused interactions. For someone not to maintain eye contact when asked an important or telling question might suggest they are lying or at the very least covering something up. When Susan Smith gave an emotional plea on TV in October of 1995 to the man who car-jacked her car and kidnapped her two sons who were in the car at the time, at no time during her speech did she look at the camera. As she begged and pleaded to the kidnapper, identified by her as a black man, her eyes were always cast down as if she was reading from a script, but there was no script. Only later was it proven that Susan Smith made up the story about the kidnapping of her two young children to cover up the fact she had murdered them in cold blood by allowing her car to roll into a lake with the children still strapped in their car seats--all because she wanted the man she was having an affair with didn't want children.

Figure 7. Susan Smith at her conviction in 1995 for the murder of her two sons Michael and Alexander.

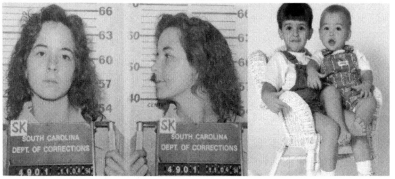

Marking Our Territory

The final component of body language is marking our territory. Dogs may mark their territory by peeing on things, but fortunately humans do not. However, we do still mark our territory just in different ways. Students in a classroom will sometimes have their books, notebooks, computers, and purses scattered to the left and right of them on the desk beside them. By doing this they are marking their territory; in other words, they are keeping others from sitting next to them. It's as if they have a sign that says, "This is my territory. Keep away!" Or maybe you are at a theater, a concert or even attending a lecture and you put some of your personal belongings in the seat next to you. Whether you are conscious of it or not, you are marking your territory and letting others know that seat or desk space is taken. Another example might include an engagement or wedding ring. That is a signal to others that person is "taken" and "belongs" to someone else--so stay away!

Interpersonal Distance

Interpersonal distance refers to the distance we like to keep others based on their relationship to us (Hall, 1966; Moore, 2010).

Figure 8. Interpersonal distance requirements.

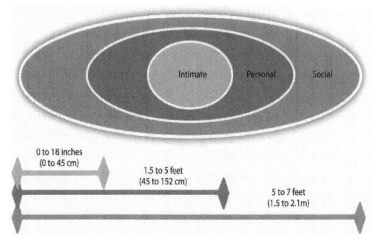

Research suggests that we Americans like to keep strangers at about six feet, friends around four feet or closer depending on the friendship, and then intimate others at around two feet or less. When this distance is violated, we may feel threatened and find a way to increase the distance. Sometimes increasing our distance as a reaction to someone getting too close to us might be automatic, you don't have to think before acting. However, sometimes there are occasions where you might have time to think about what to do if your interpersonal space is violated. If you have time to think about it before you react to the intrusion, you might want to increase the distance in a subtle way because otherwise they will know that they have made you uncomfortable and that's something you may not want them to know. Remember, their action and your reaction are both symbolic and will be interpreted. Can you imagine some situations in which you'd rather not let them know they've made you uncomfortable? Another example would include elevators. There are "unwritten" rules, scripts, when we ride an elevator with strangers. When you're riding an elevator with a stranger do you stare at them? Do you sing? Do you talk to yourself? No. The most common behavior while riding on an elevator with a stranger is staring at the control panel with the floor numbers or even staring straight ahead at the doors. If Goffman was still with us, he would probably make the argument that we do this so we can "pretend" our interpersonal space isn't being violated by being in an enclosed environment with a stranger.

Figure 9. The "script" for riding an elevator with strangers suggests that our eyes should be straight ahead, but how would we feel if a stranger on an elevator turned and stared at us?

Civil Inattention

Erving Goffman believed that as two people enter into each other's personal space, we acknowledge the other person briefly with eye contact. So, imagine walking in one direction on a sidewalk and someone is walking towards you in the other direction. Goffman suggests that for one brief part of a second both parties will acknowledge each other by making eye contact. Why is this symbolic? Because it's interpreted. Imagine a situation where you're walking on the sidewalk in one direction and someone is walking towards you in the other direction. As you lift your eyes to make that brief eye contact with the other person you notice that their eyes are glued to the sidewalk. As you get closer and closer to each other you notice in your peripheral vision that the other person never looks up from the sidewalk as they pass you. If eye contact is the symbol we are interpreting, how might you interpret the fact that they never made eye contact with you even as you entered their space? Distracted? Depressed? Low self-esteem? What if as they walked toward you on the sidewalk you noticed that not only did they make eye contact with you, but they continued to stare at you the entire time you entered each other's space and passed each other on the sidewalk? How would you interpret that? Aggressive? Sexual interest? One way or another, you will interpret the meaning of that eye contact or lack thereof.

143

Physical Characteristics

Another component of non-verbal communication is **physical characteristics**. Again, these are symbols that are interpreted. The first is our biological image. Our biological image represents those characteristics about us over which we have no control. We are born with those characteristics. Height, eye color, skin color, facial features, gender, and weight to some degree. These are things that we have no control over, but they are interpreted by others. Tall people are generally perceived to be more competent than our short people. Likewise, the research also suggests that attractive people are more favored in the workplace than lesser attractive people (Shahani-Denning, 2003; Toledano, 2013). Overweight people, according to the research, are often victims of discrimination. Research also suggests that married males are more likely to be promoted and are paid more than single males. The reason for all of these research findings is that these characteristics are interpreted, and people treat us according to those interpretations.

The number one characteristic that is associated with discrimination in the workplace may surprise you: it's gender (Verniers & Vala, 2018). The ratio of males to females in the United States is 48 to 52. As I've mentioned before, all things being equal, we should expect to see that ratio in anything we study. If we have had 44 presidents, approximately 23 or 24 of those should have been female. As we all know we have not had one female president to date. What does that suggest? Think about the last time you went to a car dealership to buy a car. How many of those sales people were female? Why would there be more males than female car sales people? Again, because gender is interpreted-women are not supposed to know about engines or anything mechanical. Would it surprise you to know that when the typewriter was first invented secretaries were males and not females, but as wages in other occupations increased males left the secretarial positions and females filled them.

Made images are those things that we have control over. We can change your hair color, we can control the type of clothes that we wear, we can choose the type of car that we want to be seen driving, or the house we live in. Again, those are all symbolic and therefore all interpreted. When symbols are interpreted and often acted upon, prejudice and discrimination may be involved. Sometimes it may seem trivial, but sometimes it is not. What is the stereotype we have about blonde women? Not overly blessed with intelligence says the stereotype. And thinking about the new car market, and without naming names, there is a particular car that you can buy new for about $14,000. If the point of a car is to get you from point A to point B safely, and the $14,000 car will do just that, why are we not all driving $14,000 cars? Why? As you sit next to a $70,000 Mercedes waiting for a light to change, how do you explain the difference between your driving a $14,000 car and they're driving a $70,000 car? Undoubtedly, you will reach the conclusion that the $70,000 car is to be interpreted as a sign of their success. So, even the cars that we drive are symbols and interpreted differentially.

Expressions given versus expressions given-off

When judging other people's self-presentations, we pay attention to two types of expressions. **Expressions given**: words and gestures that are consciously transmitted, and **expressions given-off**: *also known as nonverbal leakage*, are behaviors unintentionally transmitted.

Expressions given off are generally a better predictor of deception than expressions given. For instance, body movements such as fidgeting and shifts in body posture are good predictors among nonverbal behavior symbols. Imagine being on a job interview and you begin to sweat because you are nervous. That's not something you would like for your future employer to notice because it will likely be interpreted as you are nervous and may lack self-confidence. On the other hand, sitting up straight, eye contact maintained with the interviewer, not sweating and appearing to be calm, relaxed and comfortable almost certainly interpreted positively and as a sign that you are self-confident. Speaking with a shaky or quivering voice, an example of paralanguage, is something else to avoid because it can also be interpreted negatively as nervousness or worse as having something to hide.

The "buts"

Embarrassment and excuse-making commonly follow failed self-presentations. Using this strategy allows people to protect the impression others have of them, maintain self-esteem, and lower anxiety. Sometimes we make momentary mistakes as we manage the impression others have of us while we are on stage. Goffman says we look for excuses to justify those mistakes and to show they are just momentary lapses in the impression others should have of them and their overall impression of that person should not be altered. If someone knows in advance they may have to do or say something that may violate the impression others have of them, they might saying something like, "I normally wouldn't ask this but..," or "I normally wouldn't say this but..." In other words, they attempt to head off any potential damage to the impression others have of them by rationalizing the action in advance of that action. It's a preventative action.

On the other hand, someone might have to repair the damage to the impression others have of them after the act or comment is made, in which case they offer excuses to minimize the damage to the impression others may have of them after the fact. "You would have done the same thing if....," might be one example of minimizing the damage after the fact.

Expressions of Intimacy

Nonverbal communication, in other words, what we communicate with symbols, includes expressions of intimacy or lack thereof. The first would involve intimacy with words. As examples: Bbl versus tbl, Sie versus du, and Usted versus tu. Do you recognize any of those word pairs? All of them represent the formal form of the word "you" versus the informal form of the word "you"—first in Russian, then German, and finally in Spanish. Here in the U.S. we make no such distinction—which therefore deprives us of information that could be used to help us interpret an interaction.

For instance, imagine you were in Germany and you overheard two adults conversing on the street and they frequently used the word "Sie" as they spoke to one another. If we understand not one more word of German than the word for "you," and its formal versus informal distinction, how might we interpret the interaction between these two Germans we hear conversing on the street? How would we likely interpret their relationship? "Sie" is the formal word for "you," and "du" is the informal form of the word. So, more than likely we would conclude they were either strangers or one was perhaps a superior from their mutual workplace. In other words, that they chose to use the formal form for the word "you," was symbolic and therefore something that could be interpreted and add meaning to the situation. What if instead of two adult Germans interacting, we overheard a German child and an adult interacting and the adult kept using the informal form of the word for "you," in other words "du?" How might be we interpret that? Generally, that would suggest it was either a parent talking to his or her child or a stranger talking to a child. Again, the form of the word, a symbol, adds meaning to the situation. But "you," is not the only word for which there are formal or informal designations.

There are also special words that are symbolic and convey meaning—words that are meant for particular others but not for the general public. Being called "honey," or "darling," or "sweetie" by a waitress might not be appropriate depending on which part of the country someone is in or comes from. These are words generally reserved for significant others and therefore are supposed to hold special meaning. Imagine seeing a man and a woman in a grocery store, and the woman turns to the man and says, "Oh, honey, I forgot, could you go pick up a loaf of bread?" Because the word "honey" is symbolic, how would we likely interpret the relationship between them? Husband and wife? Boyfriend and Girlfriend? It's not likely we would think of them as strangers who just met minutes earlier while on their mutual excursions to the grocery store.

And while there is intimacy with words, obviously there is intimacy without words. Touching is the best example, but have you ever really given any thought to touching being symbolic? Imagine this scenario. You are at a party and stationed so that you have a view of the door and can see newcomers arriving at the party. In walks a man and a woman arm-in-arm. You've never seen them before, can't hear anything being said between them, but how are you likely to interpret their touching one another? Most likely you would interpret their symbolic act of walking in arm-in-arm as an indication they were together romantically. What if instead they walked in together without touching and then went their separate ways after entering the room? Strangers? Friends at best? What if after walking into the room arm-in-arm, they kissed, and as she went in one direction he went in the other. While the man walked away from her you noticed he slid his wedding ring off and put it in his pocket? How would you interpret that? Probably not positively. And while not quite touching, what about interpersonal space violation? What does it say when a man and a woman are seen sitting closely together while having lunch or dinner? Is that not interpreted as intimacy? Interestingly in Europe when a couple sits at a table or booth while having a meal, they sit side by side, but here in the US, couples are more likely to sit across from one another.

The Media and Social Interaction

Research on the impact of the media on social interaction is varied. There is no doubt that media influences our attitudes and behaviors. Media includes newspapers, magazines, television, television commercials, movies, and social media. For instance, the growth in the use of social media has been dramatic. In 2005, only five percent of the US population used social media, but in 2019 that had grown to 70 percent.

So how does social media impact our lives? Some researchers worry that social media leads to social displacement, which essentially means that it displaces face-to-face time with close friends and family. Overall, for adults, there seems to be little in the way of evidence that use of social media replaces meaningful interaction with those closest to us because we tend to keep in contact with those close friends and family members in a number of different ways--text messages, email, phone calls, and spending face-to-face time with them (Allen, 2019).

Research on social media use is less conclusive for teenagers. According to research by Common Sense Media in 2018, 81 percent of teenagers reported they used social media to keep in touch with friends and family and more than one-third used social media sites a number of times per hour. In one study (Twenge, 2016), found that high school teenagers spent "...an hour less a day engaging in in-person social interaction." She also found that students who spent less time engaging in face-to-face interactions and more time interacting with others using social media were more likely to experience loneliness. Other research (Hall, 2019) suggests that we have the chicken and egg argument reversed. Hall states that parents, educational demands, and possibly part-time work demands, restrict teens face-to-face interactions and so they use social media to make up for that lost time in face-to-face interactions with close friends and family.

While the research is varied on the use of social media by teenagers, there are both advantages and disadvantages to social media use. On one hand, it seems to be associated with self-presentation (i.e., how people work to get others to see them as they see themselves) and self-identity (i.e., the Looking Glass phenomenon that asks the question *who am I?*). On the other hand, Common Sense Media reported that 13 percent of teenagers who use social media said that they had been victims of cyberbullying, which obviously negatively affects self-esteem. Subrahmanyam (2019) reports:

> "My hypothesis is that digital interactions….[are] more fleeting and you feel good but that feeling is lost quickly versus face-to-face interaction….We tend to think about online and offline as disconnected, but we have to recognize that for youth there's so much more fluidity and connectiveness between the real and the physical and the offline and the online."

Status

Words can also symbolically represent status. Imagine a famous cardiologist who wants to reserve a table at a crowded restaurant that evening. After introducing himself as "Dr. Smith," the maître 'd accommodates him, "Well, of course Dr. Johannsen we can reserve you a table tonight at 8 p.m." even though the maître 'd just got off the phone with another potential customer who he told there were no openings at 8 p.m. What happened? Status. That's what. In our culture status can be conveyed with words: e.g., sir, Dr., Judge, Mr. President, etc.

As status can be conveyed by words, research has found that people with higher perceived status tend to talk more frequently, talk longer, talk louder, and interrupt more. Statuses are the positions we occupy in society. Positions are always going to be relative to others. For instance, your boss occupies a status or position higher than you and you may hold a status or position higher than a subordinate. At any point in our life we hold multiple statuses. For instance, if you're reading this you are obviously a student. That is a status, where on a status hierarchy, you rank higher than someone who is not a student. However, you would rank lower on that hierarchy than someone who has already graduated. What other statuses might you hold? Are you male or female? Married or unmarried? Young or old? Are you a parent? Are you Hispanic, African-American, Asian, or Caucasian? All of the aforementioned are statuses and undoubtedly several of the above apply to you—hence you occupy a number of statuses at one time.

Ascribed statuses are those that are given by society—you have no control over an ascribed status. In a monarchy, a title that is passed down from generation to the next is a great example of an ascribed status, but we are not a monarchy. On the other hand, if you are born with the last name of Kennedy, Rockefeller, or Gates, you are "given" ascribed status—people treat you differently because you are born to a recognized family name usually associated with wealth. Other ascribed statuses include race, gender, and age. Age is an ascribed status because young people rank lower on the status hierarchy than do people in their 50's, but people in their 60's or older tend to rank lower in status than people in their 50's or younger people.

The other way status is awarded is through effort. Whereas ascribed status is simply handed to someone based on certain characteristics, the other way status is awarded is through effort. For instance, while Bill Gates' children will have ascribed status, Bill Gates himself achieved his status through his own efforts. When you graduate college, that would be an example of **achieved status**—your position on that status hierarchy will be positively affected because you hung in there and earned your degree whereas other people may not have done so. Other examples of achieved status would include employee, friend, club member, etc.

Master Status

Is one status more important than others? Yes. Everyone has what is called a master status. While master statuses are the most important, a master status is determined by society and not by the individual. As I mentioned earlier, the number one reason discrimination is experienced in the workplace is because of gender. And even though gender is an ascribed status and you had nothing to do with whether you are a male or female, and though society is changing, it still places women lower on the status hierarchy than men, therefore gender may be a working woman's master status. On the other hand, the research says that married males climb to the top of the work world faster than do unmarried males—in which case marital status could be a man's master status. Again, master statuses are decided by society and not the individual.

Social Roles

Social roles are expected behaviors for people occupying specific statuses. If I were to use the example of your status as a student, I would expect that your role as student includes coming to class, taking notes, and staying awake in class. Another example might be if you were a policeman. As a policeman, I would expect your role to include obeying the law and not running red lights on your way home from work, parking in handicapped spaces, or threatening your neighbors because you didn't like the way they mowed their yard. Because we occupy a number of statuses at one time, and therefore fulfill multiple roles at the same time, we might experience role conflict.

Role Conflict

Role conflict occurs when we struggle with situations that put our roles in conflict. For instance, as a married woman with a child, you are expected to buy groceries, cook dinner, transport your children, take care of them if they are sick, and so forth. But can you see several of those roles coming into conflict? What if you have a hungry husband, a hungry child, a sick child, a clothes dryer that has just finished its cycle, and your best friend is on the phone in tears because her husband of 20 years has just left her? You certainly can't perform all the duties associated with the associated roles at one time. That's role conflict.

Role Strain

There is role strain which occurs when in a particular status there are different expectations that come into conflict with each other. For instance, what if you are a police officer and you pull someone over for speeding. Your radar gun shows the violator traveling 15 miles per hour over the speed limit. All you have to do is hand out a speeding ticket, but as you approach the violator's car you realize it's your best friend. Unfortunately, because it's on the radar, you have no choice, you have to issue the ticket, but that's not going to make your friend feel good about the friendship—in this case you are experiencing role strain.

Role Exit

Role exit is the process where you end or exit one role and start another. Divorce or widowhood would be great examples. As a newly single person someone would have to create an entirely new identity—in other words, moving from the "we" to the "I." For some this process can be difficult and lengthy.

Sapir-Whorf Hypothesis

Edward Sapir and Benjamin Wharf hypothesized that language is used to shape our perception of reality (Sapir, 1929; Whorf, 1956). Words as symbols shape our interpretations of reality. Culture uses language to shape itself, and in turn is shaped by language. The Sapir-Wharf hypothesis suggests that language is how we perceive the world. Edward Sapir and Benjamin Whorf were interested in explaining the connection between language and culture. Specifically, they wanted to investigate how our view of the world is shaped by our thoughts and how language influences our thoughts. They believed that language shaped the way we think and how we perceive the reality of our world. The most important feature of their hypothesis was that because language shapes the social reality of our world, people who speak different languages would have different views of their social world (Kennison, 2013).

As an example, let's look at how a culture's language can influence gender roles. John and Mary are best friends and have been so for most of their lives. Both of them decided they wanted to be pilots and fly for commercial airlines. So, both went to pilot school and both put in the required training. They graduated at the same time and both found jobs almost immediately with the same airline. John and Mary are still very close and will often see other at parties. Mary has noticed that when fellow party-goers talked about John they referred to him as a "pilot," but when people talked about her, they referred to her as a "female pilot." Mary wondered why people tied her gender to her job, but they didn't do the same thing to John. They performed the exact same job, so why would people refer to them differently? Mary concluded that When others referred to her as a "female-pilot" and her friend as just a "pilot," their friends were using sexist language created by their culture and this suggested that Mary was not in accord with societal views of gender roles by being a female pilot, because after all according to society, males are pilots and women are housekeepers.

Conclusion

To be human means interacting with other people. As we interact with others, we attempt to maintain a high sense of self-esteem and our self-concept intact. To do so, we manage the impression others have so that it is consistent with the image we have of our self. In doing so, we use symbols to manage the impressions others have and Erving Goffman called this the dramaturgical effect. He believed that when we were on stage we used symbols to manage the impression others have of us, but because being on stage requires a great deal of energy, he argued that like actors waiting to go on stage we needed time to recuperate and gather our resources before doing so. He referred to this time as being off stage or behind stage when we could let our guard down and not work at managing the impression others have of us because when we're off stage we are usually with close friends or loved ones where managing our impression was unnecessary.

Social interaction involves more than just communicating using symbols. It means being conscious of the many statuses we hold and the subsequent diversity of roles we play. Statuses can be earned or assigned at birth. Those statuses are always linked to what are perceived as appropriate roles that are acted out accordingly. Statuses vary in their social importance and because of that there is always one or two statuses that society considers most important. Where we fall on the hierarchy of statuses within our culture are known as master statuses. Race and gender are the two most common types of master statuses in our society. Sometimes our roles conflict with another which sets the stage for role conflict or role strain.

Finally, the Sapir-Whorf hypothesis suggests that we interpret and shape our world through the use of symbols and language is perhaps the best example of symbols.

Terms and Concepts to Know

Socialization
Social roles
Self
Self-knowledge
Social interaction
Social isolation
Feral child
Empathy
Social development
Perception
Status
Normative actions
Cultural values
Exchange
Cooperation
Conflict
Coercion
Goffman's Dramaturgical Model
Impression management
On stage/front stage
Off stage/back stage
Self-presentation
False modesty
Self-promotion
Competence
Ingratiation
Symbols
Interpretations of symbols

Encounters
Brackets
Focused interaction
Unfocused interaction
Situational awareness
Channels of communication
Verbal communication
Verbal symbols
Language
Para-language
Nonverbal communication
Body movement/body language
Survival value hypothesis
Civil Inattention
Marking our territory
Interpersonal distance
Expressions given
Expressions given-off
Expressions of intimacy
Status
Ascribed status
Achieved status
Master status
Social roles
Role conflict
Role strain
Role exit
Sapir-Whorf Hypothesis

References

Ahmet, R. (1992). Crowding effects of density and interpersonal distance. *The Journal of Social Psychology*, 132(1), 51-58.

Allen, S. (2019). Social media's growing impact on our lives. *American Psychological Association.* Retrieved January 2020 from: https://www.apa.org/members/content/social-media-research
Common Sense Media. (2018). *Social media, social life: Teens reveal their experiences.* Retrieved January 2019 from:

https://www.commonsensemedia.org/research/social-media-social-life-2018

Goffman, Erving (1959). *The Presentation of Self in Everyday Life.* New York: Doubleday.

Goffman, E. (1967). *Interaction ritual: Essays on face-to-face behavior.* Pantheon. Reprinted 1982.

Hall, Edward T. (1966). *The hidden dimension.* Anchor Books. Pp. 111-129.

Hussein, B. (2012). The Sapir-Whorf hypothesis today. *Theory and Practice in Language Studies*, 2(3), pp. 642-646.

Kennison, M. (2013). *Introduction to Language Development.* Sage.

Kitching, A., Roos, V., & Ferreira. (2014). Ways of relating and interacting in school communities: Lived experiences of learners, educators and parents. *Journal of Psychology in Africa*, 21(2), 245-256.

Pinker, S., & Bloom, P. (1990). Natural language and natural selection. *Behavioral and Brain Sciences*, 13(4), 707-784.

Siegman, A., Anderson, R., & Berger, T. (1990). The angry voice: Its effects on the experience of anger and cardiovascular reactivity. *Psychosomatic Medicine*, 52(6), 631-643.

Sapir, E. (1929). The status of linguistics as a science. *Language*, 5, 207-19.

Shahani-Denning, C. (2003). Physical attractiveness bias in hiring: What is beautiful is good. *Hofstra Horizons*, Spring 2003, 15-18. Retrieved May 17, 2018 from http://www.hofstra.edu/pdf/orsp_shahani-denning_spring03.pdf

Spitz, R.A. (1945). Hospitalism—An inquiry into the genesis of psychiatric conditions in early childhood. *Psychoanalytic Study of the Child*, 1, 53-74.

Spitz, R.A. (1946). Hospitalism; A follow-up report on investigation described in volume I, 1945. *The Psychoanalytic Study of the Child*, 2, 113-117.

Toledano, E. (2013, February 14). May the best (looking) man win: The unconscious role of attractiveness in employment decisions. *Cornell HR Review*. Retrieved May 18, 2018 from http://www.cornellhrreview.org/may-the-best-looking-man-win-the-unconscious-role-of-attractiveness-in-employment-decisions/

Twenge, J. (2013) Does online social media lead to social connection or social disconnection? *Journal of College and Character*, 14:1, 11-20.

Uhls, Yalda & Ellison, Nicole & Subrahmanyam, Kaveri. (2017). Benefits and Costs of Social Media in Adolescence. *Pediatric*s. 140. S67-S70.

Verniers C, Vala J (2018) Justifying gender discrimination in the workplace: The mediating role of motherhood myths. *PLoS ONE*, 13(1): e0190657. https://doi.org/10.1371/journal.pone.0190657

White, M. (1975). Interpersonal distance as affected by room size, status, and sex. *The Journal of Social Psychology*, 95(2), 241-249.

Whorf, B. (1956). *Language, thought and reality. Selected Writings.* Ed.: J.B. Carroll. MIT, New York: J.Wilky/London: Chapinaon & Hall.

Chapter 7: Conformity and Deviance

Setting the Stage: The Holocaust, the Salem Witch Trials, and the Native American Genocide

In 1933 Germany, Adolf Hitler became head of state of what would come to be known as Nazi Germany. Within two years, laws had been put into place denying rights to German Jews. Jews were forbidden to practice medicine, hold teaching positions at all levels in the educational system, hold political positions, marry or have sex with non-Jews, what Hitler called "Aryan Germans," and to display the Nazi flag--as if any Jew at that point would want to do so anyway. By 1938, concentration camps had been established for thousands of Jews rounded up in the aftermath of Kristallnacht and for those who opposed Nazi ideals.

In early September of 1939, on the pretense of a Polish attack on Germany, which was fabricated by Hitler, Hitler invaded and occupied the Western half of Poland while the Soviet

Figure 1. A Jewish woman and child being shot by Einsatzgruppen commando.

Union occupied the Eastern part. Jews living in the Nazi occupied were Jewish were made to wear yellow Stars of David so they could

be identified as Jews. Laws were soon passed by the Nazis and Jews were "resettled" in what became known as ghettoes. In May of 1940, Hitler invaded most of Western Europe. Then in June of 1941, Hitler invaded the Soviet Union. Now not only did all of the Jews living in the Eastern part of Poland come under his control but so did millions of Jews living in the Western Europe and the Western part of the Soviet Union that was overran by the Nazis and occupied within months of their invasion. The question became: what to do about the Jewish problem?

In January of 1942, to-ranking Nazis met in a suburb of Berlin to discuss a "solution to the Jewish problem." Though Jews in living in the Western part of the Soviet Union were being shot en masse as German Einsatzgruppen teams moved through the conquered territories, the Germans judged it to be inefficient-- especially given the millions of Jews that now lived within the territories they occupied. At that meeting in Wannsee in early 1942, it was decided the much more efficient method of killing Jews and other undesirables existed and could be put into effect within months. That method included marching unsuspecting Jews, men, women and children, into rooms where they were told to undress before they were ushered into a large "shower" room--sometimes as many as one thousand at a time. After being packed into the shower room, and the doors locked and sealed behind them, crystals of cyanide, Zyklon B, were dropped into specially constructed vents that allowed the poison to fall to the wet floor of the shower room. When cyanide is exposed to moisture it turns to cyanide--a lethal gas.

After realizing how effective the killing procedure was, and with millions of Jews living in ghettoes in Western Poland, and the hundreds of thousands of Jews living in Nazi occupied Western Europe, the Nazis put their assembly line method of murder into full gear. By the time the war officially ended in Europe in May of 1945, more than six million Jews and five million other "undesirables" had been murdered. Beginning in late 1945, high-ranking Nazis were put on trial for those murders. As they were asked to plead guilty or not-guilty, one by one they loudly proclaimed, "Nicht schuldig!"--"Not guilty!" Americans listening to the daily reports of the trials on their radios each night, could not understand how the Germans were capable of such cold-blooded murder. Each of the high-ranking Nazis claimed they were simply

Figure 2. High-ranking Nazis on trial at Nuremburg fall 1945.

following orders--orders clearly going all the way up to Hitler--who had committed suicide months earlier. Evidence was presented, video and photographic evidence, eye-witness and survivor testimony, and because the Germans were efficient record-keepers, thousands of pages of documentation were entered into evidence.

It was determined that even though they were following orders, they had a personal responsibility they failed to exercise. The orders to commit the murders were unlawful and most were found guilty and hanged for their crimes. Nazi Germany represents a good example of the dangers of both conformity and obedience. A significant number of German military personnel carried out atrocities in the name of obedience. By our standards and even those of the time were judged to be unlawful.

Most scholars agree that the Holocaust happened because Germans conformed to Nazi rule. They were motivated because they believed in Hitler's vision of a Greater Germany, the propaganda Hitler gave for Germany having lost the first world war, or they feared the consequences of not conforming to Nazi doctrine. German citizens stood by and did or said nothing as rights were taken away from Jews one by one. As their Jewish neighbors

began to disappear in the dead of night Germans looked the other way. When one U.S. soldier was asked after the liberation of Buckenwald, a Nazi concentration camp, if the German citizens of the nearby town of Weimar knew what had been going on at the camp, he responded, "They saw the trains going in but no one saw them leave. If they say they didn't know what was happening, they were lying." As Stanley Milgram said, "Behavior that is unthinkable to people acting on their own, may be executed without hesitation when we believe we have legitimately been ordered to do so" (Milgram, 1974).

As the pictures of what became known as the Holocaust were beginning to find their way into American newspapers and news segments at local movie theatres, again and again Americans asked how such a thing could have happened. Were all Germans complicit in the crimes? Didn't they know what was happening? Couldn't they have spoken out against these criminal acts? How could they stand idly by as their neighbors were dragged from their homes never to be heard from again? Why? For Americans, what happened was just incomprehensible.

The Events of Salem

A classic example of the dangers of deviance can be found in the Salem Witchcraft Trials of 1692. Allegations of witchcraft snowballed from three accusers to seven. Nineteen people were convicted of witchcraft and executed. In Salem Village, in February 1692, Betty Parris, age 9, and her cousin Abigail Williams, age 11, the daughter and niece, respectively, of Reverend Samuel Parris, 12-year-old Ann Putnam, Jr., and Elizabeth Hubbard, began to have fits that the Rev. John Hale said couldn't be caused by epilepsy.

Figure 4. Salem witch trials. Illustration from Pioneers in the Settlement of America by William A. Crafts, 1876.

The girls screamed, threw things about the room, uttered strange sounds, crawled under furniture, and contorted themselves into peculiar positions. The doctor was called and he could find nothing physically wrong with the girls. Accusations of witchcraft were leveled against Sarah Good, Sarah Osborne, and Tituba (a slave). In the case of Ann Putnam, she was probably accused because the

Putnam and Porter families were feuding and the whole community of Salem had taken sides; it was a way to get even. Sarah Good was a beggar and homeless—things that didn't go well with the ideas of the Protestant work ethic and Calvinist thought, which had affected all non-Catholic Christianity. Sarah Osborne attended church infrequently, which was interpreted as a sign that she rejected Christian beliefs, and it didn't help matters when she married an indentured servant—someone perceived beneath her class position. Tituba was a slave from the Caribbean who would tell stories of black magic to young girls as they sat around a fire at night. These girls accused her of telling them stories of demons, black magic, and witchcraft. In March of 1692, more townspeople were accused of witchcraft. Martha Corey had stated that she didn't believe the girls' accusations, but this was problematic because she was seen as a devout Christian who attended church regularly as was Rebecca Nurse, also accused. The charges against her and Rebecca Nurse were compounded by the townspeople's belief that if such upstanding people could be witches, then anybody could be a witch.

The trials began on June 2, 1692 with Bridget Bishop's case first. Bishop was described in testimony as not living a Puritan lifestyle, wearing black clothing, which was not allowed by the Puritan faith. She was convicted and sentenced to hang. She was executed by hanging on June 10, 1692. Trials immediately followed for 36 others accused of being witches and in league with the Devil. By the time the trials were ended by the Governor of Massachusetts, 19 people had been found guilty and hanged, despite pleading their innocence. Giles Corey was pressed to death with stones because he would not plead one way or the other.

The Use of Spectral Evidence

During the trials, spectral evidence was allowed in the testimony of those accusers who were "afflicted" by the Devil. Spectral evidence is when someone claims to see an apparition, which could be anything, that was interpreted as the Devil. The apparition was enough to accuse the defendant of voluntarily having allied themselves with the Devil. Only after Cotton Mather, a highly respected minister, argued against the use of spectral evidence, and the governor's own wife was accused of witchcraft, did the trials begin to lessen.

The Aftermath

There are a number of explanations for the events that occurred in Salem between February 1692 and May 1693:
1. Old feuds with disputes between the two congregations in Salem, and the new minister, Rev. Samuel Paris, was incapable of acting as a mediator between the two sides;
2. Native Americans continued to attack many English settlements up and down the East coast, resulting in a climate of fear;
3. A stage for young women to gain the attention they were denied as part of Salem's cultural values;
4. A belief that Satan was the cause of instability affecting their community—i.e., natural disasters, Indian attacks on nearby settlements, smallpox;
5. Mass hysteria;
6. A belief that Satan recruited people to work for him.

In 1695, reacting to Mather's statement, "it is better that one hundred Witches should live, than that one person be put to death for a Witch, which is not a Witch." Doubt began to increase throughout the American colonies, and in particular, Salem. Between 1700 and 1703, the Massachusetts government demanded that the convictions be overturned for three accused witches who not yet been executed. In 1711, 22 people who had been tried, convicted, and executed of witchcraft, had their convictions reversed. Martha Corey was posthumously restored to the Salem church. In December of 1711, the Governor of Massachusetts authorized compensation to the families of the 22 people who had been executed. Today, Salem is known as Danvers, Massachusetts. A number of memorials were erected by the townspeople of Salem who honestly were repentant for their actions. In the end, one thing stands out: each of the women accused of witchcraft were on the fringes of Salem society. This was enough to make other members of the community suspicious of them because of their unusual actions. For most, the world is not often kind to those seen as deviant. Martin Luther King, Jesus

Christ, Malcolm X, Joan of Arc, Mahatma Gandhi, and others serve as proof of the danger associated with being labeled a deviant.

The Native American Genocide

One of the dangers of conformity is the idea that people unthinkingly go along with the crowd or the public sentiment of the time. What if going along with that public sentiment leads to a call for genocide like what happened in Germany under the Nazis?

"The proud spirit of the original owners of these vast prairies inherited through centuries of fierce and bloody wars for their possession, lingered last in the bosom of Sitting Bull. With his fall, the nobility of the Redskin is extinguished, and what few are left are a pack of whining curs who lick the hand that smites them. The Whites, by law of conquest, by justice of civilization, are masters of the American continent, and the best safety of   the frontier settlements will be secured by the total annihilation of the few remaining Indians. Why not annihilation? Their glory has fled, their spirit broken, their manhood effaced; better that they die than live the miserable wretches that they are" (Gitlin, 2011).

The above was taken from an editorial written in the 1890s after the death of Sitting Bull. Who was the author of the editorial? L. Frank Baum. He wrote, "The Wonderful Wizard of Oz." Strange how the author of one of the most beloved children's books ever written would call for the cold-blooded murder of an entire people ... or is it?

Obedience and Genocide

Obedience, in human behavior, is a form of social influence. It occurs when a person yields to explicit instructions or orders from an authority figure. **Obedience** is generally distinguished from **compliance,** which is behavior influenced by peers, and **conformity,** behavior intended to match that of the majority. Following the Second World War—and in particular the Holocaust—psychologists set out to investigate the phenomenon of human obedience. Early attempts to explain the Holocaust had focused on the idea that there was something distinctive about German culture that had allowed the Holocaust to take place. They quickly found that the majority of humans are surprisingly obedient to authority. The

Holocaust resulted in the extermination of millions of Jews, Gypsies, and communists; it has prompted us to take a closer look at the roots of obedience—in part, so that tragedies such as this may never happen again.

In 1961, at a laboratory on the campus of Yale University, a relatively unknown psychologist decided to test a hypothesis he had developed about obedience to authority. The researcher's name was Stanley Milgram and his research stunned Americans. Milgram's research, along with later research done by fellow psychologists Solomon Asch and Philip Zimbardo, suggested that what had happened in Nazi Germany could happen anywhere--even in the United States--and because of the Salem Witch trials and the Native American genocide, had already happened here.

Before presenting the aforementioned classic research on conformity, let's look at the overall issues of deviance and conformity.

Deviance

What is deviance? **Deviance** is action or thoughts that differ from the groups to which you belong. While deviance can be found in all groups and cultures, including subcultures, we will be focusing on those thoughts and/or actions that differ from the dominant group. Every group has standard practices members are expected to adhere to—whether they are thoughts or actions. When members of the group do not adhere to those standards, they are given the label deviant. I use the word "label" because deviance doesn't really exist--it is socially constructed, and because it is socially constructed it can vary by culture and time and therefore in constant flux. For instance, most drugs were perfectly legal in the U.S. until the early part of the last century. Opium and marijuana were made illegal in the 1920's/1930's; opium remains illegal while marijuana laws are shifting towards decriminalization--as of this writing 29 states have decriminalized it for medicinal use and 11 states and the District of Columbia have decriminalized it for recreational use.

Other examples include prohibition and divorce. Alcohol was legal to manufacture, sell and consume until 1919 when prohibition, the 18th Amendment to the Constitution, made it illegal to manufacture and sell--as a private individual you could still drink it in your home as long as it had been purchased prior to prohibition going into effect. But in 1933, largely because of the lost tax revenues which amounted to billions of dollars, the 18th Amendment was repealed. So, those who drank before prohibition were not largely seen as deviant, but prohibition changed that and went a step farther by not only making it a criminal act to manufacture and sell it, but also made its consumption deviant. After the repeal of the 18th Amendment, and the sale and manufacture of alcohol was legal again, someone who drank it was no longer seen as deviant.

Divorce is another example of how deviance changes with time. The divorce rate is somewhere around 45 percent today, so you could argue it's hardly a deviant thing to do. But 50 years ago, divorce would have been considered highly deviant and earn the divorced woman a label that I dare not repeat in this text.

Deviance also varies by culture. In Japan, not bowing to someone of higher rank or status would be disrespectful and deviant. In Turkey, it would be deviant to have your hands in your pocket while talking to another or offering your left hand when attempting to shake someone's hand. In some countries, it is deviant to show the soles of your feet to another person or sitting with your legs crossed when conversing with another. Being on time is something else that varies significantly by culture. In South America and some parts of the Middle East, being late is rarely seen as deviant—twenty, thirty minutes or more is considered normal. On the other hand, being even a minute or two late for a meeting in Japan is seen as significantly deviant and disrespectful.

Who are deviants? We are all deviants in one way or another. At some point in our lives we have all broken rules or laws and therefore fall on a continuum of conformity versus deviance. Can you think of things you have done in your life that have violated **normative expectations**? Have you ever run a stop sign or red light? Worn a hat inside the house? Failed to pay a parking ticket? Cohabitated with someone with whom you had a romantic relationship? Failed to report every dollar you have earned on your tax return? Spoken out against a popular political view? Used an illicit drug? Driven after having too much to drink? These could all be considered deviant actions. On the other hand, does deviance necessarily conflict with the law? Let's go back and look at one action as an example—running a stop sign. At one point in all of our lives we have run a stop sign--in other words, not come to a full and complete stop. If most people have done it, can it still be deviant or is it conformist? Keep in mind that just because a majority of people do something, so that it becomes the new norm, doesn't mean it's legal. Even though I suspect most Americans fail to report every dollar they earned through the year on their income taxes, I doubt the IRS would shrug it off just because it was the conformist thing to do. So, even if it is the conformist thing to do, in other words, the majority perform the act, it might still be illegal. This is a list of few things, ranging from formal to informal, that are deviant in India. Which of the acts below do you think are deviant in the U.S.?

1. Cannibalism.
2. Dyeing your hair purple and wearing a spike cut.
3. Shoplifting.
4. Smoking marijuana.
5. Using hallucinogenic drugs or narcotics.
6. Selling illicit drugs.
7. Cheating on an exam.
8. Cheating on your taxes.
9. Seeing someone else cheat and not reporting it.
10. Premarital sex.
11. Gay or lesbian sex.
12. Marrying your sister/brother or first cousin.
13. Having sex with an animal.
14. Watching a pornographic movie.
15. Making a pornographic movie.
16. Extramarital sex.
17. Polygamy.

Deviance Can Lead to Innovation

Emile Durkheim believed that deviance was necessary for society. He felt that deviance would spur **innovation** and encourage different methods of problem solving. Therefore, he advocated that society be more tolerant to certain types of deviance, not crime, but rather a deviance that allowed people to move away from social norms to some degree that is not a threat to society nor will the action violate laws. *Grant (2016) expressed that notion in an article published in Harvard Business Review. He wrote that innovation is essential for business growth and that most people, given some* *degree of freedom, are capable of being innovative.* Grant goes further by actually suggesting that organizations can work towards "creating a culture of non-conformity." He proposes the following steps in the process of creating a culture of non-conformity:

> 1. Give employees the freedom to nurture and encourage their imagination.
> 2. Encourage employees to see things from the view of a competitor.
> 3. Resist having people work in groups when generating new ideas because group brainstorming tends to encourage conformity to group ideas.
> 4. Once ideas are generated, have "visionaries" evaluate and give feedback on which ideas to pursue. These visionaries should be "other innovators with a track record of spotting winners."
> 5. Value the support and maintenance of programs designed to encourage nonconformity and imagination.
> 6. Perform a delicate balancing act between the important elements of the organization: cohesion between organizational members with "creative dissent."

Dangers of Conformity and Obedience

Like Durkheim, Eric Fromm (d. 1980) believed that deviance was necessary for society. Fromm wrote, "Human history began with an act of disobedience," referring to Adam and Eve's disobedience to God. "Man has continued to evolve by acts of disobedience. Not only was his spiritual development possible only because there were men who dared say no to the powers that be in the name of their conscience or their faith, but also his intellectual development was dependent on the capacity for being disobedient to authorities who tried to muzzle new thoughts and to the authority of long established opinions which declared a change to be nonsense" (Fromm, 1981).

In 2013, approximately fifty-four percent of adult Americans (i.e., 18 years and older) were married according to a Gallop poll (Newport & Wilkie, 2013). Today, twenty-three percent of adult males and seventeen percent of adult females are single. However, 5% of adult Americans say they are not married and don't want to marry (Goodwin et al., 2009). The conformist thing to do in our society is to marry, but not only marry, but to have kids, too. In fact, we tend to deny childless couples the term "family." The conformist thing to do in America, and has been since its founding, is for a man and a woman to marry and have kids; to do anything less, is deviant. And in this case, someone who doesn't marry and/or have kids is "broken." Another example would be someone at a party who wasn't drinking. How do we think about people who don't drink? Something must be wrong with them. Maybe they're an alcoholic. What about vegetarians? Society often wants to label them "health nuts." In short, the conformist things to do are to get married, have kids, drink alcohol, and eat meat.

Before we can more fully discuss deviance, we have to define and investigate conformity. Why? Because deviance is simply non-conformity. Nothing more, nothing less. Deviance represents violations of the do's and don'ts of society. Conformity is going with the values and actions of the groups to which we belong. Just because we are expected to conform, doesn't give those overarching groups the right to insist we conform—unless conformity is tied to specific laws that those groups have put in place. Obedience is the idea of conforming to higher authorities who in theory have the legal right to enforce that obedience. But even then, the question becomes are we obligated to conform to all rules and laws put in place by the conforming majority? A good example of this would be the military. Today, U.S. "military personnel have an obligation and a duty to only obey Lawful orders and indeed have an obligation to disobey Unlawful orders, including orders by the president that do not comply with the UCMJ (Uniform Code of Military Justice, (UCMJ) 809.ART.90 (20). We will return to these topics later in the chapter.

Milgram's Research on Obedience to Perceived Authority

The world was outraged by the Holocaust as the details were revealed in the postwar months. Americans, listening to daily summaries of the Nuremberg trials on their radios in the evenings, were horrified and angered by the cold-blooded murder of 11,000,000 innocent men, women and children (i.e., Jews, Gypsies, Russian civilians, Russian POWs, people with disabilities, homosexuals, political dissidents, Jehovah's Witnesses, clergy,

Masons, union members, communists, and many, many more). Though shocked, we said it could never happen here! But one man, Stanley Milgram, wasn't so sure and decided to do an experiment on the issue of obedience to authority, and specifically on illegitimate authority.

In 1963, experiments on obedience to authority figures (1963) was done in a series of social psychological experiments conducted at Yale University by psychologist Stanley Milgram. **Obedience** is different from **compliance**, which is behavior influenced by peers, and conformity, which is behavior intended to go along with the majority. In short, obedience is a form of social influence in which a person yields to explicit instructions or orders from an authority figure.

These experiments done by Milgram measured the willingness of study participants to obey an authority figure who instructed them to perform acts that conflicted with their personal conscience. **Authority** is when a figure or institution holds a position of power that enables them to give legitimate orders because of that power. Milgram, a Yale university professor, published an ad in help wanted column of the local New Haven newspaper. In exchange for $4.50, (a lot of money back then) males who agreed to participate would work on a research project investigating the effects of punishment on learning. Subjects arrived at the laboratory in pairs at a specified time. After drawing straws, one subject would be designated "teacher" and the other as "learner." The "learner" was really a **confederate** of the researcher--in other words, someone who pretends to be a participant in the study but is really working with the researcher. The subject, the one designated "teacher," believed his role was randomly assigned. They were then taken to a room where the "learner" was strapped into a chair and wired to a shock generator in an adjacent room. The researcher explained that the "teacher" would be taken into another room where he would read a list of word pairs over an intercom system. After reading the word pairs, the teacher would give one word of the word pair and ask the learner for the matching word. When the learner was incorrect, the teacher would administer a shock. If the teachers questioned the procedure, the researcher would encourage them further to proceed with the shocks.

Figure 5. Milgram's "learner" being strapped into the chair.

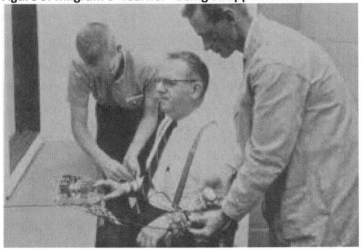

Figure 6. Milgram's "teacher" administering shocks to the "learner"

At this point, and in front of the teacher, the learner would state that he had been diagnosed with a slight heart problem and ask if that would be a problem. Again, in front of the teacher, the researcher stated that while the shocks may be painful, they were not harmful. After that the teacher was taken to the room that housed the shock generator. The shock generator consisted of 30 toggle switches each marked with a corresponding voltage which ranged from 15 volts to 450 volts. The researcher positioned himself behind and to the right of the teacher. The experiment began with the learner getting the first few questions correct, but at some point, he answered incorrectly, to which the teacher responded by stating, "That is incorrect. Fifteen volts," before pressing the corresponding switch. The question and answers continued and at some point, the teacher could hear the learner verbally reacting to the pain of the shocks. After administering a 150-volt shock, the learner screamed in pain before demanding the experiment be stopped. "I told you I had a heart problem," he yelled, "I don't want to do this anymore." At this point, all the teachers stopped and asked the researcher seated behind him for instructions. The researcher replied by reminding the teacher that while the shocks may be painful, they were not dangerous. If there was resistance on the part of the teacher, the researcher would state the following to gain compliance:

1. Please continue.
2. The experiment demands that you continue.
3. You have no choice, you must continue.

If the teacher still wanted to stop after all the verbal commands by the researcher, the experiment ended. Otherwise, it went on until the teacher had administered a 450-volt shock three times in a row.

Milgram's research assistants had predicted that only a very small percentage of "teachers" (1 percent) would actually take the voltage to the maximum 450-volts. However, at the conclusion of his research, 2/3s of Milgram's "teachers" administered the 450-volt shock to the "learners" even though the "learners" had long since stopped making any kind of noise as a response to the pain that was being inflicted on them. Milgram noted that most of those who took the voltage to the maximum amount were noticeably uncomfortable in doing so but did obey the verbal commands of the researcher (i.e., the perceived authority figure).

In researching differences between the 1/3 that refused to administer voltage past 150 volts (if they made it that far) and the 2/3s that did, Milgram found that the 2/3s were willing to let others assume responsibility for their actions whereas the 1/3 were not. In later research, Milgram found that the closer the learner was physically to the teacher, the less the maximum amount of voltage the teacher was willing to administer, and the closer the authority figure (i.e., researcher) was to the teacher, the greater the maximum amount of voltage the teacher was willing to administer. Milgram's results clearly demonstrated that a majority of his participants were willing to obey the perceived authority figure even to the point of potentially killing another.

Philip Zimbardo's Stanford Prison Experiment

Conducted at Stanford University in 1971, and influenced by Milgram's work in the 1960s, Philip Zimbardo wanted to study obedience to **perceived authority** like Milgram. Zimbardo designed an experiment where he would study the psychological effects of acting out the part of a prisoner or prison guard. Zimbardo selected 24 male university students to play the part of either a prisoner or prison guard at a mock prison he had set up in the psychology building at the university.

Zimbardo's subjects adapted to their new roles well--too well. Over a period of days, the "prisoners" began to be uncooperative when following the orders of the "guards." The "guards" reacted by becoming more authoritarian, brutal and sometimes sadistic in their treatment of the "prisoners." The "prisoners" were subjected to both physical and psychological torture at the hands of the "guards." A number of the "prisoners" reacted passively to the guards' orders and some even went so far as to verbally and physically harass other "prisoners" who would not follow orders or try to incite them to rebel against the "guards."

Zimbardo was later severely criticized for allowing the experiment to go on as long as it did, given the behaviors of both "guards" and "prisoners." However, at some point even Zimbardo realized that the experiment had gotten well out of hand and ended the research study earlier than planned. Results were interpreted to suggest that subjects, specifically the "prisoners," tended to be obedient to perceived authority especially when that perceived authority included **institutional support** (i.e., Stanford University) and others, specifically the "guards," would enforce their authority on the "prisoners" because they felt having been given the authority to act as they did because of that same institutional support.

In analyzing his results, Zimbardo concluded that environmental factors played a large part in the behaviors exhibited by his subjects. Further, Zimbardo believed that the excessive psychological and physical behaviors of the "guards" on the "prisoners" was the result of deindividuation. He attributed the deindividuation to the perceived authority they were given during the experiment and also by the **anonymity** their uniforms provided.

In a series of lectures Zimbardo gave in the decades following his research, he has eluded to the same environmental factors when looking at the misconduct by American soldiers in their capacity as guards at the infamous Abu Ghraib prison in Iraq. Again, he argues, deindividuation was responsible. **Deindividuation** is a social psychological concept that refers to the loss of self-awareness when people are in groups. In other words, when in groups our individual identities and self-concepts seem to weaken or even evaporate and thus no longer see themselves as responsible for their actions.

Milgram's and Zimbardo's Other Findings Influencing Obedience

When both Milgram and Zimbardo had finished their research, they identified four factors that influenced obedience. Those factors are:

> *1. Proximity to the authority figure.* In other words, the closer the authority figure was to the subject, the more likely they were to obey. This is one of the independent variables that Milgram manipulated in his research. When a "teacher" hesitated to administer the shock to the "learner," the authority figure would simply remind them that while the shocks were painful, they were not harmful and then told the "teacher" to continue and administer the shock. If the "teacher" didn't obey, the authority got up from his desk and stood behind the "teacher" and restated the command. If the "teacher" still refused to obey, the authority repeated the command after placing his hand on the "teacher's" shoulder. Milgram clearly demonstrated that the closer was the authority figure, the more likely the "teacher" obeyed.
>
> *2. Prestige of the experimenter.* Both Milgram and Zimbardo effectively used uniforms in their experiments. In Milgram's study, the authority figure wore a white lab coat, which symbolized their identification as a researcher. In Zimbardo's research, the "guards" wore what resembled

the type of uniform a prison guard might actually wear. Milgram and Zimbardo concluded that the uniforms provided prestige that increased obedience on the part of intended subjects.

3. *Prestige of the institution.* The research was done at a highly respectable and prestigious institution, Stanford University.

4. *Expertise.* Both Milgram and Zimbardo discovered that subjects who lacked experience or expertise in making group decisions tended to leave the decision-making to the group as a whole and whatever status hierarchy existed within the group.

In summary, Milgram and Zimbardo concluded that higher levels of perceived authority and the associated prestige, the closer to the authority figure was the subject, the lack of expertise on the part of the subjects in leading a group (i.e., rebellion), and deindividuation were all factors that increased obedience.

Solomon Asch's Conformity Experiment

Solomon Asch was a social psychologist who is known for his research on conformity and for his belief you had to study the whole to understand the part. He wrote: "Most social acts have to be understood in their setting and lose meaning if isolated. No error in thinking about social facts is more serious than the failure to see their place and function" (Asch, 1952).

In 1951, Asch conducted experiments on group conformity. Research subjects were told they would be participating in a "perceptual task," and they would be joining others in the same research project. Subjects were ushered into a room and sat at a table along with the other subjects, though unbeknownst to the primary subject the other subjects were really research confederates working with Asch on the research project. Asch designed the experiment to test whether people would go along with the group even though there was an obviously correct answer; if the subject gave an incorrect answer it would be clear that they did so because of group pressure (i.e., a desire to conform to the group). Asch put eight college-aged males in a room. Seven of the

Figure 7. Solomon Ash's Line Experiment

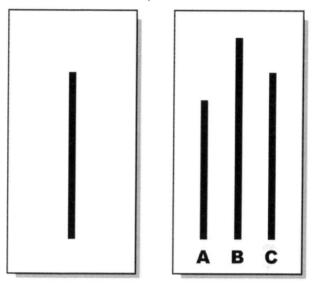

eight had been coached on what they were expected to do. The eighth person was unaware that the other seven men were different than him or had been instructed to answer in specified ways.

As the eight men sat around a table, the real subject of the experiment was deliberately sat in the last position around the table. Asch handed the first subject the first subject two placards: one with three lines of different length, labeled A, B, or C, and one with a single line, which Asch called the target line. Asch then proceeded to ask the first subject the following: "Of the three lines, A, B, and C, which is the target line closest to in length?" The seven subjects had been coached to give an incorrect answer. One after the other, each of the seven subjects gave an incorrect answer. Finally, Asch handed the placards to the eighth subject, the real subject of the experiment. Asch repeated his question: "Of the three lines, A, B, and C, which is the target line closest to in length?" Asch varied the research and on some occasions his research confederates were told to **unanimously** provide the correct answer and sometimes the incorrect answer. Asch found that about one-third of the real subjects went along with the group and gave the incorrect answer though there could have been no doubt that it was the incorrect answer. To verify his results, Asch performed a similar experiment with a **control group** where there was no pressure to conform, in other words all the other subjects stated what they felt was the correct answer even if it wasn't. Asch reported the error rate as one-percent in the control group where it had been around 37 percent in the experimental groups.

Why did the participants conform even though they must have known they were giving the incorrect answer? When the real subjects were debriefed after the experiment, most said they knew they were giving an incorrect answer but did so to go along with the group out of fear they would be ridiculed by the group. Only a few subjects believed they were giving the correct answer. Asch concluded that people conform for a number of reasons:

> 1. they want to fit in with the group (**normative influence**),
> 2. they believe the group is better informed than they are (**informational influence**).
> 3. group size affected conformity. Conformity is decreased as the presence of deviance is increased. This is true up to five acts of deviance. In other words, as the number of people deviate from a group norm increases, the less likely someone will conform to group norms simply for the sake of conforming. "The most robust finding [of Asch's research] is that conformity reaches its full extent with 3-5 persons, with additional members having little effect" (Hogg & Vaughan, 1995).
> 4. difficulty of the task (the more difficult the task, the more people will conform largely because of self-doubt).
> 5. the presence of high-status group members (i.e., people are more likely to conform with someone they perceive as having high status).
> 6. answering in private. When subjects were allowed to answer in private, conformity decreased dramatically.

Research by Heerdink et al. (2015) wanted to revisit Asch's finding that people will conform because they don't want to stand out and/or be ridiculed. The researchers wanted to investigate whether anger could influence people to conform. So, where Asch found that subjects were more likely to conform when the presence of deviance (i.e., other group members who disagreed with the group) was low, Heerdink et al. found that as the degree of anger increases in the group to deviants, the greater the likelihood the real subject feels rejected. The authors believe that the rejection felt on the part of the subject will lead to **anti-conformity** unless:

> 1. the deviant or deviants seek forgiveness from the group and seek reacceptance, and
> 2. re-conforming becomes a "strategic behavior aimed at gaining reacceptance from the group."

Sherif and the Autokinetic Effect

Years before Milgram and Zimbardo's famous experiments on obedience to authority, Muzafer Sherif wanted to investigate how many people would change their opinions in order to conform with the group. In his 1936 experiment, subjects were placed in a dark room and asked to fix their gaze on a small dot of light 15 feet away projected onto a screen. Subjects were then asked to estimate the amount the dot of light had moved during a specific period of time, even though in reality the dot never moved. Years before researchers had discovered something called the **autokinetic effect**, a belief that motion occurred when in fact it was really a visual illusion and no motion in fact had occurred.

On the first day of Sherif's experiment, each subject perceived the dot of light had moved differently--some saying it had moved greater distances with others perceiving it had moved very little. However, beginning on the second day and running through the fourth day of the study with the same subjects, Sherif found that the group tended to agree on the perceived movement of the light. Because the light had not moved at all during the five-day experiment, Sherif concluded that the group's perceptions were influenced by a desire to conform to group norms. Sherif then went on to suggest that was the same process used by society in determining social norms.

Motivations Underlying Conformity and Compliance

Unconscious influences or social pressure, overt or direct, may cause someone to conform. A general awareness of public attitudes towards social norms, whatever they may be, may be enough to cause someone to conform to those norms--others do not even have to be around in order for just the knowledge of those social norms to lead to conformity. The two major motivators that lead to conformity are normative influence and informational influence. An example of normative influence would be when a person conforms to social norms so that they may be accepted by the overall group or society. As a rule, most people do not want to be isolated or rejected by society for failure to follow prescribed norms. Today in the US, body size and structure have become important issues. Fat-shaming has become a target for social psychological investigation. While views of the ideal weight for a given height and gender tend to be well-known within a society, normative influence takes over so that a significant number of people try to conform to those standards--even if those standards are unrealistic and difficult to achieve for a sizeable proportion of Americans. People try to fit that rigid body stature so that they fit in, gain social acceptance, and keep from being socially rejected or having sanctions placed on them. **Sanctions** can be in the way of labels, "You need to lose weight," to the workplace where the research clearly shows that overweight people are less likely to be hired than are normal-sized people (Vanhove & Gordon, 2013).

But what if people are uncertain about what particular or specific social norms are? This is where informational influence plays its part. Informational influence is the result of people asking people in their social environment questions about those specific norms. They feel normative influences to be accurate sources of information about what is or isn't the reality of the particular social norm in question.

Examples of this can be found in the workplace. What if John graduated college and found a good job working as a computer programmer with a specific company. Consequently, because he is judged to excel at his job, he garnishes substantial pay raises and is promoted. After several years, John would do well to seek out a new job commensurate with his experience and pay grade as a future employer would likely be influenced by how well John's current or former employers thought so well of him. In fact, this is one of the chief goals of obtaining a good recommendation from your peers or preferably your employer for people who want to move up the ladder. But on the other hand, if Mary is generally not regarded as highly motivated, a good learner, or a valuable worker by her present employer and therefore hasn't received a raise in sometime and has been in her current rank within the company for longer than is typical, it is likely future employers would look on this negatively as it is a sign their peers do not hold high views of her. Likewise, if Tom has been out of work for some time, prospective employers might be unwilling to hire him because it could indicate other employers were not impressed by his skills or work history.

Factors Influencing Conformity

Research has found a number of factors that are thought to increase the likelihood of conformity in a group--some of which have already been offered by Milgram, Zimbardo and Asch. Those are:

1. Group size. Generally, larger groups are more likely to conform to group or overall social norms and beliefs than in smaller groups.
2. Unanimity. When a group's response to a situation or norm is unanimous, group members are more likely to conform to those group norms or decisions. This can be associated to a phenomenon that we will discuss later called groupthink.
3. Cohesion. Generally, the more **cohesive** the group, and the tighter the bonds between group members, the less tolerant the group is of diverse opinions or behaviors and group members are more likely to conform to those group norms or beliefs.
4. Status. Group members are more likely to conform when they belong to high-status groups. One example of this is the high status held by Nasa and the team members who, when provided with a caution from the manufacturer of potential weakness in a rocket seal when exposed to cold weather, engaged in group think, ignored warnings by the manufacturer of the particular rocket part, and decided to launch the space shuttle Challenger despite the warnings on a cold day in January 1986. Seven crew members were killed.
5. Culture. Collectivist cultures tend to exhibit much higher levels of group conformity when compared to individualistic

cultures like the US and most of the industrialized world.

6. Gender. In 1985, a University of California at Berkeley social psychology professor obtained permission to recreate Stanley Milgram's experiment done in the early 1960s. To gain approval from the university's Institutional Review Board, he had to stop the experiments after people were willing to administer a 150-volt shock to "learners," who like in Milgram's experiment, were actually research confederates and not really shocked. Unlike Milgram, the researcher used a mix of both males and females in his study. *His research showed that slightly more women than men were willing to administer the maximum 150-volt shock.* The possible explanation for this is that women in our culture are more likely to do what they are told when it is a male telling them to do something. Other research that seems to confirm the latter found that women were more likely to conform when they were being watched or surveilled, but less likely to conform when they weren't.

7. Age. As a rule, younger people are more likely to obey to commands by older people than when given commands by their age peers.

8. Importance of stimuli. One important research finding found that people are less likely to conform for the sake of conformity when the specific task they are trying to achieve is important--the more important the task, the less likely people will conform and instead more likely to give their true opinion. One study that looked at passenger plane safety signals, a situation that could lead to passenger deaths, found that subjects were less likely to conform to group decision-making probably because people's lives were at stake should they make the wrong decision.

9. Minority influence. **Minority influence** has nothing to do with racial or ethnic minority conformity, but everything to so with minority factions within a particular task group. In this case, the influence is largely informational and conformity is the result of three factors: (a) consistent adherence to a position, (b) the degree of defection from the majority, and (c) the status and self-confidence of the minority members.

Factors Influencing Compliance

Factors that influence compliance include the following:

1. Group strength. The strength of the group, or rather its importance in the life of the group member, has a dramatic effect on compliance. The more important the group, the greater the likelihood of compliance to group norms.
2. Immediacy. The degree which group members are physically and emotionally close to the group member, the greater the likelihood of compliance.
3. Number. Simply put, the larger the group, the greater the likelihood of compliance. However, Asch's research suggests that the likelihood of compliance because of group size only holds true to a certain point. After that point is reached, group size seems to have little effect on compliance. Adding one person to a group made up of five or six people is likely to affect compliance but adding one person to a group of fifty or sixty does not.
4. Similarity. The more alike someone feels they are to other group members, let's say their **ingroup**, a feeling of shared values, beliefs, and behaviors can lead to greater compliance. Ingroups are those that we identify with-- usually on some superficial characteristic, whereas **outgroups** are made up of everyone else--people we think we have nothing in common. We will return to the idea of ingroups versus outgroups when we discuss prejudice.

Other Techniques to Achieve Compliance

In addition to the above factors that have been found to increase compliance, the following represent other sources of compliance to group norms. They are:

Foot-in-the-Door Technique

Research has found that if you want someone to make a fairly large compliance to some request, it is more effective to ask them to comply with smaller requests in the beginning. If the subject agrees to a small compliance, another slightly more intensive compliance is requested. If the subject makes that latter compliance, another more instance request for compliance be asked and probably obtained. Because someone complies with the smaller requests, it increases the chance they will conform to the next more intense request, and so on until they will almost certainly comply with the intended act of compliance because they feel obligated to do so. Telemarketers often employ this technique. The moral here is if you want someone to do something significant and important for you, start small and work your way up.

Door-in-the-Face Technique

This technique takes a completely opposite approach to the foot-in-the-door technique. Here someone begins with a large request for compliance that they know the subject will refuse. However, at that point a smaller and more reasonable request for compliance is made. Generally, this technique is considered highly likely to obtain compliance to the smaller request. For instance, let's say John has managed to save enough money to put a down payment on a car because he is working a part-time job. He wants his parents to pay for his car insurance as he will be able to make payments on the car because of his part-time job. John asks for his parents to either outright pay for his new car or help him make the payments. They refuse. He then asks if that will at least pay for his car insurance to which they agree. It's akin to a spider luring a fly into its web and then pouncing! But it is highly effective and too many parents have been victims of this door-in-the-face technique.

Low-Ball Technique

There is a scene in the movie Fargo where a man and a woman have come into pick up the new car they ordered. The salesman informs them that the car has come in with a special paint sealant to prevent rust, though the couple did not order it because it increased the cost of the vehicle by hundreds of dollars. In the end, the couple grudgingly pays the difference and leaves with their car. This is low-balling in practice. By offering someone at a reduced price or commitment and gaining their compliance, someone comes along and at the last-minute asks for more. The subject is more likely to agree to the additional cost or commitment because they've already complied with the first request and at this point, they have more time and effort involved in the exchange to simply walk away.

Ingratiation Technique

The non-scientific word for this tactic is called schmoozing. The schmoozer ingratiates (flatters, points out how much they are alike, agrees with their opinion about something) themselves to someone. In truth, the schmoozer has a goal or agenda which is to get someone's compliance. So, the next time someone sits down in your office, compliments your office decoration, seems to agree with your opinions about things, and points out how much alike you are, beware! That could be a schmoozer in sheep's clothing!

Norm-of-Reciprocity Technique

Humans almost have a need to repay a debt. If someone does a favor for you, it is natural for you to want to return the favor. In fact, it is a social norm to do so. Consequently, if someone does you a favor you are more likely to comply to some request they have made as a way of paying them back.

Controversy and Obedience Experiments

Though both Milgram and Zimbardo's research was heavily criticized for ethical reasons, and those criticisms led to institutional review boards at every college and university in America, there findings still serve as powerful reminders as to what man is capable of doing in the name of obedience and compliance. But in truth, there is always going to be controversy over social psychological research because of the subjects they attempt to tackle. Likewise, there will always be debate as to how their research and other controversial research should be interpreted, but that's what science does--it offers facts and then puts them up for discussion and debate. It is only in this way that any scientific discipline grows and matures while building the body of knowledge for its discipline.

Concepts and Terms to Know

Obedience
Compliance
Conformity
Deviance
Normative expectations
Innovation
Authority
Perceived authority
Legitimate authority
Confederate
Institutional support
Anonymity (as part of a group or crowd)
Deindividuation
Prestige
Unanimity
Control group
Normative influence
Informational influence
Anti-conformity
Autokinetic effect
Sanctions
Cohesive/cohesion
Minority influence
Ingroup
Outgroups
Foot-in-the-Door Technique
Door-in-the-Face Technique
Low-Ball Technique
Ingratiation Technique
Norm-of-Reciprocity Technique

References

Asch, S. E. (1952). Group forces in the modification and distortion of judgments. In S. E. Asch, *Social Psychology* (pp. 450-501). Englewood Cliffs, NJ, US: Prentice-Hall, Inc.

Fromm, E. (1981). *On disobedience and other essays.* Seabury Press.

Gitlin, T. (2011). Patriotism. *The Chronicle of Higher Education.* Retrieved January 2017 from https://www.chronicle.com/article/An-Era-in-Ideas-Patriotism/128493

Goodwin, J., Jasper, J., & Polleta, F. (2009). *Passionate politics: Emotions and social movements.* University of Chicago Press.

Haney, C., Banks, W., & Zimbardo, P. (1973). A study of prisoners and guards in a simulated prison. *Naval Research Review*, 30, 4-17.

Haney, C.; Banks, W. C.; Zimbardo, P. G. (1973). Interpersonal dynamics in a simulated prison. *International Journal of Criminology and Penology,* 1, 69–97.

Heerdink, M., van Kleef, G., Homan, A., & Fischer, A. (2015). Emotional reactions to deviance in groups: the relation between number of angry reactions, felt rejection, and conformity. *Frontiers in Psychology*, 6(1). Retrieved May 2017 from https://www.frontiersin.org/articles/10.3389/fpsyg.2015.00830/full

Hogg, M. & Vaughan, G. (1995). *Social psychology: An introduction.* Prentice Hall.

Milgram, S. (1963). Behavioral study of obedience. *Journal of Abnormal and Social Psychology*, 67, 371-378.

Milgram, S. (1965). Some conditions of obedience and disobedience to authority. *Human Relations*, 18(1), 57-76.

Milgram, S. (1974). *Obedience to authority: An experimental* view. Harper-Collins.

Sherif, M. (1936). *The psychology of social norms.* Oxford, England: Harper.

Van Kleef, G. A., van den Berg, H., & Heerdink, M. W. (2015). The persuasive power of emotions: Effects of emotional expressions on attitude formation and change. *Journal of Applied Psychology*, 100(4), 1124-1142.

Vanhove, A., & Gordan, R. (2013). Weight discrimination in the workplace: a meta-analytic examination of the relationship between weight and work-related outcomes. *Journal of Applied Psychology,* 44(1), 12-22.

Zimbardo, P.G. (2007). *The Lucifer effect: Understanding how good people turn evil*. New York: Random House.

Chapter 8 Groups

A **group** consists of two or more people who interact with one another. An interaction is defined an exchange of information that has the potential to change an attitude, belief or behavior of one or both parties. To speak of a group means that members are **interdependent**. In other words, they must work together to keep the group together and to accomplish the group's goals. Also, members of a group are aware of their membership in those groups to which they belong. We belong to many groups at any one time in our life--some of which we are a member of for life and some of which come in and out of our life as we progress through the **life course**. Some examples include our family, close friends, friends, co-workers, social clubs to which we belong, members of our church if we go to church, and even your fellow classmates in this class. Some groups expand and contract as we go through the life course. For instance, your family may grow when a member marries and not only adds a new wife or husband to the group, but their family intertwines with your family. On the other hand, divorce and death may reduce the size of your family group.

Social psychologists study groups because virtually all of our activities occur in groups of one kind or another. The "loner" or the person who isolates him or herself from others, and therefore doesn't belong to any group, is a person who most likely has a mental illness which impairs his or her ability to interact with others. Even so, it is very unhealthy for people to remain isolated. Do you suppose it was just an accident that Tom Hanks' character in Castaway the movie created a surrogate human being out of a volleyball named Wilson? No, it was not. Tom Hanks' character knew that if he didn't have someone to "talk" to, he would go crazy. In fact, maybe you'll remember the scene before Wilson came along where Hanks' character tried to kill himself out of loneliness and despair. Wilson kept him alive.

While psychologists would be interested in individual behavior free from human interaction and their environment; sociology, studies groups relatively free from biological needs or traits. The social psychologist studies groups as a creation of both psychological traits and the exigencies of the social environment. It truly is the middle ground between the two disciplines. Social psychologists investigate groups, organization, communities and culture as a whole as well as the various subcultures within that dominant culture.

One of the first questions we need to ask is why are groups so important? What is the significance of belonging to a group? What are the consequences, both good and bad, of belonging to a group? Is being a member of a group good or bad? Are we members of just one group or many? Do our group memberships change as we age? (and we actually belong to many groups at one time and this peaks during mid-life). In the end, we are left with one clear and indisputable truth about groups: as humans, we have a need to belong (Baumeister & Leary, 1995). We will explore that need and all it entails.

Research reports that upwards of 50 percent of Americans regularly performed activities with others in groups (Putnam, 2000). Other research has found that as humans we don't respond well when we are alone and not part of a group. College students are less likely to feel lonely and isolated if they are part of a cohesive, productive, and satisfying group. It is human nature that makes us want to belong (Buote et al., 2007). Further, people who are part of a group, and accepted for who they are, are far more likely to feel satisfied. However, when they are rejected for group membership they are more likely to feel unhappy, sad, depressed and lonely (Williams, 2007). One study using magnetic imaging reported that people who were excluded from group membership actually experienced the same kind of pain sensations as though they were physically injured (Eisenberger, Lieberman, & Williams, 2003).

Groups versus social categories

When speaking of groups there are two concepts which sound as if they are groups but are not. A **social category** is made up of people who share an attribute in common, for example gender, but they do not interact as a group. You may interact with a women's club because you are female, but you do not interact with all women, therefore, to call gender a group would be a misnomer. Ethnicity would be another example of a social category. You may be Hispanic, and think of yourself as part of a larger and encompassing group, but in reality, while you may know and interact with other Hispanics, you do not interact with all Hispanics-

-not to mention that Hispanic itself has a broad definition--Mexican Americans, Cuban Americans, Puerto Ricans, and other Spanish speaking peoples. There are many social categories based on gender, race, ethnicity, religion, location, and social class. So, these are not examples of groups but rather of social categories.

Social aggregates are collections of people who happen to be in the same place at the same time but are not typically a group because just because two or more people are in the same place at the same time doesn't mean they interact or especially have a meaningful interaction. Any time you are part of a crowd, which is a collection of people you do not know, you are part of social aggregate and not part of a group. Some examples social aggregates and not groups include waiting at a bus stop with other travelers, standing in line to buy tickets for a sports event, sitting in the stands watching that sporting event. Since there is no common identity or meaningful interaction these are social aggregates.

How do groups develop?

Groups constrict and expand over time as situations and tasks change. If you think of your family as a group, at some point you are likely to marry. When you marry your new husband or wife becomes a new member of your family group. Likewise, so do your in-laws. So, the size of your "family" group has increased, as has your wife's or husband's. Several years down the road, you have children, which further increases the size of your "family" group. Perhaps one day your parents decide they want a divorce. While the size of your family remains the same, the cohesiveness of the group may change. On the other hand, if one or both of your parents remarry, your "family" group now increases to take in not only your parent's new spouses, but their children and parents. In these types of situations, the family group increases dramatically. Likewise, perhaps a parent or sibling dies, the family group is now more constricted. This tends to be the pattern over the life course. As we age, our family group constricts ever more with the passing of time as members die off.

Human society depends on the existence of groups. Without the ability to form groups, we could not exist as a species. We would have come and gone from the world as a species thousands of years ago. We really don't take the time to stop and think of ourselves as a member of a particular group, let alone that we are actually members of many groups at the same time. In order to form groups, we need something or somethings in common with other members of our species. We need to be able to talk or communicate somehow with others of our species. We need to be similar in some ways--we eat, drink, get sick, and myriad other things that make us similar. We also need to realize that we need and are needed by others so that we develop an understanding that we are in fact interdependent. Again, as fully independent species, man would not long have survived after he came onto the scene. Finally, groups provide us with an identity as part of those groups to which we belong, which in turn shapes our **self-concept**.

Tuckman and Jensen (1977) developed a model of group formation. They called it, "**Stages of Group Development**." In it, they propose four stages of development: (1) **forming**, (2) **storming**, (3) **norming and performing**, and (4) **adjourning**.

The forming stage is just that--the formation of a new group. Depending the on the particular group, it can be formed over some period of time, as would be the case of development and growth of a new family, or in a very short period of time, as would be the case of a task group put together by a college professor in which students were given a task to complete as a group. Students in the task group might begin by introducing themselves and then sharing ideas on how to complete the task. There is discussion about how to solve the problem. Each group member begins to understand their specific role in the group and the relationship he or she has with the other members. Some members may occupy more important roles than others depending on their knowledge and skills, but all develop an identity as group member.

The storming stage. During this stage, group members begin to express themselves more. They offer strategies or procedures on how to accomplish a task and the other members evaluate their suggestions. Likewise, the other group members are expressing their own ideas. At this point, group members may try to establish their rank in the group by forcibly reasserting their ideas in attempt to get the group to accept his or her solution as the best. This stage is called the storming stage because this is when disagreement first arises in the group with members competing

Figure 1. Stages of group development.

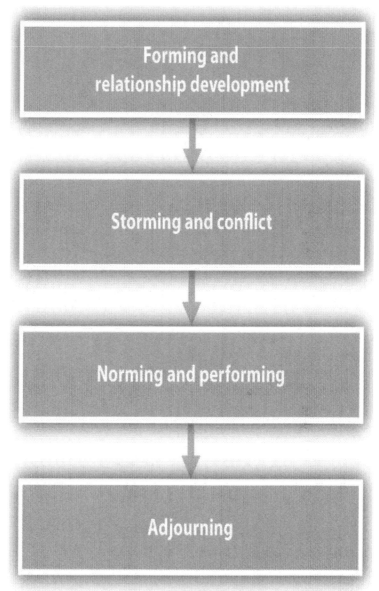

with one another for their ideas to be accepted as the best. Still, even though group members may be at odds with each other as to whose idea is the best solution to solve the assigned task, they still share their identity as group member. Sometimes problems may occur that cause group members to have to work out other ways to solve the tasks at hand, and unfortunately, this can lead to intergroup conflict. Hopefully, group members will work out a new solution to solving the task assigned to them, but that doesn't always happen. In fact, research reveals that most task related work groups don't get past the storming stage because of conflict (Kuypers, Davies, & Hazewinkel, 1986).

While the research suggests that many task related groups don't make it past the storming stage, other groups manage to handle the conflict constructively. Conflict can sometimes be beneficial as it may put pressure on group members to resolve the problem rather than disband. Like people, some groups work better when stressed, but sometimes if the conflict becomes just so extreme and intense that group members really can no longer even work together, they may disband (Rispens & Jehn, 2011). If group conflict at low to mid-levels can actually increase task performance, a lack of conflict can actually decrease group performance on a task. Group members that are disinterested, lack motivation, and perhaps because they just don't like talking to people they don't know well, are unable to achieve the assigned task and are therefore unproductive (Tjosvold, 1991). To meet the challenge at hand, group members need to feel like they can express their ideas without automatic rejection by other group members, present novel views of how to achieve the assigned task, but involves an open, honest and free discussion between group members.

The norming and performing stage. This stage involves the more formal creation of norms, roles, and procedures to which the group needs to adhere in order to accomplish their goal. Only after developing these standardized rules and duties can the group move on to the performing stage. In the performing stage, because the group has set down specific roles, rules, and procedures to accomplish the assigned task, group members will be able to work together effectively and efficiently. Once this has happened, and the group is functioning successfully as a cohesive group, their identity as a group member is enhanced and the group is likely to more than successfully meet their assigned goal or task.

The adjourning stage. As the group reaches completion of their assigned task, group members begin preparing for the breakup of their group. In some cases, such as when group members have other things competing for their time and effort, the group's end is not stressful. On the other hand, because group members have formed a cohesive group in order to solve their assigned task, they may still have a strong sense of identity with the group and this can cause separation anxiety--much like when a parent drops their child off at daycare. Group members are used to seeing each other, spending time together, often intensely working out a problem, and in between chatting about their personal lives. Often group members form friendship bonds which makes the adjourning stage more difficult. They may exchange contact information, schedule a time to get together again, so that whatever was created between them when they working as part of a unified group, remains, but unfortunately, that is seldom the case. Life moves on and so do these people who were at one time members of a highly successful group capable of solving an assigned task.

There are many types of groups with many goals and reasons for their existence. To say the above model works the same in every group, would be inaccurate. In general terms, the model is valid, but when it is specifically used to examine any one particular group, the fit may not be as tight or as representative of the stages. Further, not all stages present themselves in the same linear way that the model suggest. Some groups may go through the storming stage, fall back to the forming stage, and then move forward to the norming and performing stage. In some cases, groups may skip an entire stage. It just depends on who makes up the group and what the goal is for that group. Still, even though it is a general model for describing stages of group development, the research reports the model as having been proven successful when applied to a wide-range of groups (Johnson & Johnson, 2004).

So, what do groups do for us?

Being part of a group fulfills our need to belong, to socialize and interact with others. Being a part of a group gives us access to information, helps us understand the issues and events that confront us, helps us to define ourselves, and gives us the help we need to accomplish shared goals or objectives--things which we might not be able to accomplish by ourselves. As part of a group, we also learn to work together and quickly learn that a group is far more productive, efficient and powerful than working alone. The Amish know this well. They are known for their "barn-raisings." When newlyweds are given their plot of ground on which they will live and farm, members of the Amish community come together as a group to build the barn--a task that would take a single person perhaps one year to build, can be built by group of Amish working together in a single day. The lesson we should take away from that is that working as part of a cohesive team increases the likelihood we will succeed at whatever task or tasks we have chosen to take on.

People also use groups when they have important decisions to make and need the advice and input of others. And while groups provide help and assistance, guidance, and fulfill our needs as social creatures to interact with others, they also limit us. Being part of a group means following the rules and procedures set down by the group as whole. Also, it is important to note, regardless the size of the group to which we belong, while we as individuals have the power to influence the group, the group has the power to influence us.

Group affiliation

Groups provide us with information we might not otherwise have access to. Grannovetter (1973) wrote that we actually have access to even more diverse information through what he referred to as "the strength of weak ties" (see Figure 2). So, it's not just about the information that our group members have that we might find useful, but it's also information that members of our group have access to in their membership in a group of which we ourselves don't belong. Groups provide information, physical and emotional help when we need it, and make up part of our **social support network**. All very important to our health and well-being.

Social Comparison

One of the reasons we join groups is so that we may develop sense of self or self-concept, and one of the ways we do this is through a process of **social comparison**. People want to know if the view they have of themselves is actually shared by others. This is where social comparison comes into play. Festinger (1954) reported that people often join groups so they can "evaluate the accuracy of their personal attitudes and beliefs." In research done

Figure 2. Grannovetter's strength of weak ties.

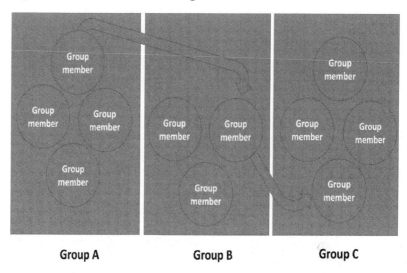

Group A   Group B   Group C

by Schachter (1959) he found that when given a choice of either waiting alone for some task to begin or waiting with others, the overwhelming majority preferred to wait with others. Again, we have a need to be part of a group.

I often ask my students to differentiate a friend from a good friend. Usually, they arrive at the most important difference: a good friend will care so much for you that they will risk the friendship by showing just how much they care. A friend might not risk telling you something you don't want to hear, whereas a good friend will take that risk if they think it's in your best interest. While we may join groups where we think they will provide us with an accurate and objective view of ourselves, we are also more likely to join groups in which we perceive the other members to be slightly inferior to us in some way--it builds our ego, and the ego is a fragile thing. This tendency to seek out the less fortunate so we can feel better about ourselves, is called **downward social comparison**.

Self-Concept and Group Membership

In 1970 Los Angeles, a 13-year-old girl was brought into a social services office by her grandmother. The child couldn't speak, read nor knew how to interact with others. In this case, the child who they named **Genie**, had been kept chained to a potty chair

197

during the day and locked into a crib at night from the age of four to the age of 13. Her only interaction with others was when her grandmother brought in her food and water, but seldom said anything to the girl. When social workers found out her story, they immediately took custody of Genie and began working with her to try and restore the mental damage that had been done by years of isolation. In the end, they were largely unsuccessful in repairing the damage and Genie remained in a nursing home for the rest of her life only being able to speak several words; she was totally incapable of being independent. Imagine if you had been the social worker who first discovered Genie, and you took her into a room away from her grandmother, and asked this question of Genie: who are you? Let's say for one moment that Genie could speak in order to answer you, but what would she say? Genie would have absolutely no idea what you were talking about because she would not have developed anything that resembled a self-concept.

Our **self-concept**, who we are, is the result of the comparisons we make with others in our culture and especially within the groups to which we belong. Our membership in groups plays a large part in our self-concept. We are defined by our likes and dislikes, by those personality traits that make us unique, but also by the people we are around--our friends, our family, and the groups to which we belong. Make no mistake about it, we are judged by those things and labeled accordingly. Once we begin to think of ourselves as part of a group, that our identity is influenced by those group memberships, we are no longer an "I" or "me," but a "we."

Research has found that when we identify with a group, when we think of ourselves as that "we" and we put ourselves into categories. As part of a group of which we have categorized stereotypically, we begin to identify ourselves with those stereotypes, we then assign those characteristics of what it means to be a member of that group to ourselves, and just like that, we have stereotyped ourselves (Hogg, 2001).

Our sense of self-worth is also highly influenced by our group memberships. The type or quality of the groups to which we belong influences our esteem of the group and consequently our own self-esteem (Crocker & Luhtanen, 1990). If for some reason we find that our self-esteem is threatened or being attacked, we can always revert back to comparing ourselves to those groups of which we are members that we regard as having high status so that the result is that our self-esteem is repaired and we feel slightly superior to others again. In fact, a very simple reason some people are prejudice is because by seeing their group as superior to others, it allows people to look down on people who belong to other groups and our self-esteem increases (Crocker & Major, 1989). Leary and Baumeister (2000) add that if we feel our self-esteem appears to be going down-hill, which threatens our continued membership in a particular group, we look for ways to increase our self-esteem, self-concept and overall value to the group so that we restore to ourselves to the good graces of the group. This enhances our strong belief in our worthiness to belong in that group (Leary & Baumeister, 2000).

Groups, Roles and Selves

Group action. A lot of research has focused on effective work teams. Though that research has been done for 30 years or more, it still points to a lais·sez-faire leadership style as being one of the best especially when in industries that require a lot of thinking outside the box and creative support. Findings of that research show that an informal and relaxed atmosphere are conducive to this type of creative freedom, but there are constructive constraints, which is not typical in the American workplace. For instance, research on groups has found that more productive groups are more likely to exhibit the following characteristics:

> 1. There is a lot of "on-task" discussion where all members of the group are expected to participate;
> 2. The tasks assigned to the group are well-defined, have goals, and are achievable;
> 3. Respect for each member of the group results in group members listening and paying close attention to what other members of the group are saying or suggesting;
> 4. A single person does not dominate the conversations;
> 5. While there is disagreement, group members are always respectful to their fellow group members and respond constructively to any suggestions others make;

6. There can be criticism, as long as it is respectful, honest, and constructive--the criticism is of the idea and not the member expressing the idea;

7. There is complete openness to new ideas and they are expressed freely without fear of instant condemnation;

8. Assignments are clear;

9. Leadership shifts constantly as no one person has the power or status to decide on a plan of action; groups are democratic in that regard.

10. Finally, group members understand the rules and procedures for this kind of work environment.

Group structure

Every group has norms with which they operate to accomplish their goal. Those norms may be **implicit**, obvious but not necessarily openly expressed, and explicit, formally stated. **Prescriptive norms** essentially dictate how group members are expected to perform and act. **Proscriptive norms** are just the opposite, they are formally stated policies and procedures by which group members are expected to behave. For instance, if you were to start work for a large company, your first day or two would be spent in workshops where you would learn both prescriptive and proscriptive norms of that organization. One of the chief proscriptive norms you would almost certainly learn is what constitutes sexual harassment.

All groups foster cohesiveness--it is the glue that holds the group together. Sometimes, depending on the group and their goals, cohesiveness may be forced on group members because it binds them together and has the potential to improve overall group performance--unless there is resistance in the group to the near tyrannical nature this can sometimes take. Also, the more attractive group membership appears to us, the more we are willing to pay or put up with in order to join the group. The more that we have "paid" to get into the group, the more committed we are to the group and its goals. Consequently, the smaller the group size, the more cohesive are the members and the more important the actions of any single group member the more cohesive it becomes.

Also, threats from outside the group tend to make the group more cohesive--again, picking up on work by Simmel (1922).

Primary Groups

Social psychologists recognize two specialized groups based on who the other members of the group are. The first is a **primary group**. Primary groups are usually small in size, highly cohesive, share close personal bonds and the group tends to persist through the life course. Members of the group care for one another, share many activities together, and spend long periods of time together. The goal of the primary group is actually to endure and maintain the relationships they have with one another. The best example of a primary group is the family, though there can be other primary groups. Characteristics of primary groups include:

1. Shared concern about the other members of the group, spend a great deal of time together, assist in the development of the self, offer a safe haven for its members, and provide emotional and physical assistance to its members.
2. Families are usually the best example of a primary group.
3. Unlike other types of groups, the goal of the primary group is to stay together and maintain the bonds that unite them.
4. Charles Cooley was the first to coin the term *primary group* in his book, Social Organization: A Study of the Larger Mind (1909).
5. Sometimes close friends, life-long friends, can also serve as primary groups as they perform many of the same functions as do families.
6. Love, caring, concern and support are characteristics of primary groups, which is why the family is the best example of a primary group.
7. Examples of primary groups would obviously include the family, but also intimate relationships, support groups for people struggling with mental health, grief, or additional problems.

Charles Cooley

In his book, *Social Organization: A Study of the Larger Mind* (1909), Cooley introduced the term primary group. He maintained that they played an important role in the development of the self. Cooley went on to suggest that the concept of primary group was so important, not just in the development of the self, but that the closeness and comfort of ties that we often attempt to create primary groups in settings other than the family. For instance, within organizations sometimes people will develop the same kind of close and supportive relationships that are characteristic of families. Further, the whole concept of **fictive kin** ties into this almost innate need within us to form these strong, enduring and supportive ties with others who are not related to us by blood.

Secondary Groups

Secondary groups are typically large groups to which we belong where work tasks are the reason for the existence of the group. Other characteristics of **secondary groups** include:

1. Relationships tend to be impersonal and work related, members interact on a more formal level, and usually membership in the group is temporary.

2. Ties between members are weak, usually lack emotional support, and are not committed to the long-term survival of the group.

3. Charles Cooley coined the term secondary group because they tend to develop later in life, whereas primary groups usually are formed at birth, and have less influence on the development of the self.

4. Members tend to have little personal information about other members.

5. Group members typically exchange things--money for service, studying for a university degree, and athletic teams.

6. Secondary groups are completely goal-oriented.

7. Member's roles are typically more interchangeable and fluid.

8. Unlike primary groups, members of secondary groups choose to be members of the group.

In-Groups and Out-Groups

In-groups are the groups with which we associate ourselves. We feel that we are alike in some way albeit probably superficial way. **In-groups** are those groups with which we identify. **Out-groups** on the other hand, are groups made up of members who we perceive to be different than us, though again, in usually superficial ways. Basically, an outgroup is made up of members who are not part of our in-group. Research on in-groups and out-groups has found the following:

1. We have a preference for members of our in-group over those in our out-group.
2. We have an overwhelming need to feel slightly, or in some cases of mental illness, a need to feel greatly superior to others. While a little bit of egotism has been shown to be healthy, too much leads to arrogance, overconfidence, and can be associated with some mental illnesses like narcissism. Therefore, when looking at our out-groups, we will find something about them that makes them inferior to our in-group and gives us the ability to look down our nose at them and see them as more different from us than they really are. It leads to a feeling among members that their in-group is superior to all others and therefore their way of thinking is right, moral and justified. Just ask a Ku Klux Klan member. One typical tactic used by an in-group against an out-group is to dehumanize them. A classic example of this historically was the treatment of Jews in Nazi propaganda as vermin that needed to be exterminated. Even today we see Muslim Americans and undocumented aliens being dehumanized because they scare members of an in-group. Dehumanization is a very effective tactic because it suggests that the out-group is less than human and therefore doesn't deserve to be treated as a human.

3. This feeling of difference between a person's in-group and their out-group, and the superiority that goes along with it, can in some cases lead to violence.

4. A member of an in-group tends to look at their in-group and develop the opinion that they are diverse while members of an out-group are often perceived as "all alike."

5. Prejudice is highly associated with out-groups.

6. Likewise, the perception of all out-group members being alike, leads to generalizations which are a key component of stereotypical thinking and are associated with prejudice.

7. In-group bias refers to the favorable attitudes people have about members of their in-group as opposed to members of an out-group. The term ***in-group bias*** was coined by Henri Tajfel in his social identity theory.

8. In-group bias leads to the **homogeneity effect** which is the belief that members of the out-group are far more alike than they really are and are more alike than members of the in-group.

As I've noted, in-group bias, favoritism and the homogeneity effect all are characteristic of **prejudice**. As a reminder, prejudice is a negative, rigid, generalization about people in an out-group; we are not prejudice towards members of our own in-group. These negative and rigid attitudes are based solely on membership in an out-group, are usually intense, and that intensity of dislike or hatred towards members of an out-group can often lead to violence.

Reference Groups

As previously mentioned, groups influence how we perceive ourselves. When we use groups and the members of those groups to evaluate ourselves, by comparing ourselves to those other members, it is called a **reference group. Social comparison theory** suggests that by comparing ourselves to others in those groups, we define our self. Merton (1957) suggested that we find groups, or specific group members whom we idealize and who occupy the same role that we wish to eventually occupy, serve as models for us as we develop a more concrete self. Thus, we form our self-identity. The central belief of social comparison theory is that within us is a drive to develop accurate evaluations about our self by comparing ourselves to those respected and admired others.

Reference groups essentially become a person's frame of reference and a source for shaping their identity to match that reference group or person.

Social Networks

A social network consists of people who are in constant interaction with one another. They are connected through direct or indirect social relationships, casual acquaintances to close family members, and from which we receive **social capital.** Social capital is the expected benefit, economic or social, that we expect to derive from the preferential treatment we receive from members of our social

Figure 3. A social network diagram showing both nodes and ties.

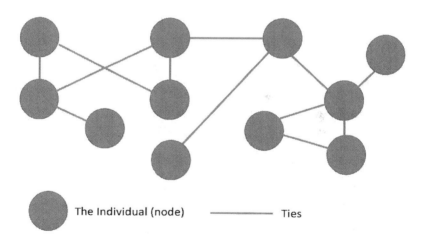

The Individual (node) ———————— Ties

network. The study of social networks is referred to as social network analysis or social network theory. Social network theory sees these ongoing and intertwined social relationships in terms of nodes and ties. Nodes represent that individual who occupies a position within the social network and the ties are relationships between nodes--in other words, between individual actors within the social network.

205

Research has repeatedly found that social networks operate on many levels of closeness--from the family with its unshakeable and close bonds to the level of nations. Social networks provide us with a variety of diverse information that can be used to solve problems, achieve goals, overcome threats, and in the case of war, achieve victory.

Social psychologists are interested in studying social networks because of their potential for intense influence on individuals. Social networks should be considered in some sense as tools needed to form relationships, influence others and be influenced by others, achieve an intense level of cohesion, and ultimately increase their social support network.

There can be many different kinds of ties between nodes as seen in Figure 3. A social network simply ties all the nodes together. Some nodes have very dense ties with other nodes, and some nodes have weak ties, but they are all part of a social network. Networks are often used to value the social capital of each individual member of the social network. Social capital is the strength, power, prestige that the individual brings to the social network with him or her. With that they can be awarded preferential treatment and more say in the rules and procedures that are in place for each social network.

Online Communities

Online communities are relatively new--only having been on the scene since the early 1980s--maybe even later if you look at the birth of Facebook. Community itself is an old concept. However, what has modernized the term is the advent of the online community, which has made our world much smaller. In the past, your community consisted of your family, any other farmers who lived nearby, and members of the town which you went to on occasion for supplies. Consequently, interaction between community members was done face to face. That definition has become completely outdated with the advent of the Internet--save for communities like the Amish. Generally, you no longer have to be physically proximate to interact with others in your "community."

Online interactions are not face to face, but is a virtual place where members join together in groups of hugely diverse tasks. The Internet is a great source for information, but that also can be a weakness since anyone can post anything to the Internet. Some online communities involve little cost--the price of an Internet connection, while other communities require much greater expense in the way of games, apps, dating sites, and a host of other costly necessities to participate in the online community. Online communities have also become an additional form of communication between people who know each other in real life--Facebook or Twitter would be good examples. Most of the time members communicate through keyboards, but today they may communicate vocally and visually. The popularity of online communities has skyrocketed as they provide near instant communication with members of the communities to which we belong.

Finally, online communities have completely changed the face of doing business in the US. Once upon a time, you used to drive to your local shoe store for a pair of shoes, then to a clothing store for new pants, and finally on your way home maybe you would stop and pick up groceries for dinner. Not anymore. Many retailers have had to enter into the online community in order to survive. Whereas for years Amazon has promised its paying Prime members delivery within two days, Walmart has now had to do the same thing in order to compete...or die. In fact, if you check out prices on Walmart and Amazon you would find the majority of items are priced identically.

Types of Social Influence Related to Group Membership

Social facilitation

Generally speaking, most people perform better when they're being watched. Being watched makes us anxious--"I have to do well or people will think less of me" and that helps to enhance our performance on some task. So, whether it's playing pool, solving a math problem on the whiteboard in front of the class, playing baseball, or any other kind of activity, we perform better when there is an audience watching us perform. This is another example of how stress can actually lead to improved performance in most people, but certainly not all.

Social loafing

It is common for people to think that putting people together to work on a task as a group results in more accomplishments and higher quality accomplishments because you are combining the skills and abilities of the individuals who make up a particular group. Unfortunately, that is not always the case with some members of the group contributing less than expected and sit back and let others do the majority of the assigned task. **Social loafing** refers to the fact that most people do not exert themselves on easy task performance when working in a large group because their performance, or lack thereof, is less noticeable because of the size of the group. In other words, our performance declines as the group size increases.

Consequences of social loafing include poor cohesiveness of the group which can lead to a splintering of the group with those who are performing the majority of tasks (the "in group") versus those who are performing a minimum of assigned tasks (the "out group"). The result of this could lead to resentment by the in group towards the out group which results in splintering of the task group and therefore the group is less cohesive which negatively affects productivity.

What Are the Causes of Social Loafing?

1.Group Size. Basically, the larger the group, the easier it is for some group members to sit back and let others do the work. When in large groups, we are often anonymous--lost in the size of the group.
2. Poor Motivation. If a group member doesn't feel motivated to accomplish the assigned group task, they are far more likely to let others do the majority of the work. College students often see this when assigned to group work. Poorly motivated students who don't like group work and don't want to be in a project that requires group work, are almost always poorly motivated which results in social loafing.
3. Task Value. If a group member doesn't believe in the value of the assigned task, and see their time as being wasted, they are less likely to participate in working

towards task completion and thereby force others to pick up the slack.

4. Feeling as if Their Contribution Doesn't Matter. If a group member doesn't feel that their efforts really matter for task completion, they are less likely to contribute to the group's task.

Deindividuation

Deindividuation is essentially when, largely because of group size, we become anonymous--we are just one person among a crowd of people. The larger the crowd or group, the more anonymous we become. **Deindividuation** refers to that lack of

Figure 4. Social facilitation effect.

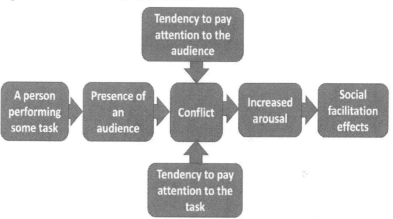

personal identity and with that also makes us do things in groups we would not otherwise do on our own. It takes away our individual responsibility, moral restraints we would otherwise have as an individual on our own, and accountability for our actions. It diminishes our self-awareness as we lose our personal identity in that large group or crowd. This is most likely to occur when we are in large groups and are aroused by distracting activities. Riots are often a good example. What some people do in riots, when they feel deindividualized, they might never do on their own.

Group polarization

When we are in a group and have been assigned a task to perform or a problem to solve, group members have their own ideas on how to perform the task and these are presented during discussion. If other people in the group, especially those we regard as having information or experience in regards the task, support our idea, and enough others support our idea, the group likely takes on more cohesiveness. In other words, what is seen as normative versus deviant, takes over. Dissent with the proposed plan to accomplish the task is diminished and strengthens the ideas in regard successfully completing the assigned task. This often leads to a risky shift--choosing a solution that is much riskier than any one individual would be willing to take on their own--and too often, the risk doesn't pay off.

Conformity

First, **conformity** implies that people will change their behavior or attitude to go along with the group even if they don't agree with the group's behavior or attitude towards some assigned task. In other words, we yield to a feeling of group pressure focused on us to conform. Factors that influence conformity include:

1. group size,
2. cohesiveness of the group,
3. the perception of a legitimate authority that supports the particular activity even if as an individual we perceive it to be wrong,
4. the perception of the institution or environment in which we are expected to conform,
5. the physical distance of any victim of our conformity, and
6. the physical distance from us of the perceived authority figure.
7. group unanimity has a very large effect on conformity.

Obedience

Obedience is simply following the commands of others who someone feels has the legitimate authority to issue the commands. Sometimes we are more likely to obey if the perceived authority figure takes on the responsibility for our actions, and sometimes we obey out of fear of the consequences for us if we don't obey.

Compliance

Compliance is simply doing what is asked of you to do-- sometimes this may be in the way of a simple request and sometimes it may be in the way of a command. If a command, it may be a case of obedience.

Normative social influence

All groups have norms. Following those norms, or fitting in, makes us feel better, be like the other members of the group, and helps make the group more cohesive.

Informational social influence

If we are part of a group, believe the group has the right view of things and is competent, we are more likely going to go along with the group--especially when there is an important task to be accomplished or the group is in battle with out-groups.

Groupthink

Groupthink is when several members of a group tend to dominate a groups discussion when thinking of ways to solve a task. The result is usually a poor decision-making process and a solution that does not adequately solve the assigned task.
Factors leading to groupthink include:

1. A high level of group cohesiveness
2. Isolation of the group from outside influence
Dominate and influential leaders

4. Typically occur in high stress situations--pressure to perform

Characteristics of groupthink include:

1. Feeling invulnerable
2. A belief in the superiority of the group and its strong belief it has the best solution to the assigned task
3. A tendency to ignore or devalue information that opposes the task solution being supported by the majority of members
4. A strong push for group conformity
5. The stereotyping of groups outside their own

Brainstorming

Brainstorming is a term we routinely hear when there is an assigned task that as part of a group we are expected to accomplish or solve. Creativity is a good thing, but it has been shown in groups that brainstorming, especially when the groups lack good leadership, most often leads to fewer novel ideas for solving the assigned task than more ideas. Not only does brainstorming lead to fewer new or novel solutions to the assigned task, but it also results in less innovation--in other words, it reduces creativity. In the end, it is clear that more innovation and creativity is associated with the individual working alone than when he or see brainstorms as part of a group.

Terms and Concepts to Know

Group
Interdependent
Life course
Social category
Social aggregates
Stages of Group Development
Forming stage
Storming stage
Norming and performing stage
Adjourning stage

Group affiliation
Social support network
Social comparison
Downward social comparison
Genie
Self-concept
Implicit norms
Prescriptive norms
Proscriptive norms
Primary group
Secondary group
In-groups
Out-groups
In-group bias
Homogeneity effect
Reference group
Social comparison theory
Social networks
Social capital
Online communities
Social facilitation effect
Social loafing
Deindividuation
Group polarization
Conformity
Obedience
Compliance
Normative social influence
Informational social influence
Groupthink
Brainstorming

References

Baumeister, R., & Leary, M. (1995). The need to belong: Desire for interpersonal attachments as a fundamental human motivation. *Psychological Bulletin*, 117(3), 497-529.

Buote, V., Pancer, S., Pratt, M., Adams, G., Birnie-Lefcovitch, S., Polivy, J., & Wintre, M. (2007). The importance of friends:

Friendship and adjustment among 1st-year university students. *Journal of Adolescent Research*, 22(6), 665–689.

Crocker, J., & Luhtanen, R. (1990). Collective self-esteem and ingroup bias. *Journal of Personality and Social Psychology,* 58(1), 60-67.

Crocker, J., & Major, B. (1989). Social stigma and self-esteem: The self-protective properties of stigma. *Psychological Review*, 96(4) 608-630.

Eisenberger, N., Lieberman, M., & Williams, K. (2003). Does rejection hurt? An FMRI study of social exclusion. *Science*, 302(5643), 290-292.

Festinger L (1954). A theory of social comparison processes. *Human Relations*, 7(2), 117–140.

Grannovetter, M. (1973) The Strength of Weak Ties. American *Journal of Sociology*, 78(6), 1360-1380.

Hogg, M. (2001). A Social Identity Theory of Leadership. *Personality and Social Psychology Review*, 5(3), 184-200.

Johnson D., Johnson R. (2004). *Assessing students in groups: Promoting group responsibility and individual accountability.* Thousand Oaks: Sage.

Kuypers, B., Davies, D., & Hazewinkel, A. (1986). Developmental patterns in self-analytic groups. *Human Relations*, 39(9), 793–815.

Leary, M., & Baumeister, R. (2000). The nature and function of self-esteem: Sociometer theory. In M. P. Zanna (Ed.), *Advances in Experimental Social Psychology,* Vol. 32, pp. 1-62). San Diego, CA, US: Academic Press.

Merton, R. 1957. *Social theory and social structure.* New York: Free Press.

Putnam, R. (2000). *The collapse and revival of American community.* Simon & Schuster.

Rispens, S., & Jehn, K. (2011). Conflict in workgroups: Constructive, destructive, and asymmetric conflict. In D. De Cremer, R. van Dick, & J. K. Murnighan (Eds.), *Social psychology and organizations* (pp. 185–209). New York, NY: Routledge/Taylor & Francis Group.

Schachter, S. (1959) *The Psychology of affiliation.* Stanford:

Stanford University Press.

Simmel, G. (1922). *Conflict and the web of group affiliations.* Translated and edited by Kurt Wolff (1955), Glencoe, IL: Free Press.

Tjosvold, M. (1991). *Team organization: An enduring competitive advantage.* Chichester, UK: John Wiley & Sons.

Tuckman, B., & Jensen, M. (1977). Stages of small-group development revisited. *Group Organizational Studies*, 2, 419-27

Turner, J., & Tajfel, H. (1986). The social identity theory of intergroup behavior. *Psychology of Intergroup Relations*, 7-24.

Williams, K. (2007). Ostracism: The kiss of social death. *Social and Personality Psychology Compass*, 1(1), 236-247.

Chapter 9: The Development of Prejudice

Prejudice on the Rise

According to the Associated Press, 51 percent of Americans, express explicit anti-black attitudes and that compares with 48 percent in a similar 2008 survey (NPR, 2012). Further, in national poll conducted by Quinnipiac University (NDTV, 2017), 63 percent of those polled said that hatred and prejudice had increased since the November 2016 election. Also reported was that 77 percent of those polled said that **prejudice** against minority groups in the US was a serious or somewhat serious problem. Mirroring the latter finding, 70 percent of those polled reported anti-Semitism to be on the rise--up from an earlier poll in February 2017.

Figure 1. Anti-Muslim Discrimination. Pew Research Center, 2017.

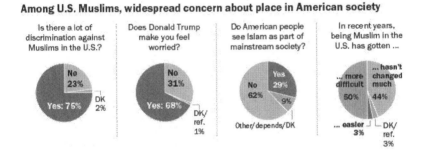

Discrimination against Muslims and Hispanics is also on the rise. In a recent Pew poll (Pew, 2017) 48 percent of Muslims polled said they had been the target of anti-Muslim discrimination in the past year and 75 percent of Muslims polled stated they felt there was a lot of anti-Muslim discrimination directed at them. The poll went on report that 82 percent of Muslims interviewed said "they were either very concerned (66%) or somewhat concerned (16%) about extremism in the name of Islam around the world. This is similar to the percentage of the U.S. general public that shares these concerns (83%), although Muslims are more likely than U.S. adults overall to say they are *very* concerned about extremism in the name of Islam around the world (66% vs. 49%). Surprisingly, the same poll found that 92 percent of those interviewed agreed with the statement: "I am proud to be an American."

Figure 2. Proud to be an American. Pew Research Center, 2017.

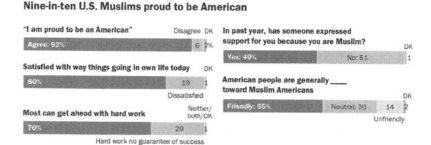

Nine-in-ten U.S. Muslims proud to be American

Prejudice and Discrimination Defined

The first thing we need to do is to define what **prejudice** is and how it differs from discrimination. Prejudice is:

1. A negative attitude held against others simply because they are members of a group different from the group that you belong to.
2. Prejudice is an attitude whereas discrimination is the behavior.
3. Common features of prejudice include negative feelings, stereotyped beliefs, and a tendency to discriminate against members of the group.
4. Prejudices are usually negative statements finding fault with the group at which the prejudice is directed. A prejudice person may know little or nothing about the group of which they are prejudice.

Discrimination is a behavioral and intentional act of withholding services, benefits, and other things in general. **Individual discrimination** is denial of services or other things by an individual towards people to whom someone has prejudicial feelings towards the group to which that person belongs. **Institutional discrimination** is when those acts of denial of service or other things are sanctioned by the state. For instance, laws that existed prior to the Civil Rights Movement forcing blacks to sit in the back of the bus, drink from separate drinking fountains, use different bathrooms and more are examples of institutional discrimination.

In short, *prejudice is a negative, irrational and rigid attitude that is generalized to entire group of people who are perceived as different from the person who is prejudice.* Prejudice is largely based on stereotypes. Whereas prejudice is the attitude, discrimination is the act.

Ingroups and Outgroups

Prejudice is directed at people from outside of their own group, their **ingroup,** which included people we perceive to be like us in some way. People simply have more knowledge about their own group, so they don't use heuristics to make judgments about them. **Heuristics** are rules that people use to make decisions, judgments, and solve problems, usually because they don't have enough information about members of another group. Heuristics are akin to unwritten rules, stereotypes, guesses, judgments, and profiling. While these internal rules often work well, they can sometimes lead to systematic errors in judgement or cognitive biases. Therefore, when evaluating members from other groups, or **outgroups**, individuals may have access to limited information and refer to predetermined ideas to make predictions about behavior.

Research has found that **ingroup favoritism**, which is a type of bias, or preference for members of the group one belongs to, can occur even when the outgroup had no prior social meaning to them; in other words, people they had no prior contact with. Research has shown that when subjects, who had been randomly assigned to groups based on some insignificant factor like tossing a coin, subjects displayed ingroup favoritism and exhibited preferential treatment to the other members of their group. Even though those group ties were the result of random assignment and essentially meant they had nothing more in common than that random assignment.

Outgroup Homogeneity

The **outgroup homogeneity effect** is the perception that members of an outgroup are more similar, mentally or physically,

218

than members of the ingroup. In other words, people think that members of their ingroup tend to be more diverse, different and unique--just the opposite of how they think of members of their outgroups. Anything that makes one person different from another can essentially serve as an indication of who is assigned to the outgroup. This kind of assignment can be seen during war when it is typical to dehumanize the enemy and to lump him or her into a category based on appearance. During the Iraq war, American soldiers often referred to the enemy as "towel heads" or "camel jockeys," during the Vietnam War the enemy was referred to as "gooks," "slant eyes," and during World War II German soldiers were referred to as "krauts" by American soldiers. To reiterate, *any person perceived as different from another and in some way different from the "ingroup" by default becomes a member of the outgroup.*

Stereotypes

Stereotyping is associated with prejudice. To stereotype someone is to put that other person you perceive as different from you into a category. By putting people into category, we are essentially saying that everyone in that category is exactly alike. It leads to group distortions, myths and unsupported truths. It blinds us and leads us to believe that members of the group to which we belong are made up of a collection of unique and distinct individuals, while members of the group to whom we are prejudice are thought to be all alike. This kind of **social categorization** leads to a complete distortion of the group and the uniqueness of its members and is known as the **outgroup homogeneity effect.**

Functions of Stereotypes

Stereotypes can have positive functions. Those include:

1. They allow people to quickly process new information about an event or person.
2. They organize people's past experiences.
3. They help people to meaningfully assess differences between individuals and groups.

4. They help people to make predictions about another person's behavior.

Dangers of Stereotypes

Stereotypes can lead to distortions of reality for several reasons:

1. They cause people to exaggerate differences among groups.
2. They lead people to focus selectively on information that agrees with the stereotype and ignore information that disagrees with it.
3. They tend to make people see other groups as overly homogeneous, even though people can easily see that the groups they belong to are heterogeneous.

Prejudice

It is easy to be prejudice towards people you don't know. For instance, Aging Watch, is a website setup to inform the public about elder stereotypes, identifies five characterizations of the elderly in the media:

1. Elders are portrayed as helpless victims,
2. Elders who defy negative stereotypes are presented as bizarre and comical,
3. Growing old is equated with inevitable deterioration and decline,
4. They are demonized as a group, and
5. Elders are underrepresented and ignored (Aging Watch, 2010).

Often the media portray seniors either as frail and needing help getting off the floor, or as leading an active but well-to-do lifestyle. The reality is somewhere in between for many seniors. While the media may target the elderly as being weak and needing help with activities of daily living (e.g., the walk-in tub, emergency communication devices, hearing aids, assisted living communities), they target younger people for very different products (e.g., cars, real estate, soda, foods, alcohol).

Prejudice can sometimes appear as positive when in fact it is still a prejudice based on a stereotype. For instance, if you live in Miami or New York and need a doctor, your family might suggest that you go to one of those "Jewish doctors" because "they're so smart and make the best doctors." Or if you're looking to hire someone to do computer programming you might want to hire an Asian because the stereotype says they're smart and studious.

Prejudice is rigid. Once learned or adopted, prejudice is very difficult to eliminate or often even reduce. Stereotypes are not easily changed. Even when people encounter instances that disconfirm their stereotypes of a particular group, they tend to assume that those instances are atypical subtypes of the group. For example, Ben stereotypes gay men as being non-athletic and not into sports. When he meets Dave, an athletic gay man who loves football, he assumes that Dave is not truly representative of gay people. Or, Frank stereotypes Mexican-American males as heavy drinkers who love their cerveza, but Juan doesn't drink, and therefore he thinks Juan is different. In other words, they make exceptions. He or she is "different." They're not like the "rest."

Prejudice is irrational as people's perceptions are influenced by their expectations. For example, Liz has a stereotype of elderly people as being mentally unstable. When she sees an elderly woman sitting on a park bench alone, talking out loud, she thinks that the woman is talking to herself because she is unstable. Liz fails to notice that the woman is actually using the hands-free device on her cell phone.

Prejudice is a destructive phenomenon, and it is pervasive because it serves many psychological and social functions. Prejudice allows people to avoid doubt and fear. For example, Rachel's parents came from a working-class background but are now wealthy business owners. Rachel might develop a dislike of the working class because she does not want to be identified with working-class people. She believes such an association would damage her claim to upper-class social status. Prejudice also provides people **scapegoats** to blame in times of trouble. For Example, Glen blames his unemployment on foreign nationals whom he believes are incompetent but willing to work for low wages.

Prejudice can boost self-esteem. For example, a poor white farmer in the nineteenth-century South could feel better about his own meager existence by insisting on his superiority to African-American slaves. Evolutionary psychologists suggest that prejudice allows people to bond with their own group by contrasting their own groups to outsider groups. For example, most religious and ethnic groups maintain some prejudices against other groups, which help to make their own group seem more special.

Prejudice also legitimizes discrimination because it justifies one group's dominance over another. For example, pseudoscientific arguments about the mental inferiority of African Americans allowed whites to feel justified in owning slaves. People commonly hold prejudices about individuals of a particular social class, sex, sexual orientation, age, political affiliation, race, or ethnicity (Adorno & Frenkel-Brunswik, 1993). Researchers are interested in knowing what prejudices are held by people, the intensity of those prejudices, and how they were learned or adopted. With this information social policy makers can work to develop programs that will reduce prejudice.

Stereotype Threat

Stereotype threat refers to actions on the part of someone who is stereotyped by people in a given society that seems to confirm the stereotype. Someone who is stereotyped doesn't have to believe in the stereotype, but they do have to be aware of its existence. As long as a person is aware of the stereotype and believes they might fit that stereotype, though they themselves do not believe in the truth of the stereotype, a stereotype threat may be said to exist. Research has shown that when people believe their actions may confirm the stereotype, their performance in specific tasks may suffer.

In one study done with white and black college students, researchers divided the students into two groups. The control group, which in this case was identified as the non-stereotype threat group, was told they would be completing a problem-solving exercise but that it did not measure their ability to solve the problem but rather focused on how they solved the problem. In the experimental group, which was identified as the stereotype threat group, students were asked to complete a verbal aptitude test from the Graduate Record Exam. These latter students were told that their performance would be an indication of their intelligence. Researchers found that the black students in the stereotype threat group performed less well than did the white participants but performed equally as well as white students in the non-stereotype threat group (Steele et al., 1995; Steele, 1997).

Do People Who Are Prejudice Always Discriminate?

People who are prejudice have been found not to necessarily express their prejudice. This could largely be explained by their reluctance to be "politically incorrect." But it could also be explained by the weak link between attitudes and behavior. It might be easy for someone to say they don't like members of a particular outgroup, but would they display that prejudice in the way of discrimination when face-to-face with a member of the particular outgroup they are prejudiced towards? In an experiment by LaPiere (1936), he found that as he and his Chinese traveling-partner attempted to stay at hotels, only one hotel refused them service, but when he contacted the hotels by mail asking if they would serve Chinese, many hotels indicated that they would not provide service to Chinese. The moral here is that people with prejudiced attitudes do not always display discriminatory behavior (Farley, 2000).

Measuring Prejudice

So, if people who are prejudice may be afraid or unwilling to display their prejudice, how then do we measure prejudice? Imagine coming to this statement on a survey designed to measure prejudice:

I am prejudice. (Circle one) YES or NO

How would you answer it? Do you suppose anyone would answer, "Yes?" Probably not. Even members of the KKK or Aryan Nation would not think of themselves as prejudice, but as "realistic" or "justified," but not prejudice. Ok, so there might be a problem in trying to measure it directly. There might be a few people who would answer yes, but most people aren't going to think of their attitudes as prejudice. So, we still haven't come up with an effective way to measure prejudice. How about we use the following to measure prejudice?

I would marry someone of a different race.
(Circle one) YES or NO or MAYBE

Couldn't we say that someone was prejudice if they answered "no?" The logic here being that we select people for dating based on how attractive we find them as individuals and not as members of a group. For instance, John is 22 years old, single, and white. Let's say I lined up 10 single white women in front of him. Should I assume that John would want to date a woman simply because she was white? Of course not. Some of them may be too old for John. Some may be too short or too tall. Some may have a prettier smile than others. Some may be underage. In other words, John will choose to date someone he finds attractive ... and attraction is an individual appeal that comes from seeing what that individual person looks like. For John to say that he would only date someone of the same race, negates the importance of individual attraction. John would literally have to say that all members of a 'race' look alike to him and that all members of that 'race' are not attractive to him. Which is simply nonsense.

The Bogardus Scale

Maybe, we could measure prejudice by asking people with which of the following statements they agree. This is an adaptation of the Bogardus Social Distance Scale (Bogardus, 1947), a way of measuring how close or accepting of another group we are. The general idea is that the more prejudice we are, the more distance we want to keep between ourselves and members of the other group. Can you figure out how it works? Respondents are asked whether they would admit members of minorities to a variety of situations, ranging from close kinship by marriage, to living close by as neighbors, or to exclude them from the country. The general idea is that the more prejudice someone is, the more distance they want to keep between their self and members of the other group.
Let's intensify the scale by using it to measure prejudice towards someone of a different race. So, someone who circles "1" but not "2" or above, is someone who doesn't want people of a

different race being close to them, while someone who circles "6" would be someone who is comfortable with having someone of a different race near them.

Read each question below and then circle "Yes" or "No" for each statement.

1. It's ok for someone of a different race to live in this country. YES or NO
2. It's ok for someone of a different race to live in my state. YES or NO
3. It's ok for someone of a different race to live in my city. YES or NO
4. It's ok for someone of a different race to live in my neighborhood. YES or NO
5. It's ok for someone of a different race to live next door to me. YES or NO
6. It's ok for someone of a different race to marry my son or daughter. YES or NO

What do you think? Does this do a better job of measuring prejudice towards someone of a different race? It's still not perfect, is it?

Interestingly enough, the research says that 39 percent of Americans polled in a national Pew poll (Bialik, 2017) reported that increasing intermarriage (i.e., interracial and interethnic) is "good for society," which is up from 24 percent in 2010. The most likely to agree with that statement were adults under the age of 30, those with a college degree, and who identified as progressive or Democrat.

Another significant change in the number of Americans who would oppose an interracial or interethnic marriage in their own family--down from 31 percent in 2000 to only 10 percent today. The most significant shift in opposing an interracial or interethnic marriage in their family was noted among non-blacks. As of 2017, only 14 percent of non-blacks reported that they would oppose interracial or interethnic marriage in their family, which is down from 63 percent in 1990.

Causes of Prejudice and Discrimination

One simple explanation for the social development of prejudice relates to Karl Marx's work. Simply put, the powerful have the ability to discriminate. In fact, given the definition of discrimination, that it is basically the power to withhold, power and authority are necessary ingredients for discrimination. Further work by C. Wright Mills and his Power Elite, and you now have all the ingredients for near **institutional discrimination**. According to him, the rich and powerful make the laws and those laws favor

Figure 3. Intermarriage across the U.S. Pew Research Center, 2015.

Across metro areas, huge variation in intermarriage rates

Share of newlyweds with a spouse of a different race or ethnicity, by metropolitan area (2011-2015)

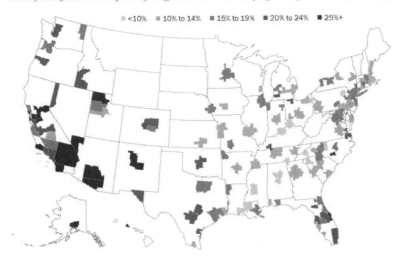

themselves. Consequently, it is easy for them to develop negative attitudes about those they do not interact with, do not understand, and question their work ethic since they are not "up there" with them. In fact, it is not uncommon for the rich and powerful to develop negative attitudes towards the very people who have suffered under their oppression. Most slave owners in the US at the end of the American Civil War had negative attitudes about their slaves.

Religion and the Development of Prejudice

Study after study has found that while some religions are more tolerant of other religions and religious beliefs, many are not. Prejudice and religiosity are highly correlated (Lundblad, 2001) as is religiosity and racism (Hall, et al., 2009). One study (Brown-Iannuzzi et al., 2018) reported that "Theists often receive the benefit of being stereotyped as trustworthy and moral, whereas atheists are viewed as untrustworthy and immoral." One study (Allport, 1967) found that churchgoers were more prejudice and non-churchgoers and people with an extrinsic religious orientation (i.e., put their religiosity on display) were more prejudice than people with an intrinsic religious orientation (i.e., felt no need to outwardly display their religiosity).

By its very nature, religion has to promote prejudice. For a religion, denomination, sect, or cult to survive it must convince its members that it offers the right path and that other religions do not follow the right path--for a religion to say anything different would certainly lead to its demise.

Historically, many wars fought have invoked the name of God or outright fought that war in God's name. During the Crusades, a series of wars fought to free the Holy land of Muslim "infidels," between 1096 and 1291, it is estimated, because counting the dead was not a common practice until the 1700s, that around one million people died--Christians, Jews, and Muslims.

Realistic Conflict Theory

Another potential cause of prejudice is intergroup competition. **Realistic group conflict** occurs when people compete over scarce resources. As a consequence, ethnocentrism, which is the belief that your race or ethnic group is superior to others, raises its ugly head.

Realistic conflict theory advocates that scarce resources lead to competition to secure those resources for a particular group and this in turn leads to increased levels of prejudice and discrimination. The good news is that the research by Allport (1967) and others shows tensions between the groups can be decreased or even eliminated if the groups learn to cooperate to achieve a common goal; for instance, obtaining the resource and dividing it evenly between groups.

Sherif's Robber's Cave experiment demonstrated the realistic conflict theory in action and how tensions could be reduced, which supported Allport's later research.

In the Robber's Cave experiment, 24 boys, ages 11 and 12 years, were divided into two groups so that physical, mental and social skills were roughly equal. All the boys came from lower middle-class Protestant families and where white. None of the boys had met prior to the study. Researchers passed themselves off as camp personnel.

The two groups were housed separately at the camp, but over time as the two groups became aware of each other, both groups urged camp personnel to organize some kind of competition between them. While the two groups were not encouraged by researchers to disrespect the other group, nevertheless it happened. Name-calling was common when the groups were brought together in the mess hall. At one point, tensions were so high that the boys almost got into a physical brawl.

Researchers had two hypotheses they wanted to test. The first was: If two in-groups, formed there at the camp, were brought into functional relationship under conditions of competition and group frustration, would attitudes and appropriate hostile actions in relation to the out-group and its members arise and be standardized and shared in varying degrees by group members? The dramatic and near-violent actions of the boys when they were divided and competing for rewards, supported Sherif's hypothesis.

Sherif's second hypothesis was: when individuals having no established relationships are brought together to interact in group activities with common goals, they produce a group structure with hierarchical statuses and roles within it. To test this, camp personnel created two problem situations that ultimately led to the two groups working together to solve.

These two problem situations resulted in teamwork and intergroup cooperation. In the end, tensions between the groups was virtually eliminated when they were brought together as equals to solve a common problem.

Social Identity Theory

Social identity theory stresses the importance to humans to

be part of a social group and that group is made up of people we perceive to be like us in some way. Our self-concept is in part shaped by the social groups to which we identify. Research has found that we begin to think in terms of "us" versus "them" beginning in pre-school (Buttelmann & Bohm, 2014; Dunham et., 2013). Research has also found that people with low self-esteem are more likely to identify with a social group of which they are a member (Hogg, 2014). The problem is when the boundary between an individual's self-concept and of his or her membership in their ingroup merges and becomes one. Once our identities merge, we conform to group norms regardless of whether they support or are in opposition to overall cultural and societal norms. Therefore, social identity theory suggests that people:

> 1. categorize others - in that we find it useful to put people, ourselves included, into categories;
> 2. identity with others - in that we associate ourselves with certain groups (our ingroups); and
> 3. compare - in that we contrast our groups (ingroups) with other groups (outgroups) and we are favorably biased towards our own group.

Social Learning Theory

Perhaps the simplest explanation of the development of prejudice centers on social learning theory. Social learning theory suggests that prejudice, just like any other value, belief, or norm, can be learned through the process of socialization. Children raised in families where there is expressed attitudes of prejudice, are likely to themselves have prejudiced attitudes towards outgroups. Likewise, peer relationships are another socializing agent where attitudes of prejudice can be transmitted and learned.

Conformity Theory

Another source for the development and maintenance of prejudice is associated with our desire to conform. If prejudice is socially accepted, if it is the norm of an ingroup, the group to which you identify, members of the group will tend to conform to group norms. Whether out of a need to hate or simply a need to conform, people want and need to conform so they can be liked and accepted by other ingroup members (Pettigrew, 1958; Campbell & Pettigrew, 1959; Agnew et al., 1994).

The Justification-Suppression Model

The justification-suppression model of prejudice suggests that people are conflicted between expressing their disdain and prejudice for an outgroup while trying to protect their self-concept. In other words, they seek a way to express their prejudice towards a particular outgroup but in a way they feel will not likely damage the image others have of them and their own self-concept. The result is that this leads to internal tension between the self-concept and their biased and prejudiced view of the outgroup and so they attempt to rationalize their prejudice toward the outgroup. As I've mentioned, even a KKK member would not think of themselves as prejudice, though we know differently. Their self-concept isn't likely going to include that negative self-statement. More than likely they will have rationalized their dislike for outgroup members, which means unless you're white and Protestant, you're in their outgroup. For instance, their hatred of Jews would be because of their belief there is a world-wide Jewish monetary conspiracy (the one Hitler used by the way). Their hatred of blacks would likely be because of their belief that blacks damage the white Protestant gene pool by intermarriage with white women and are responsible for the high crime-rate in America. Their hatred of Catholics would be based on the belief that the Pope controls America and that Catholics are more diverse ethnically than are white Protestants.

In the end, the justification-suppression model suggests that people who are prejudice towards an outgroup will find what they believe to be rational justifications for their prejudice that allow them to maintain a positive self-concept.

Social Dominance Theory

Social dominance theory suggests that within every society are a number of group-based hierarchies. Further, when these groups come into competition for scarce resources, like employment and affordable housing, the more dominant groups will attempt to create myths that effectively legitimize their moral claim to the specific scarce resource. These "legitimizing myths" are prejudicial in nature.

Research has found that contact between competing groups reduces prejudice because it enhances knowledge about a competing group (i.e., an outgroup), reduces anxiety about interactions between groups, and increases empathy for the competing group (Allport, 1967).

Personality Dynamics

A despised and hated outgroup promotes a desire to belong to an ingroup and increases the cohesiveness of the ingroup. Ingroup: those people we think of as being like us in some way (usually based on very superficial characteristics).
Outgroup: those people not in our 'ingroup.' The best way to increase the conformity and cohesion of a group is to find an outgroup that can be made a 'threat' (Simmel, 1955).

Adorno's Authoritarian Personality

Theodore Adorno's theory on the authoritarian personality suggests personality needs or deficits that exist within people can precipitate the development of prejudice. Adorno believed that children raised in authoritarian homes where there is an absence of love, discussion, and freedom of thought, and harshness of discipline, are often insecure. Adorno (left) suggested that these

children, and later as adults, often repressed their hostilities and impulses and projected them to outgroups. Adorno believed that such people tended to be inflexible and have a rigid way of thinking about life; i.e., they found ambiguity difficult to tolerate (Adorno & Frenkel-Brunswik, 1993).

Adorno's research suggested that people who tended to be prejudice against one outgroup, were more likely to be prejudice against other outgroups. There does appear to be research supporting Adorno's theory when looking at the prejudices held against blacks, gays and lesbians, women, AIDS victims, the homeless, and even fat people (Bierly, 1985; Crandall, 1994).

Cognitive Sources of Prejudice

A cognitive source of prejudice, categorization involves the way that people categorize or organize the world by clustering objects into groups. Race, gender, and sexual orientation are powerful ways of categorizing people. By itself, categorization is not prejudice, but it does provide a foundation for prejudice. Essentially, it is easy and "efficient" for people to use stereotypes (a form of categorization) when:

> 1. they don't have a lot of time to think about a present encounter (Kaplan et al., 1993),
> 2. they are preoccupied (Gilbert & Hixon, 1991),
> 3. they are physically and/or emotionally tired (Bodenhausen, 1990),
> 4. they are aroused or upset emotionally (Haddock et al., 1993), and
> 5. when they are too young, inexperienced, and egotistical to appreciate diversity (Biernat, 1991).

Scapegoating

Displacement and scapegoating are psychological mechanisms associated with prejudice and discrimination. In displacement, feelings of hostility are directed against objects that are not the real origin of anxieties. People project anxieties and insecurities onto scapegoats.

Simmel (1955) points out that external conflict can bring together people who would otherwise have nothing to do with one another. Conflict might even cause enemies to join together against an outside foe. In other words, the quickest way to solidify a group, to increase the bonds between members of a group, is to impose an external threat. Hitler used this very effectively by targeting Jews, Gypsies, and other undesirables and making them out to be significant threats to Germany's existence as a "racially pure" nation.

Evolutionary Psychologists

Evolutionary psychologists suggest that prejudice allows people to bond with their own group by contrasting their own groups to outsider groups. Examples could include:

1. Most religious and ethnic groups maintain some prejudices against other groups, which help to make their own group seem more special.
2. Prejudice legitimizes discrimination because it apparently justifies one group's dominance over another.
3. Pseudoscientific arguments about the mental inferiority of African Americans allowed whites to feel justified in owning slaves.

Racism

There are several different kinds of racism: individual racism and institutional racism. **Individual racism**, often referred to as "old-fashioned" racism, is someone who thinks their race or ethnicity is superior to that of others. The idea is that a member of a particular ingroup considers their ingroup as superior to all other or specific other outgroups, involves blatant, negative, and rigid stereotypes and oppose racial inequality. This is the most commonly seen type of racism. But, as I've noted about prejudice, while others may see the actions and beliefs of someone as being racist, most racists do not see themselves that way. Like prejudice, people who hold racist beliefs rationalize their beliefs in order to maintain a positive self-concept. But again, like prejudice, actions speak louder than words.

"**Modern racism** is a combination of egalitarian values and negative feelings toward Blacks and produces negative reactions toward Blacks that are explained away as being due to other causes. **Aversive racism**, arising from a conflict between positive and negative beliefs about Blacks, produces the desire to avoid encounters with Blacks because such encounters remind one about the conflicting attitudes" (McLeod, 2008).

Institutional racism is when racist practices of discrimination are put into place by society as laws. The last country to officially end institutional racism was South Africa in 1994. Prior to that, the American South maintained institutional racism under the Jim Crow laws through the 1960s.

> "And nowhere was the iron grip of that system—known as Jim Crow to some of us—stronger than in Mississippi. That grip manifested itself most notoriously in the murder of Emmett Till, a 14-year-old black boy, in 1955. That year, Till was tortured and lynched by white men after allegedly making lewd comments toward a white woman. His mutilated corpse became one of the first mass-media images of the violence of Jim Crow, and the trial of his killers became a pageant illuminating the tyranny of white supremacy" (Newkirk, 2017).

Figure 4. Emmett Till (left); Emmett Till's body as it lay in his open casket.

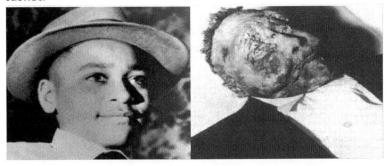

Figure 5. Emmett Till's parents looking on at his corpse in the mortuary (left); Emmett Till laying on his bed earlier that year.

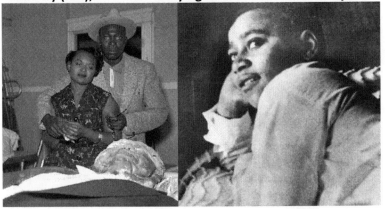

In Mississippi in 1955, a white woman accused a 14-year-old black boy by the name of Emmett Till of having whistled at her as she walked by him. That night Emmett Till was abducted, tortured and lynched--lynching can be death by any number of means and does not necessarily mean someone was hung. His mother took her son's body to her native Chicago and chose for Emmett's brutalized body to be displayed in an open casket at his funeral. It was her way of showing America what injustice still lurked in the hearts and minds of many Americans. As a result of his As a result of his death, there were protests across the US providing impetus for the growing civil rights movement. The white woman who accused Till of having whistled at her, later admitted she lied. Emmett Till had done nothing except being in the wrong place at the wrong time in a part of the country where justice was in the hands of a white mob.

Sexism

Sexism defined is simply prejudice towards a specific gender, usually towards women. The components of these stereotypical notions of women include beliefs, emotions, and behavior. People holding prejudiced beliefs about women would generally believe that women are not capable of performing specific tasks that are "better suited" for men, are incapable of performing as well as men intellectually, are more emotional, and are natural nurturers.

Research on sexism in the US began at about the same time as the **National Organization of Women** was formed in the early 1970s. Its creation spearheaded that research (as well as research on domestic abuse).

It should be noted that research done on attitudes towards women since the 1980s, demonstrates that while women are generally viewed more favorably than men on a number of characteristics or traits, those characteristics or traits are often highly **genderized**. In other words, the roles women are expected to occupy roles in society that fit those positive characteristics or traits: because women are better nurturers and caregivers (so says the stereotype), their work roles in society are seen as correspondent--daycare workers, teachers, and nurses. The problem of course is that those roles are typically low-status and low-pay.

The term **"benevolent sexism"** was the label assigned by researchers Glick and Fiske (2001) to describe outwardly positive stereotypes held about women but that were essentially patronizing; e.g., even though women are the more friendly, nurturing, and supportive sex, they still need a strong man to help and protect them. The term **"hostile sexism"** was coined by Glick et al. (1996) and refers to the negative stereotypes about women who hold positions of power in society. Research has shown that societies that exhibit the most benevolent sexist beliefs, tend to also score the highest on hostile sexism (Eagly & Mladinic, 1989).

Anti-gay Prejudice

While the US Supreme Court effectively legalized gay marriage in the case of Obergefell versus Hodges, anti-gay prejudice and discrimination still exist in the US. In the early 1970s, George Weinberg (1972) coined the term **homophobia** in his book "Society and the Healthy Homosexual" to describe the fear that heterosexuals feel about being near homosexuals. A fuller description of homophobia would be an "aversion to gay or homosexual people or their lifestyle and culture" (*American Heritage Dictionary*, 1992 edition). Today, the term probably can be described more succinctly: an irrational fear of gay men and women (Merriam-Webster Dictionary, 2018).

Herek (2000) was the first to use the phrase **sexual prejudice** to refer to negative attitudes about someone based on their sexual orientation. The term would apply to gays, lesbians, bisexuals, and heterosexual. Note that Herek was also first to recognize that as a backlash to the mistreatment homosexuals felt inflicted on them by heterosexuals, he recognized that homosexuals could be prejudiced towards heterosexuals. However, it is clearly recognized that far more often than not the prejudice is directed towards homosexuals, bisexuals and now transsexuals than towards heterosexuals.

Like other types of prejudice, there are three primary components of anti-gay prejudice: (a) an attitude, (b) it is aimed at specific group, and (c) it is negative, irrational, a generalization and

Figure 6. Attitudes towards same-sex marriage. Percentage of US adults who favor/oppose same-sex marriage (2001-2017). Pew Research Center, 2017.

Year	Favor	Oppose
2001	35%	57%
2003	32%	59%
2004	31%	60%
2005	36%	53%
2006	35%	55%
2007	37%	54%
2008	39%	51%
2009	37%	54%
2010	42%	48%
2011	46%	45%
2012	48%	43%
2013	50%	43%
2014	52%	40%
2015	55%	39%
2016	55%	37%
2017	62%	32%

often involves hostility and dislike. Herek (2000) concluded:

1. Conceptualizing heterosexuals' negative
2. Attitudes toward homosexuality and bisexuality as sexual prejudice – rather than homophobia – has several advantages. First, sexual prejudice is a descriptive term.
3. Unlike homophobia, it conveys no a priori assumptions about the origins, dynamics, and underlying motivations of antigay attitudes.
4. The term explicitly links the study of antigay hostility with the rich tradition of social psychological research on prejudice.
5. Using the construct of sexual prejudice does not require value judgments that anti-gay attitudes are inherently irrational or evil.

Figure 7. LGBT demographics. Older Americans much less likely to identify as LGBT. Percent of each group identifying as LGBT. Pew Research Center, 2017.

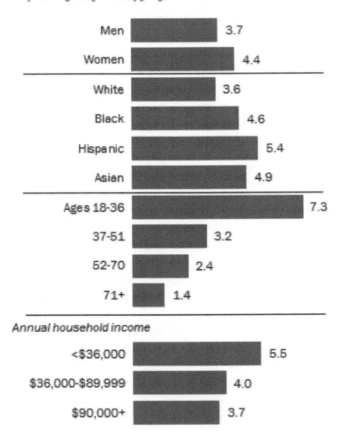

Older Americans much less likely to identify as LGBT

% of each group identifying as LGBT

Group	Percent
Men	3.7
Women	4.4
White	3.6
Black	4.6
Hispanic	5.4
Asian	4.9
Ages 18-36	7.3
37-51	3.2
52-70	2.4
71+	1.4

Annual household income

Income	Percent
<$36,000	5.5
$36,000-$89,999	4.0
$90,000+	3.7

Have attitudes towards homosexuals changed in recent years? A poll by the Pew Research Center in June 2017 found that 62 percent of those surveyed supported same-sex marriage--up from 35 percent in 2001.

Anna Brown (2017), in reporting June 2017 findings of the Pew Research Center, reported key findings of their research on L.G.B.T. Americans.

1. Americans are becoming more accepting in their views of LGBT people--from 51 percent in 2006 to 63 percent in 2016.

2. Bisexuals make up the largest proportion of LGBT people in the US--estimated at 40 percent of the LGBT population.

3. Gay men and lesbians are more likely to have "come out" when compared to bisexuals.

4. Slightly more women report being lesbian than males reporting to be gay, proportionally there are more Hispanics, Asians and Blacks who report being LGBT than whites, there is a direct positive correlation between age and those who identify as LGBT, with people aged 18 to 36 the most likely, and slightly more who identify as LGBT report household incomes of $36,000 and less.

Combating Stereotypical Thinking

Can stereotypical thinking be changed? The answer is yes...and no. Stereotyping is normal, and in some situations, important. Think of it as an automatic process that guides how we behave in a very complicated world. In other words, stereotypes can be functional. We have stereotypes for virtually everything in our social world, especially for those things we have not yet experienced. In some sense, they are like scripts. If you have ever gone on a cruise, you know what to expect if you were to go on another cruise in the future. But what if you've never been on a cruise before but are looking forward to it? Why would someone be looking forward to something they've never experienced? The answer is because they have a stereotype or a script of what going on a cruise means. They know there will be lots of food, lots of alcohol, a large onboard swimming pool, exciting ports of call, and so forth. Where did their stereotype come from? From talking to people who have been on a cruise, from seeing pictures of happy people on a cruise, or from watching commercials and movies. Stereotypes give us some foundation for what we can expect, but they are only the foundation. Once you take your first cruise, you will almost certainly modify your stereotype so that if conforms more to your actual experience. So, stereotypes serve an important preliminary function, but they must be subject to modification based on actual experience. This is what separates stereotypes as functional versus dysfunctional.

Stereotypes becomes dysfunctional when (a) people hold onto their stereotypes without ever having the opportunity to experience the situation or interaction with members of an outgroup which the stereotype is about, and (b) people do not allow a positive interaction to modify their stereotype about that specific outgroup.

So, while it is normal to stereotype and categorize, it is also normal to analyze and differentiate so there is potential to change a hitherto accepted stereotype as accurate. We have the capacity to gauge whether a stereotype accurately depicts members of an outgroup, and if it doesn't, to change our thoughts about members of the outgroup. But that takes mental work, and while we might find it difficult to believe, there are people who don't want to expend the time and energy to think and challenge their previous notions about members of particular outgroups in this case.

Reducing Prejudice

There is no research that shows prejudice is an innate trait or characteristic. Prejudice clearly seems to be learned, or in the case of personality deficits, created by poor parenting styles. While the bad news is that prejudice lurks among us, the good news is that what is learned, can be unlearned or changed.

There are a number of different factors involved in trying to change someone's stereotype or prejudice of a specific group. In one study of 515 research studies on prejudice, researchers found three important mediating factors when there is intergroup contact: (1) the contact increases the knowledge about members of the outgroup, (2) the contact reduces the fear and anxiety about contact with members of the outgroup, and (3) the contact increases empathy of members of the outgroup (WikiBooks, 2017).

Allport's Theory of Contact

Allport's Theory of Contact suggests that contact between groups will reduce prejudice if the two groups meet on the basis of equal status and pursue common goals. Intergroup contact appears more effective in reducing prejudice than communication and education. This "contact hypothesis" receives support in public housing projects where people have to live in close proximity to each other. It also receives support in the military. It appears, for example, that school desegregation is associated with decreasing levels of prejudice (Farley, 2000). This is the philosophy behind school busing. The contact has to be more than superficial. Casual contact will have little impact on reducing prejudice.

The contact hypothesis suggests that four conditions must be in place for reducing prejudice:

1. The groups must be of equal status--a level "playing field" must exist between the groups;
2. The groups must have sustained and close contact with one another over an extended period of time;
3. The groups must cooperate to achieve common goals;
4. The groups must have normative systems in place that place a value on equality.

Over time, Allport added additional requisites for the successful use of the contact hypothesis. Those include:

1. the groups have equality in terms of legal status, economic opportunity, and political power,
2. authorities advocate equal rights,
3. the groups have opportunities to interact formally and informally with each other, and
4. the groups cooperate to reach a common goal (Allport, 1979).

However, for instance, the authoritarian personality is an example of prejudice that results from personality disorders. People with a prejudice deeply rooted in their personality are more likely to reject self-analysis; and if they don't think they have a problem, they won't seek therapy.

How to Reduce Prejudice: Communication

Communication is another way to reduce prejudice, but it has its strengths and weaknesses. Strengths include persuasive communication refers to any form of communication (written,

verbal, visual) specifically intended to influence attitudes. Anti-prejudice communications are successful depending on who is giving the message (i.e., credibility of the communicator). The message must be understood and remembered. Its limitations are that people who receive and understand anti-prejudiced messages tend to be people who are already anti-prejudiced (Farley, 2000), and people who are highly prejudiced tend to not "hear" the messages. Further, prejudiced people tend to not view themselves as prejudiced. Therefore, when the message is heard, it is assumed that it applies
to someone else.

In addition to communication, education can help to reduce prejudice, but again like communication, it has its strengths and weaknesses. Strengths include that education is most successful when it causes the least amount of stress and does not put people on the defensive. One way to facilitate a positive environment is to make students feel that they are participants in the process (Farley, 2000). But education by itself has difficulties reducing prejudice, in part, because there is some self-selecting taking place in that the most prejudiced people probably do not take the courses designed to increase the understanding of majority/minority issues. On the other hand, required courses in inter-group relations might avoid the problem of self-selection. If a person is prejudiced as a result of social learning, then education (combined with change of environment) may be successful in reducing prejudice.

Strengths:
1. Persuasive communication refers to any form of communication (written, verbal, visual) specifically intended to influence attitudes.
2. Anti-prejudice communications are successful depending on who is giving the message (i.e., credibility of the communicator).
3. The message must be understood and remembered.

Limitations:
1. It appears that people who receive and understand anti-prejudiced messages tend to be people who are already anti-prejudiced (Farley, 2000:38-42)
2. People who are highly prejudiced tend to not "hear" the

messages.

3. Further, prejudiced people tend to not view themselves as prejudiced. Therefore, when the message is heard, it is assumed that it applies to someone else.

How to Reduce Prejudice: Education

Strengths:

1. Education is most successful when it causes the least amount of stress and not put people on the defensive. One way to facilitate a positive environment is to make students feel that they are participants in the process (Farley, 2000:42-45).

Limitations:

1. Education has difficulties reducing prejudice, in part, because there is some self-selecting taking place in that the most prejudiced people probably do not take the courses designed to increase the understanding of majority/minority issues. On the other hand, required courses in inter-group relations might avoid the problem of self-selection.

2. If a person is prejudiced as a result of social learning, then education (combined with change of environment) may be successful in reducing prejudice.

How to Reduce Prejudice: Therapy

Communication, education, and intergroup contact are not effective when a prejudiced person suffers from personality problems. Many argue that personality problems are best dealt with through therapy (either individual or group therapy). The goal of therapy is to:

1. Resolve the problem that caused people to be prejudiced in the first place.

2. Convince prejudiced people that prejudice is not an appropriate way of dealing with one's insecurities or problems (Farley, 2000).

Limitations:
1. The authoritarian personality is an example of prejudice that results from personality disorders and these people reject self-analysis; and if they don't think they have a problem, they won't seek therapy.

A Final Word on Prejudice

There is no one theory that can exclusively be used to explain the development of prejudice. However, taken together, these many theories presented in this chapter, because of their basis in research, suggest some possible explanations. If we know why prejudice attitudes are developed, we can implement procedures and public policies to reduce or eliminate them in the future.

Concepts and Terms to Know

Prejudice
Discrimination
Individual discrimination
Institutional discrimination
Ingroup
Heuristics
Outgroups
Ingroup favoritism
Outgroup homogeneity effect
Social categorization
Stereotype threat
Scapegoats
Intergroup competition
Realistic group conflict
Individual racism
Institutional racism
Modern racism
Aversive racism
National Organization of Women
Genderized
Benevolent sexism

References

Adorno, T., Frenkel-Brunswik, E., & Levinson, D. (1993). *The authoritarian personality: Studies in Prejudice.* Norton Publishing.

Aging Watch. (2010). *Elder stereotypes in media and popular culture.* October 2010. Retrieved April 20, 2018 from http://www.agingwatch.com/?p=439.

Agnew, R. (1994). Delinquency and the desire for money. *Justice Quarterly,* 11, 411-427.

Allport, G. W., & Ross, J. M. (1967). Personal religious orientation and prejudice. *Journal of Personality and Social Psychology,* 5, 432-443.

Bierly, M. (1985). Prejudice toward contemporary outgroups as a generalized attitude. *Journal of Applied Social Psychology,* 15(2), 189-199.

Biernat, M. (1991). Gender stereotypes and the relationship between masculinity and femininity: A developmental analysis. *Journal of Personality and Social Psychology,* 61(3), 351-365.

Bodenhausen, G. (1990). Stereotypes as judgmental heuristics: Evidence of circadian variations in discrimination. *Psychological Science,* 1(5), 319-322.

Haddock, G., Zanna, P., & Esses, V. (1993). Assessing the structure of prejudicial attitudes: The case of attitudes toward homosexuals. *Journal of Personality and Social Psychology,* 65, 1105-1118.

Bogardus, E. (1947). Measurement of personal-group relations. *Sociometry.* 10(4), 306–311.

Bialik, K. (2017). Key facts about race and marriage, 50 years after Loving v. Virginia. *Pew Research Center.* Retrieved March 26, 2018 from http://www.pewresearch.org/fact-tank/2017/06/12/key-facts-about-race-and-marriage-50-years-after-loving-v-virginia/

Brown-Iannuzzi, L., McKee, S., Gervais, W. (2017). Atheist horns and religious halos: Mental representations of atheists and theists. *Journal of Experimental Psychology,* 147.

Buttelmann, D., & Böhm, R. (2014). The ontogeny of the motivation that underlies in-group bias. *Psychological science,* 25(4), 921 – 927.

Campbell, E. & Pettigrew, T. (1959). Racial and moral crisis: The role of Little Rock ministers. *American Journal of Sociology*, 64(5), 509-516.

Crandall, C. (1994). Prejudice against fat people: Ideology and self-interest. *Journal of Personality and Social Psychology*, 66(5), 882-894.

Dunham, Y., Srinivasan, M., Dotsch, R., & Barner, D. (2013). Religion insulates ingroup evaluations: the development of intergroup attitudes in India. *Developmental Science,* 17(2), 1-9.

Eagly, A. & Mladinic, A. (1989). Gender Stereotypes and Attitudes Toward Women and Men. *Personality and Social Psychology Bulletin*, 15, 543-558.

Farley, J. (2000). *Majority - minority relations* (4th Ed.), Upper Saddle River, New Jersey: Prentice Hall.

Gilbert, D. T., & Hixon, J. G. (1991). The trouble of thinking: Activation and application of stereotypic beliefs. *Journal of Personality and Social Psychology,* 60(4), 509-517.

Glick, P. & Fiske, S. (2001). An ambivalent alliance: Hostile and benevolent sexism as complementary justifications for gender inequality. *The American Psychologist,* 56, 109-18.

Glick, P. & Fiske, S. (1996). The ambivalent sexism inventory: Differentiating hostile and benevolent sexism. *Journal of Personality and Social Psychology*, 70 (3), 491–512.

Hogg, N. (2014). From uncertainty to extremism: Social

categorization and identity processes. *Current Directions in Psychological Science,* 23(5), 338 – 342.

LaPiere, R.T. (1934). Attitudes v's actions. *Social Forces*, 13, 230-237.

Lundblad, R. (2001). Social, religious, and personal contributors to prejudice. *Faculty Publications - Grad School of Clinical Psychology.* Paper 72. Retrieved March 30, 2018 from http://digitalcommons.georgefox.edu/gscp_fac/72

National Public Radio. (October 31, 2012). *Is racial prejudice on the rise?* Retrieved April 2018 from https://www.npr.org/2012/10/31/164029897/is-racial-prejudice-on-the-rise

NDTV. (March 10, 2017). *Hatred, prejudice on rise in Donald Trump's America.* Retrieved April 2018 from https://www.ndtv.com/world-news/hatred-prejudice-on-rise-in-donald-trumps-america-poll-1668132

Pettigrew, T. (1958). Personality and sociocultural factors in intergroup attitudes: a cross-national comparison. *Journal of Conflict Resolution*, 2(1), 29 – 42.

Pew Research Center. (2017). *U.S. Muslims concerned about their place in society, but continue to believe in the American dream.* Retrieved March 2018 from http://www.pewforum.org/2017/07/26/findings-from-pew-research-centers-2017-survey-of-us-muslims/

Simmel, G. (1955). *Conflict and the web of group affiliations.* Glencoe, IL: Free Press. First published 1922.

Steele, C. (1997). A threat in the air: How stereotypes shape intellectual identity and performance. *American Psychologist*, 52(6), 613-629. Retrieved May 2018 from http://psycnet.apa.org/record/1997-04591-001

Steele, C., & Aronson, J. (1995). Contending with group image: the psychology of stereotype and social identity threat, in Zanna, Mark P. *Advances in Experimental Social Psychology*. Amsterdam: Academic Press, 34, 379–440

Chapter 10: Attraction, Intimacy and Love

In this chapter, we will look at money, well, maybe not directly at money but we will be looking at the biggest money maker the world has ever seen: love. Ah, love! In a recent USA poll (February 4, 2018), Americans spent $19.6 billion dollars on Valentine's Day cards, flowers, candy and other gifts. That's more than the annual GPD for many countries around the world. If you want to make money, peddle love. Over four hundred years ago, a very astute man by the name of William Shakespeare, wrote: "If music be the food of love, play on." One researcher found that approximately 60 percent of top Billboard songs between 2002 and 2005 were about love (Keen, 2007). Between 2017 and 2020 approximately 65 percent of all songs will be about love. Try typing love into your Google search engine and see what you get. I did it. I had 2,300,000,000 hits. That's two trillion three hundred million hits. Yes, love really is a money maker.

Of all the words in the English language, the word "love" is without a doubt one of the most used and abused. People will talk about how they love that, and love this, and then tell someone "I love you." But just what does love mean? What should it mean? According to a Huffington Post article (Paul, 2012):

> "Sanskrit has 96 words for love; ancient Persian had 80, Greek three, but English only one....we are close to dying of loneliness because we have only one word for love. Of all the Western languages, English may be the most lacking when it comes to feeling."

And it is largely because we only have one word for love in the English language that I would argue it has lost its meaning. So, this chapter is about finding that lost or confusing meaning about what love actually is. Can you love your car? Can you love your house? Did you really love your vacation to Hawaii? Can you love a robot? What about a sex doll? By the time you tell that significant other that you love them, the meaning of what you're trying to say could easily get lost in the overuse of the word love.

Attraction

Why are people attracted to one another? Is the old saying about opposites attract true? Are we attracted to friends in much the same way we are attracted to people we have a romantic eye for? These are a few of the questions that we will address as we look at the overall phenomenon of attraction. Even when choosing our friends, the role of attraction is involved. Research has found that **first impressions** of facial attraction is important among children aged 10 to 16 years of age. It is thought that it is seen as advantageous even in youth that having attractive friends represents a social advantage (Zarbatany & Marshall, 2015).

There are a number of factors we need to investigate in order to speak about the forces of attraction relating to romance and love. When investigating attitudes people develop, one of the most interesting is interpersonal attraction. Physical attraction has the greatest effect on first impressions. Research has found that we initially judge a person's attractiveness in a "blink of an eye" and draw a more complete picture, or "size them up" in about three seconds (Schab, 2017). While people typically say that they do not think attractiveness plays an important role in immediate interpersonal attraction, the research says otherwise. Finding someone, anyone, physically attractive has a direct and positive correlation on being judged more favorably (Goddard, 2012).

When looking at what's important to a woman in deciding what man to date, she is most likely to identify his **physical attractiveness** to be the first criteria. However, after physical attractiveness, women are likely to identify other more intangible factors as being important—e.g., sense of humor, personality, would he make a good provider, would he make a good father, would he make a good husband, and many other things. Like women, men are just as likely to identify physical attractiveness as being the first criteria in identifying someone to date. However, and unlike women, other more intangible criteria are much less important. It would be like asking a man what's most important in deciding to date a woman and he answers, "Her looks." So, we respond by asking, "Ok, what next?" He responds by saying, "Her looks." "Ok, ok," we say, "but what after that?" After pausing for a second he says, "Her looks." Eventually the research suggests he would identify those intangible criteria like women have named, but again, they tend to be given much less importance by men.

Research has found that the more in love a woman is with a man, the better looking he gets (Wargo, 2011). Why? Because she has gotten to know him and discovered that he possesses many of those intangible criteria identified above. Unfortunately, the research does not support that the same holds true for men.

Looking for Mr. or Mrs. Right

So, who are we looking for? What makes them appealing to us as a potential dating partner? Thousands of pages have been written about the process of mate selection, and even more when taking into consideration that most young people in the US don't want to get serious about a relationship (i.e., getting married) until their mid-20s and see dating as a recreational activity until that time. But what follows are some of the more important findings of research on who we look for in someone to date:

1. Research shows that there is an expectation that males look for females to date who are slightly shorter than them. The "**male taller bias**" has been supported in the literature time and time again (Gillis and Avis, 1980; Graziano, Brothen, and Berscheid, 1978).
2. Research has also found that the more similar are potential couple in things like attitudes, beliefs, other personality traits and behaviors in general, the more attracted to the other person they will feel. The old adage applies here: birds of a feather flock together. Also, people like people who like them, so this too increases similarity and the likelihood of something more developing (Berscheid and Walster, 1974).
3. The "**matching hypothesis**" (Berscheid and Walster, 1974), suggests we want to date people we judge to be about as attractive as we are or better. Further, research suggests that we are attracted to people who we perceive as similar in values and behaviors. There is little evidence that "opposites attract" and no evidence that suggests "opposites" stay together in the long run.
4. According to research done by the University of Pennsylvania (2006), men's **first impressions** of women,

aside for their looks, are largely driven by "observable characteristics" that are interpreted as indications of both their demeanor and personality. Those characteristics include the way she dresses, wears her hair, carries herself, and the way she makes and/or maintains eye contact. This is a page right out of Erving Goffman's work on the **Presentation of Self in Everyday Society** (1956). Dury et al. found that **nonverbal communication** (i.e., those characteristics already mentioned) and **body language** were significant in influencing initial impressions by men of women. Interestingly, many researchers believe that "first impressions cannot be scientifically determined due the highly subjective nature of the elements of social desirability."

5. Studies have found that humans, especially men, are attracted to people who have symmetrical faces. **Facial symmetry** would be where the two sides of a person's face are in proportion to each other. Women seem to value facial symmetry a little less than do men. Research has also found that men are more attracted to women with a waist to hip ratio of 0.7. To calculate your hip to waist ratio, measure your waist and divide that by your hip measurement. It seems men subconsciously still prefer women with "child-bearing hips" for biological reasons: women with wider hips are less likely to die during childbirth and thus the man's genes are passed down to a large number of offspring (BBC Fisher, 2014).

6. Other research by Jones et al. (2014) found that humans have a subconscious preference for their own face when it comes to mate selection. Perrett used a system of facial morphing to turn a subject's face into the face of an opposite sex person. His research found there was a preference for his or her own face as morphed into someone of the opposite sex. While Perrett admits he doesn't know the reason for this, he suggests it might be because the morphed faces remind us as how we looked in childhood.

While it may be difficult to scientifically predict who one person will find physically attractive, the role of physical attraction is of paramount importance to people when looking for someone to date. Simply put, we pursue relationships with those we find attractive (Luo and Zhang, 2009; Kurzban and Weeden, 2005; Thao et al., 2010). There is some debate in the literature as to whether men or women are more affected by the attractiveness of another. Research by Lippa (2007) found that both gay and straight males were consciously aware of how important physical attractiveness was when compared to women. However, other research has found that the role of physical attraction to be equally important to both men and women. Again, when looking at traits such as personality, education, and intelligence, physical attractiveness is paramount (Eastwick et al., 2011; Eastwick and Finkel, 2008; Luo and Zhang, 2009; Kurzban and Weeden, 2005; Sprecher, 1989; Thao et al., 2010).

So, while research clearly emphasizes the importance of physical attractiveness, do we really want a 10? Research by Langlois (2006) found that while lacking in physical attractiveness was associated with a more negative evaluation of the that person,

Figure 1. Who do we want to date relative to our appearance?

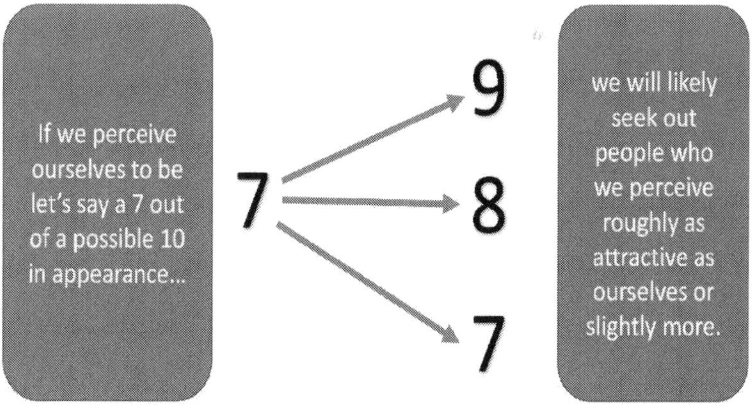

If we perceive ourselves to be let's say a 7 out of a possible 10 in appearance...

9
8
7

we will likely seek out people who we perceive roughly as attractive as ourselves or slightly more.

people perceived as moderately attractive were judged to have significantly more potential dating value to subjects. Langlois' research seems to confirm research done by Dion et al. (1972) which showed that potential dating partners perceived as attractive or moderately attractive were perceived more positively than those judged to be less attractive.

So, why do we seem to "settle" for someone moderately attractive than to hold out for that special person we find highly attractive. Maybe it's because the old expression is true: a bird in hand is worth two in the bush. Or maybe we have issues with insecurity and we're afraid of that perfect 10. A 10 would be that trophy boyfriend/girlfriend that we've always dreamt of. But the reality is that a 10 would almost certainly be "high maintenance" and leave us constantly wondering if they were remaining true since they would have so many more options than we might perceive ourselves as having. But there is more to it than that.

Research suggests that we are likely to perceive that 10 as a luxury, while we view the 7, 8 or 9 as a necessity. Though we might say that the physical attractiveness of a potential dating partner is not important to us, the research definitely says otherwise. But that could be interpreted as finding an extremely attractive dating partner might not be important to us but finding a moderately attractive dating partner is. Unfortunately, actually defining what is considered to be "moderately" attractive is nearly impossible to do from a research perspective because people and their perceptions and needs vary so widely. Research found that people who judge themselves as being highly attractive, that "10" I've spoken about, tend to see only other 10s as physically desirable, while people who judge themselves as moderately attractive (i.e., the 7, 8 and 9s they encounter), will likely have a greater range of those they perceive to be appealing to them (Montoya, 2008). Again, and possibly related to similarity, the research says that relationships more likely to survive have partners who consider themselves to be equally attractive (Feingold, 1998; Fugère et al., 2015).

Finally, the research suggests that we associate physical appearance with positive or negative personality qualities. Those who are perceived as most attractive are often thought of as having a better and happier life than those judged unattractive (Dion et al., 1972; Griffin and Langlois, 2006).

But no matter our personal level of attractiveness, or our partner's, as we get to know, like, and respect each other more, our attraction naturally grows and deepens (Kniffin and Wilson, 2004). The longer we know each other, the less important physical attractiveness becomes to beginning and maintaining a long-term relationship (Hunt et al., 2015). In conclusion, while physical attraction plays a large part in who we find desirable, other things mediate that perception but are less tangible. We will investigate those non-tangible elements later in this chapter.

Intimacy

We need to begin our investigation of love, and all the things that go with it, by looking at **intimacy**. What does it mean when we refer to being intimate with others? Intimacy means much more than just who we have sex with. Intimacy exists in your self-concept because it implies you have included someone in that self-concept that you care for and are therefore are intimate with. **Attributions**, which are statements or beliefs we have about ourselves and others, have been found to be more similar to ours when we speak about people we know and are close to us versus strangers or people we don't know well (Green et al., 2006). Generally, intimate others are included in the way we allocate our resources--time, energy, and money, but we make more of distinction in how we allocate resources to strangers or people we don't know well. The implication that we would be less likely to allocate our resources to them than to intimate others.

Social exchange theory suggests that when dealing with strangers or people we do not know well, we are more concerned with the ratio between our costs and rewards, but that we are less concerned about that ratio when dealing with intimate others. Further, because intimate others are part of our self-concept, those intimate others are also part of the **self-schemas** we have about what it means to be intimate with another. Intimacy means that we are close to some people. We feel that closeness in the way we interact with them, in the way we confide in them, trust them, provide for them, and share with them. This is why our intimate others are part of our self-concept. They are important to us and to our identity.

Researchers have identified four different types of intimacy. Those are physical, emotional, cognitive, and experiential (Blumin, 1989).

1. Physical intimacy is sensual proximity or touching (Proxemics 2016). More examples of physical intimacy would include hugging, kissing, holding hands or sexual acts. |

2. **Emotional intimacy** is the result of trust entering the relationship. Personal bonds have been formed by the partners. The couple confides deep emotional feelings to one another and a sexual union between the partners almost certainly has developed (Giddens, 1990).

3. **Cognitive intimacy** occurs when the couple feel free to express their opinions with one another and therefore enter into meaningful, intellectual, and interesting conversations.

4. **Experiential intimacy** occurs when the couple just enjoys spending time with each other even to the point of not speaking. Enjoying some activity together even if they performing activities but are proximate to each other (Healthy Place, 2008).

Finally, communication has a large part to play in the longevity of romantic relationships. Research by Gottman (2010) reported that in a longitudinal study he was able to predict the success or failure of a relationship with 93 percent accuracy by analyzing problem-solving strategies of romantic couples. He did this by viewing couples, and recording their body language and emotional reactions, as they rehashed a previous argument in his presence.

Romantic Relationships

As we grow close to certain others who are not related to us, and as we begin to think of them as being in our circle of intimacy, a **romantic** relationship may start to develop. Most research suggests that relationships, for both heterosexuals and homosexuals, begin as friendships and advance from there (Cannoni & Bombi, 2016). Eventually, if the intimacy grows, the relationship takes on the characteristics of a romantic relationship, which consists of much greater levels of intimacy and intensity (Kropp et al., 1994). Somewhere in that process the relationship goes from one of friendship to one of dating (Hendrick & Hendrick, 1993). And despite the popular belief that women fall in love more quickly than do men, research has found the opposite to be true (Harrison & Shortall, 2011). Why is that hard to believe? Because even though the research says men fall in love more quickly, that doesn't necessarily mean they tell the woman they are love with--men are far more likely to keep their emotions hidden than are women.

Before we discuss the factors associated with dating, let's dispel some myths about romantic relationships.

> 1. Myth: Historical views of the meaning of love have not changed. False. The primary reason people marry today in the US is because they fall in love (see Figure 6). But five hundred years ago, or less, love had nothing to do with it. Marriages were arranged, and still are in many parts of the world. Sadly, if the primary reason people marry in the Western world is because they fall in love, the primary reason they divorce is because they fall out of love.
> 2. Myth: People who are in marriages that were arranged are less happy than people who marry for love. False. Couples whose marriage was arranged and live in that same culture exhibit much higher marital satisfaction than do couples who marry for love in the Western world. Why? Because they don't marry for love. They marry for other more tangible reasons and for a more stable form of love. If they fall in love, they consider it a blessing, but it is not an expectation.
> 3. Myth: You have to love yourself before you can love another. Sorry. There is no research evidence to back that up. People with low self-esteem are just as capable of loving another person as our people with high self-esteem.
> 4. Myth: All you really need for a relationship to work is love. All you need is love and everything will work out in the end. False. It takes two people to make a relationship work, but once one of the partners falls out of love, the game is over and a breakup is in their future.

Where do we find people to date?

There are a number of factors that influence who we date.

Some or obvious and some more subtle. Those factors include:

1. Propinguity or proximity. Research consistently shows that the majority of Americans choose to date someone who is physically proximate to them. When you think about where you are likely to meet people, you understand that for the most part we socialize with people who live in our community or within a short distance of us. We meet at parties, at work, at school, at church and at the grocery store. All venues that are near to us.

2. Familiarity. Akin to proximity, because we tend to meet people who are proximately to us, we are also more likely to meet new friends in the same way. Often times friendship turns into romantic relationships.

3. Social networks. Again, there is some overlap with proximity. If Karen knows Susan and Robert, and Susan and Robert don't know each other and both are not in current relationships, Karen may introduce Susan and Robert to each other. Social networks are a primary place for people to meet and form new friendships or more romantic ones. Having a large social network is always advantageous in a number of different ways.

4. Values. Study after study has found that when looking for someone to date, we want someone who shares our values.

5. Dependability. We want to be involved romantically with someone we can count on. Someone who will be there for us--in good times and in bad.

6. Emotional stability. Almost always we want to find people to date who are emotionally stable. We don't want to be involved with someone who boils bunny rabbits on the stove out of anger and rejection. No one deliberately seeks out others for a romantic relationship that is depressed, OCD, bipolar or schizophrenic, but if they do, it's probably because they suffer from the same illness. Unfortunately, relationships like the aforementioned don't tend to work.

7. Intelligence. Generally, we look for people who are intelligent. We want that special person we have a romantic interest in to be able to hold intelligent conversations with. Perhaps some men do deliberately look for a "trophy wife" whose intelligence is unimportant, but I think we guess as to the quality of their relationship beyond the bedroom.

8. Sociable. We want to date and possibly marry someone who has social skills. Someone who is able to hold their own at dinner parties or around others for a casual night of entertainment or conversation. We want to date people who friendly and likeable.

9. Attractive. While we will address the notion of attractiveness a little later, research indicates that we seek out others who are about as attractive as we think we are.

10. Healthy. Sadly, we want people who are physically healthy. Perhaps we can't deal with the stress of having to live a life with someone who is unhealthy, or maybe we cannot imagine being with someone who is physically impaired in some way (Weeden and Sabini, 2005).

11. Good personality. Closely associated with sociability, we seek out persons to date who are friendly, have a sense of humor, are genuine, not vain, and easy to get along with.

12. Similar religious background. Depending on how we were raised, and in what religion we were raised, and how important religion is to us, we are likely to seek out someone of the same religious background or affiliation. There is logic to this in that the couple simply will have more in common and have a similar set of values. However, as it is often said that love is blind, some couples do not share similar religious values. While this may not be an important issue to them, it may in all likelihood be an issue to their parents.

13. Similar social status. We often seek out others romantically who are from the same social class or background. One of the most obvious reasons for this is because of social networking, that is who we are most likely going to be around socially. Having the same social background in common does provide more things in common, a similar view on life, attitudes in general, and likely produces a more secure and stable relationship. Again, while Susan might be dating Robert, Susan's parents might have a problem with the relationship because Robert comes from the "wrong side of the tracks."

14. Similar race or ethnicity. This particular factor in who we date has been changing dramatically in recent years. According to a recent poll by the Pew organization (2014), around two-thirds of Americans now view interracial marriage and marriage outside of one's ethnic group as acceptable.

15. Age. Generally, society expects people to date and marry roughly their own age. Today the average difference in age between newly married young couples is less than two years on average. In your grandparent's day, it was probably closer to five years difference, and further back in time the difference in age could even be greater. Society sometimes imposes sanctions on people who violate this rule--sanctions aren't violations of the law, but rather informal punishments--speaking badly about someone, spreading gossip, derogating someone. When Anna Nicole Smith, aged 21, married J. Howard

Figure 2. J. Howard Marshall, 89, and his new wife Anna Nicole Smith, 21.

16. Height. This where the "male taller" norm can be seen. It is almost always the case that men are expected to be taller than the women they date and marry. The unwritten law of social interaction seems to be that the male must be

at least as tall or taller than the female in order for any meaningful relationship to develop (Cameron, Oskamp, & Sparks, 1977; Martel & Biller, 1987). As a case in point, Gillis and Avis (1980) calculated that the male should be shorter than the female in 2 of every 100 couples based on random chance. Their data showed this configuration actually occurred only once among 720 couples thus it is abundantly clear that the male-taller bias is in full operation. But what is not clear is the psychological selection process used in abiding by this "cardinal principle" of date selection (Stulp et al., 2013).

1. **Endogamy.** Endogamy refers to dating someone of the same race or ethnicity, but like was stated above, more and more Americans are discarding this as criteria when seeking someone to date.

2. **Exogamy.** Exogamy requires that people date and marry people outside of particular groups. For instance, there are strict taboos against dating one's own kin or close relatives. There are no European countries that prohibit marriage between first cousins; Canada and Mexico also allow marriage of first cousins. The US is the only country in the Western world that sometimes prohibits the marriage of first cousins: 26 US states allow first cousins to marry. Apparently, there is still scientific debate as to whether marriage to a first cousin produces more miscarriages or less. The jury is still out on that.

3. **Incest taboo.** First cousins aside, it is illegal in all 50 states and US territories to marry a sister or brother.

4. **Homogamy.** This refers to the tendency to date and marry someone who has similar personal characteristics as do they.

Where do we meet that future significant other?

According to research done by Rosenfeld (2009), he reported that approximately 28 percent of Americans in current relationships said they had met through friends, 24 percent said they had met at a bar or restaurant, and 23 percent said they had met online. The most dramatic increase was in the number of people reporting that they met their significant other through an online source (e.g., social media and online dating service). See figure 4 below. Research on gays and lesbians finds that 60 percent of those surveyed indicated they found their significant other online (e.g., social median and online dating sites or apps). Other venues for gays and lesbians to meet include LGBTQ events and fundraisers, personal growth classes, volunteering.

Sternberg's Components of Love

There are many different views as to the components of what we call "love." One such view is that of Robert Sternberg (1986) who reports three components of love that can be represented by a triangle. He believes love consists of (a) passion, (b) intimacy, and (c) commitment (see Figure 1, below), and if the couple have all three of the former components of love, he believes them to be in a state of consummate love. Steinberg describes this latter type of love as rare.

Sternberg goes on to say that evidence of love, and the particular stage or stages of love they are in, can be found in the mutual respect and understanding the couple shares as they enjoy each other's company.

Barnes and Sternberg (1997) later elaborated on his model of love to include specific characteristics for each aspect of consummate love, which if you will remember is the highest expression of love but that it a rarity. In this new model of love, the researchers believed that each of the three components had the potential to interact with each other and produce a total of seven possible types of love experiences. Each corner of his model identifies the specific type of love, and because the corners interact with each other, the result is the creation of very different types of love. He does not attempt to include "non-love" into his model as it simply doesn't belong.

Sternberg identifies the seven types of love as:

Figure 4. Sternberg's triangular theory of love.

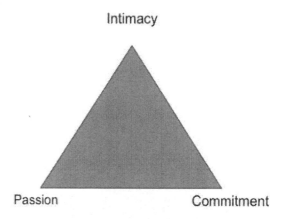

1. Liking. Liking or friendship but this love while it does contain intimacy doesn't include passion or commitment to the relationship. Obviously, this would include friends and possibly acquaintances, but not romantic partners.

2. Infatuated love. Imagine a passionate relationship without intimacy or commitment. Call it "puppy love," "lust," or a "hook-up," it is all about infatuation. The relationship may start to develop into something deeper, but again it may not. It is common in Western cultures for relationships to start with this stage of infatuated love, and hopefully develop into something more stable and meaningful as intimacy may develop within the relationship. But many do not advance beyond this point and the relationship, to whatever degree it is in fact a relationship, dies. Passionate love, often referred to as the lustful component of love, is almost entirely emotional in nature. Chemicals and hormones are released into the bloodstream providing an emotional "high" and is the behavioral pleasure aspect of love. It is that form of love that is intense and has been described as a "raging fire." It is a state of "intense longing."

3. Empty love. Empty love is just as it sounds--there may be a commitment to stay together, but there is no fire--no passion or intimacy. This is a typical scenario for divorce in

Western cultures. Put in street terms, the spark is gone--the couple simply stay together because it's easier than going their separate ways. This is even more true if there are children involved. On the

Figure 5. Sternberg's elaborated triangular theory of love.

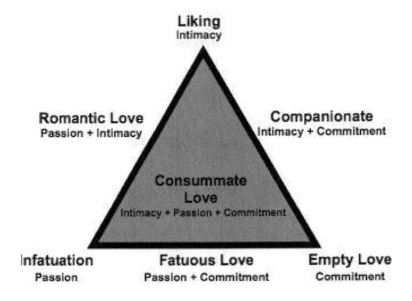

other hand, in cultures that practice arranged marriages, this is often the starting point of the marriage. The marriage is arranged by the couple's parents, maybe even years earlier when they were children, and when they get married, they do not know enough about each other for virtually any kind of love to exist. Yet, in arranged marriages it is expected that love will come in time. Research has found that couples in arranged marriages, and within their own culture, tend to score higher on marital satisfaction than do couples in the West. So, while in the US and Western countries empty love may represent the end of a relationship, in many if not most parts of the world it is only the beginning of what has the potential to be a relationship filled with love and affection.

4. Romantic love. Often times this kind of love is characteristics of "flings" or "affairs." There is passion and intimacy, but there is no commitment to a long-lasting relationship.

5. Companionate love. Companionate love is pretty well as it sounds. There is caring, affection and commitment, but it lacks passion. As time passes, partners decide to stay together not because they are necessarily happy or satisfied in their relationship, but because they have strong feelings of affection and caring for their partner and they feel it would be wrong to abandon them. It is also comforting to them because they know their partner feels that same sense of caring and commitment. There is probably nothing scarier to many people than growing old alone. This kind of relationship is a response in some sense to that state of anxiety. Oddly, companionate love has also been used to describe the love felt towards family members, and perhaps even towards close friends. If passionate love is described as a "raging fire," companionate love can be described as the steady red glow of the fire as it changes into a steadier state and longer-lasting type of fire. As previously written, Sternberg says of passionate love that it is made up of both intimacy and commitment to each other. Companionate love is typically found in long term relationships and is characterized a steadier and more stable relationship than is found in passionate love. There is a deeper respect for each other, affection and intimacy that found in passionate love.

6. Fatuous love. "Love at first sight," "a flash in the pan." This is when two people, probably having just met, fall madly in love and get married or decide to move in together and cohabitate. There is passion and commitment but no intimacy. These types of relationships typically are very short-lived. The modern romantic type of love, which is typically found in Western societies, comes from intimate and passionate forms of love being present but the relationship lacks commitment. Fatuous love has both passion and commitment but lacks intimacy.

7. Consummate love. It would not be correct to call this type of love perfect love, because consummate love is an ideal and not a reality. It is better described as a complete form of love. It is the kind of love truly committed partners strive for. This type of couple, even after many years of being in their committed relationship, still enjoy sex, they see their partner as the best partner they could have, lucky they have the partner they do, can't imagine themselves happy with another partner, manage to resolve conflict without building resentment, and the positive view of their relationship is shared completely with the other spouse (Sternberg, 1998). Sternberg wrote that as difficult as it is for couples to reach this stage of love, it is harder to maintain it than achieving it in the first place. Of this he wrote, "Without expression, even the greatest love can die" (Sternberg, 1987). Sternberg wrote that while this was as near the perfect expression love as is humanly possible, it is an ideal love, a love that takes a lot of energy to make work and to maintain. In fact, he believed this stage of love was very rarely permanent. For instance, if passion between the partners disappears for whatever reason, he suggested that the couple's love would turn into companionate love. Consummate love is the most mutually satisfying stage of love because it has all the previously identified components that make up this deep ideal type of love. So, while some couples do manage to reach this stage of love, and those that do may even manage to maintain it, it is far more an occurrence in movies and television than in real-life (Rothwell, 2012).

Why do people marry?

In a 2013 Pew Poll (Cohn, 2013) reported, "Among married people, 93% say love is a very important reason to get married; 84% of unmarried people say so. Men and women are equally likely to say love is a very important reason to get married." See Figure 6.

Online Dating

Online dating is a huge money-making industry in the US and around the world. Match.com alone reported 7 million paid subscribers in 2018--up from 3.4 million subscribers in 2014. The

Figure 6. Why get married? Percent saying each is a very important reason to marry, by marital status. Pew Research Center 2013.

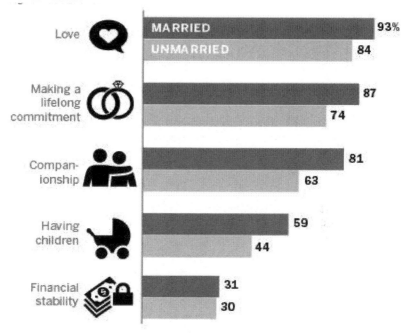

"hook-up" site Tinder reported 1.6 billion "swipes" per day in 2018, which leads to 1.5 million "dates" per year. The most popular dating apps at the Apple Store are Tinder, Bumble Match, Plenty of Fish and Zoosk with Tinder heading the pack. While the convenience of using an online dating site, or a similar app, to find potential dating partners certainly fits with our busy lifestyle, one of the downsides is that the potential risk for being rejected before or after a date is a real likelihood. One major downside to this trend is that some research has found a link between mobile device addiction, including the hunt for Mr. or Mrs. Right (for tonight or beyond) has been associated with depression and anxiety (Lleras, 2016). People using these dating apps have been found to have lower levels of self-esteem than those that don't use them.

Research on online dating as reported by the Pew organization (Smith and Anderson, 2016) found that:

1. Online dating has lost much of its stigma with 59 percent

of Americans reporting that it is a good way to meet people;

2. Online dating has dramatically increased among those under age 25 and those in their 50s and 60s;

3. One-third of those who said they have used online dating sites say that it never resulted in a date;

4. Approximately 20 percent of people who have used online dating sites say they had others help them write their profile;

5. Only five percent of Americans who used online dating sites say that it resulted in a relationship.

Positive Features of Online Dating

Why do people choose to search for a mate through an online dating site?

1. Dating sites allow members to meet more people than they would without such sites.

2. People can easily browse other members' profiles before deciding to communicate.

3. Members can communicate anonymously and with reduced fear or social awkwardness.

4. The effect of geography is mitigated, and members can meet people from distant locations.

5. Dating sites that offer free or moderately priced services allow users to meet other singles in a convenient, inexpensive way.

6. Members can determine if there is any chemistry before pursuing the relationship in real life.

Negative Features of Online Dating

Now that we have looked at the positive features of online dating, let's take a look at the dark side of online dating:

1. There are too many profiles from which to choose and it leads people to make comparisons on the basis of these flawed profiles.

2. The choices of partners can become confusing and overwhelming.

3. Without a clear plan, online daters can get stuck endlessly "shopping" for the perfect partner, rather than actually starting a satisfying relationship.
4. Matching is a difficult process and testing may not be accurate for everyone. In addition, people may present differently in person or change over time. So, matching may overlook potentially good partners in the process.
5. Communication through computers is lacking some of the information provided in face-to-face interaction. As a result, it is harder to evaluate a potential match online. Also, some of the cues and features that build attraction (like touching) cannot be accomplished through a computer. So, such computer mediated communication may have an artificial and unemotional quality.

Love and Health

Is being in love good for you? And if it is, why is it? According to a 2007 Health and Human Services (World Health Organization, 2007) report, people who are not in love have significantly higher rates of depression and anxiety disorders than do people in romantic relationships. Further, the report noted that high levels of social support, which is a large component of being in a romantic relationship, improved the overall prognosis for patients with cancer and post-heart attack.

Other research (A&Z Pharmaceutical, 2016) reported the following benefits of being love:

1. It makes you feel better. Love releases endorphins, nature's pain killer, which results in a state of euphoria among those in love. Further oxytocin, the cuddling hormone, is released which makes us feel better;
2. It can lower blood pressure probably because you are "calmer and more at peace," and it reduces stress because the person in love has someone to share their problems with;
3. It can ease chronic pain as "intense feelings of love ...activate the same areas of the brain as painkillers;"
4. It decreases the chance of becoming depressed if someone is not already depressed at the time the romance

begins. Researchers believe this is because being in love is a boost to self-esteem, which in turn lowers the risk that someone becomes depressed; and,

5. Overall, it prolongs life. Generally, the research shows that people who are married, in committed relationships are likely to outlive those that are single. Again, love seems to be a protective factor.

6. And other research (Pappas, 2017) found that the unloved are more likely to commit suicide.

Still other research (Jensen, 2015) reports the following on the effects of love on the body:

1. Love "at first sight" is real. It takes a person one-fifth of a second to fall in love due to the release of a protein associated with the nerve growth factor;

2. Those butterflies you in your stomach are cause by spikes in adrenaline, which both men and women have;

3. Your pupils will dilate when you look at your lover, likewise, we are drawn to people who have wide pupils;

4. Falling in love will cause changes in your brain's chemistry and dump specific chemicals into your bloodstream (as discussed earlier);

5. Because of the release of oxytocin into the bloodstream of lovers, you will have fewer headaches when you are in love;

6. Again, like mentioned earlier in the chapter, people in love will often feel high because of the release of dopamine into the bloodstream which mimics the same effects as cocaine and methamphetamines;

7. People in love have been found to feel better simply by being shown a picture of their lover because there is greater blood flow to the part of the brain responsible for feeling pleasure. Just looking at a picture of your beloved can reduce moderate pain by as much as 40 percent;

8. Holding hands with your lover can "calm your nerves and reduce physical pain;"

9. Because falling in love can cause serotonin levels to drop by as much as 40 percent, people in love can demonstrate

the same symptoms as someone suffering from obsessive-compulsive disorder;

10. You're likely to feel the same kind of pain because of a breakup as you would if you were in physical pain because pain effects the brain in the same way;

11. While more common among women, there really is something called "broken heart syndrome," also known as stress-induced cardiomyopathy.

Overall, love and intimacy are critical for our emotional and physical well-being. In contrast, isolation, loneliness, hostility, anger, depression, and similar feelings often contribute to suffering, disease, and premature death (Mayo Clinic, 2016).

Will Love Endure?

As I've already noted, it takes two to make a relationship work, but only one to make it fail. Thinking positively about your lover results in a more satisfying stable emotional state. Being biased toward your lover, while bias itself may not be a good thing, it does make someone feel better about the relationship and can create a self-fulfilling prophecy. In thinking about exchange theory, when one member of a couple feels their costs and rewards from the relationship are about equal to their partner's, there is greater satisfaction with the relationship. So, will your relationship endure and thrive? It depends on you...and your lover. No one person can make a relationship work.

Terms and Concepts to Know

Attraction
Attractiveness
Male Taller Bias
Matching Hypothesis
First Impressions
Presentation of Self in Every Day Society
Non-Verbal Communication
Body Language
Facial Symmetry
Intimacy

Attributions
Self-Schemas
Romantic Relationships
Different Types of Intimacy
Sternberg's Triangular Theory of Love
Sternberg's Elaborated Theory of Love

References

A&Z Pharmaceutical, 2016. *How does love affect your health?* Retrieved May 1, 2017 from http://azpharmaceutical.com/love-affect-health/

Barnes, M., & Sternberg, R. (1997). A hierarchical model of love and its prediction of satisfaction in close relationships. In R. J. Sternberg & M. Hojjat (Eds.), *Satisfaction in Close Relationships* (pp. 79-101). New York, NY, US: Guilford Press.

Berscheid, E; Walster, E (1974). Physical attractiveness. *Advances in Experimental Social Psychology*. New York: Academic Press. 7: 157–215.

Blumin, S. (1989). *The Emergence of the middle class: Social experience in the American city,* 1760-1900. Cambridge University Press.

Cameron, C., Oskamp, S., & Sparks, W. (1977). Courtship American style: Newspaper ads. *The Family Coordinator, 26*(1), 27-30.

Cannoni., & and Bombi, A. (2016). *Friendship and romantic relationships during early and middle childhood.* Sage. Retrieved March 13, 2017 from http://journals.sagepub.com/doi/abs/10.1177/2158244016659904#articleCitationDownloadContainer

Cohn, D. (2013). Love and marriage. *Pew Research Institute.* February 13, 2013. Retrieved May 2, 2017 from http://www.pewsocialtrends.org/2013/02/13/love-and-marriage/

Dion, K., Berscheid, E., & Walster, E. (1972). What is beautiful is good. *Journal of Social Psychology*, 24, 285-290.

Eastwick, P., Eagly, A., Finkel, E., & Johnson, S. (2011). Implicit and explicit preferences for physical attractiveness in a romantic partner: A double dissociation in predictive validity. *Journal of Personality and Social Psychology*, 101(5), 993-1011.

Eastwick, P., & Finkel, E. (2008). Sex differences in mate preferences revisited: Do people know what they initially desire in a romantic partner? *Journal of Personality and Social Psychology*, 94, 245–264.

Feingold, A. & Mazzella, R. (1998). Gender differences in body image are increasing. *Psychological Science*, 9(3), 190-195.

Fugère, M., Cousins, A., & MacLaren, S. (2015). (Mis)matching in physical attractiveness and women's resistance to mate guarding. *Personality and Individual Differences,* 87, 190-195.

Giddens, A. (1990). *The Consequence of Modernity*. Stanford University Press.

Gillis, J., & Avis, W. (1980). The male-taller norm in mate selection. *Personality and Social Psychology Bulletin*, 6(3), 396-401.

Goddard, N. (2012). Core psychology (3rd ed.). *Psychology,* 63-82.

Goffman, E. (1956). *The presentation of self in everyday life*. Anchor Books.

Fisher, H. (2014). *The science of love. BBC science: Human body and mind.* Retrieved June 30, 2017 from https://www.bbc.co.uk/science/hottopics/love/

Graziano, W., Brothen, T., & Berscheid, E. (1978). Height and attraction: Do men and women see eye-to-eye? *Journal of Personality,* 46(1) 128-145.

Green, V., Pituch, K., Itchon, J., & Sigafoos, J. (2006). Internet survey of treatments used by parents of children with autism. *Research in Developmental Disabilities*, 27, 70-84.

Griffin, A. M., & Langlois, J. H. (2006). Stereotype directionality and attractiveness stereotyping: Is beauty good or is ugly bad? *Social Cognition*, 24(2), 187–206.

Ha, T., Overbeek, G., & Engels, R. C. M. E. (2010). Effects of attractiveness and social status on dating desire in heterosexual adolescents: An experimental study. *Archives of Sexual Behavior, 39*(5), 1063–1071.

Harrison, M., & Shortall, J. (2011). Women and men in love: Who really feels it and says it first? *Journal of Social Psychology*, 151(6), 7270736.

Hendrick, S. & Hendrick, C. (1993). Lovers as friends. *Journal of Social and Personal Relationships,* 10(3), 459-466.

Hunt, G., Hopkins, M., & Lidgard, S. (2015). Simple versus complex models of trait evolution and stasis as a response to environmental change. *PNAS,* April 21, 2015, 112(16), 4885-4890.

Jenson, K. (2015). *What's social about social media? Social media and society.* May 11, 2015. Retrieved February 17, 2017 from http://journals.sagepub.com/doi/abs/10.1177/2056305115578874 #articleCitationDownloadContainer

Jones, B., Little, A., Burt, D., & Perrett, D. (2004). When facial attractiveness is only skin deep. *Perception,* 33, 569–576.

Keen, C. (2007). Love still dominates pop song lyrics, but with raunchier language. *University of Florida News*, May 31, 2007. Retrieved March 4, 2018 from http://news.ufl.edu/archive/2007/05/love-still-dominates-pop-song-lyrics-but-with-raunchier-language.html

Kniffin, K. M., & Wilson, D. S. (2004). The effect of nonphysical traits on the perception of physical attractiveness: Three naturalistic studies. *Evolution and Human Behavior, 25(2),* 88-101.

Kropp, P. R., Hart, S. D., Webster, C. W., & Eaves, D. (1994). *Manual for the Spousal Assault Risk Assessment Guide.* Vancouver, BC: British Columbia Institute on Family Violence.

Kurzban, R., & Weeden, J. (2005). Hurry date: Mate preferences in action. *Evolution and Human Behavior,* 26, 227-244.

Langlois, J. (2006). Pretty faces: Easy on the brain? *Developmental Psychology,* 23(3), 363-369.

Luo, S., & and Zhang, G. (2009). What leads to romantic attraction: similarity, reciprocity, security, or beauty? Evidence from a speed-dating study. *Journal of Personality,* 77(4), 933-964.

Martel, L. F., & Biller, H. B. (1987). *Stature and stigma: The biopsychosocial development of short males.* Lexington, MA, England: Lexington Books.

Montoya, R., Horton, R., Kirchner, J. (2008). Is actual similarity necessary for attraction? A meta-analysis of actual and perceived similarity. *Journal of Social and Personal Relationships,* 25(6), 889-922.

Paul, S. (2012). The Truth About Love. *Huffington Post,* August 6, 2012. Retrieved May 2, 2018 from https://www.huffingtonpost.com/sheryl-paul/love-is-loss-and-other-li_b_1614066.html

Rauh, S. (2016). Ten Surprising Health Benefits of Love. *WebMD.* Retrieved May 4, 2017 from https://www.webmd.com/sex-relationships/features/health-benefits#1

Smith, A., & Anderson, M. (2016). Five facts about online dating. *Pew Research Institute.* March 29, 2016. Retrieved April 2, 2017 from http://www.pewresearch.org/fact-tank/2016/02/29/5-facts-about-online-dating/

Sprecher, S. (1989). The Importance to males and females of physical attractiveness, earning potential, and expressiveness in initial attraction. *Sex Roles,* 21(9), 591-607.

Sternberg, R. J. (1986). A triangular theory of love. *Psychological Review, 93*(2), 119-135.

Sternberg, R. (1987). Liking Versus Loving: A comparative evaluation of theories. *Psychological Bulletin*, 102, 331-345.

Sternberg, R. (1998). Styles of Thinking and Learning. *Canadian Journal of School Psychology,* 13(2), 15-40.

Stulp, G., Buunk, A., & Pollet, T. (2013). Women want taller men more than men want shorter women. *Personality and Individual Differences,* 54(8), 877-883.

University of Pennsylvania. First impressions of beauty may demonstrate why the pretty prosper. *Science Daily*, 25 January 2006. <www.sciencedaily.com/releases/2

Wargo, E. (2011). Beauty is in the mind of the beholder. *Association for Psychological Science,* April. Retrieved, May 20, 2018 from https://www.psychologicalscience.org/observer/beauty-is-in-the-mind-of-the-beholder

Weeden, J., & Sabini, J. (2005). Physical attractiveness and health in western societies: A review. *Psychological Bulletin*, 131, 635-653.

Zarbatany, L., & Marshall, K. (2015) Are first impressions of inknown Children and early adolescents affected by the facial attractiveness of their best friend? *Merrill-Palmer Quarterly*, 61(4:2). Retrieved April 10, 2018: https://digitalcommons.wayne.edu/mpq/vol61/iss4/2

Book References

A&Z Pharmaceutical, 2016. *How does love affect your health?* Retrieved May 1, 2017 from http://azpharmaceutical.com/love-affect-health/

Adorno, T., Frenkel-Brunswik, E., & Levinson, D. (1993). *The authoritarian personality: studies in prejudice.* Norton Publishing.

Aging Watch. (2010). *Elder stereotypes in media and popular culture.* October 2010. Retrieved April 20, 2018 from http://www.agingwatch.com/?p=439.

Agnew, R. (1994). Delinquency and the desire for money. *Justice Quarterly*, 11, 411-427.

Ahmet, R. (1992). Crowding effects of density and interpersonal distance. *The Journal of Social Psychology*, 132(1), 51-58.

Ajzen I. (1991). Organizational behavior and human decision processes volume. *Sociometry,* 50, 2, 179-211.

Ajzen, I. (1971). Attitudinal vs. normative messages: An investigation of the differential effects of persuasive communications on behavior. *Sociometry*, 34, 263-280.

Ajzen, I., & Fishbein, M. (1970). The prediction of behavior from attitudinal and normative variables. *Journal of Experimental Social Psychology,* 6, 466- 487.

Ajzen, I., & Fishbein, M. (1973). attitudinal and normative variables as predictors of specific behaviors. *Journal of Personality and Social Psychology,* 27, 41-57.

Ajzen, I., & Fishbein, M. (1974). Factors influencing intentions and the intention-behavior relation. *Human Relations,* 27, 1-15.

Ajzen, I., & Fishbein, M. (1977). Attitude-behavior relations: a theoretical analysis and review of empirical research. *Psychological Bulletin,* 1977, 84, 5, 8-918.

Ajzen, I., & Fishbein, M. (1980). *Understanding attitudes and predicting social behavior.* Prentice-Hall.

Ajzen, I., Darroch, R., Fishbein, M., & Hornik, J. (1970). looking backward revisited: a reply to Deutscher. *The American Sociologist,* 1970, 5, 267- 273.

Allport, G. (1954). *The Nature of Prejudice.* Addison-Wesley.

Allport, G. W., & Ross, J. M. (1967). Personal religious orientation and prejudice. *Journal of Personality and Social Psychology,* 5, 432- 443.

Asch, S. E. (1951). Effects of group pressure upon the modification and distortion of judgment. In H. Guetzkow (ed.) *Groups, leadership and men,* 177-190. Pittsburgh, PA: Carnegie Press.

Asch, S. E. (1952). Group forces in the modification and distortion of judgments. In S. E. Asch, *Social Psychology,* 450-501. Englewood Cliffs, NJ, US: Prentice-Hall, Inc.

Asch, Solomon E. (1946). Forming impressions of personality. *The Journal of Abnormal and Social Psychology,* 41, 3, 258.

Bandura, A. (1977). *Social learning theory.* Englewood Cliffs, NJ: Prentice Hall.

Barnes, M., & Sternberg, R. (1997). A Hierarchical Model of Love and its Prediction of Satisfaction in Close Relationships. In R. J. Sternberg & M. Hojjat (Eds.), *Satisfaction in Close Relationships* (pp. 79-101). New York, NY, US: Guilford Press.

Baumeister, R., & Leary, M. (1995). The need to belong: desire for interpersonal attachments as a fundamental human motivation. *Psychological Bulletin,* 117(3), 497-529.

Berscheid, E; Walster, E (1974). Physical attractiveness. *Advances in Experimental Social Psychology.* New York: Academic Press. 7: 157–215.

Bialik, K. (2017). Key facts about race and marriage, 50 years after Loving v. Virginia. *Pew Research Center.* Retrieved March 26, 2018 from http://www.pewresearch.org/fact-tank/2017/06/12/key-facts-about-race-and-marriage-50-years-after-loving-v-virginia/

Bickman, L. (1974). The social power of a uniform. *Journal of Applied Social Psychology, 4*(1), 47-61.

Bierly, M. (1985). Prejudice toward contemporary outgroups as a generalized attitude. *Journal of Applied Social Psychology, 15*(2), 189-199.

Biernat, M. (1991). Gender stereotypes and the relationship between masculinity and femininity: A developmental analysis. *Journal of Personality and Social Psychology, 61*(3), 351-365.

Blau, P. (1964). Justice in Social Exchange. *Sociological Inquiry, 34*(2), 193-206.

Blumin, S. (1989). *The emergence of the middle class: social experience in the American city,* 1760-1900. Cambridge University Press.

Boden, J., Fergusson, D., & Horwood L. (2008). Does adolescent self-esteem predict later life outcomes? A test of the causal role of self-esteem. *Development and Psychopathology, 20*(1), 319-339.

Bodenhausen, G. (1990). Stereotypes as judgmental heuristics: evidence of circadian variations in discrimination. *Psychological Science, 1*(5), 319-322.

Bogardus, E. (1947). Measurement of personal-group relations. *Sociometry.* 10(4), 306–311.

Brown-Iannuzzi, L., McKee, S., Gervais, W. (2017). Atheist horns and religious halos: mental representations of atheists and theists. *Journal of Experimental Psychology, 147.*

Buote, V., Pancer, S., Pratt, M., Adams, G., Birnie-Lefcovitch, S., Polivy, J., & Wintre, M. (2007). The importance of friends: Friendship and adjustment among 1st-year university students. *Journal of Adolescent Research,* 22(6), 665–689.

Bushman, B. (1988). The effects of apparel on compliance: a field experiment with a female authority figure. *Personality and Social Psychology Bulletin*, 14(3), 459-467.

Bushman, B., & Baumeister, R. (1998). Threatened egotism, narcissism, self-esteem, and direct and displaced aggression: Does self-love or self-hate lead to violence? *Journal of Personality and Social Psychology*, 75(1), 219-229.

Buttelmann, D., & Böhm, R. (2014). The ontogeny of the motivation that underlies in-group bias. *Psychological Science,* 25(4), 921 – 927.

Cameron, C., Oskamp, S., & Sparks, W. (1977). Courtship American style: Newspaper ads. *The Family Coordinator, 26*(1), 27-30.

Campbell, E. & Pettigrew, T. (1959). Racial and moral crisis: The Role of Little Rock ministers. *American Journal of Sociology,* 64(5), 509-516.

Campbell, W. & Sedikides, C. (1999). Self-threat magnifies the self-serving bias: A meta-analytic integration. *Review of General Psychology,* 3(1), 23-43.

Campbell, W., Bosson, J., Goheen, T., & Kernis, M. (2007). Do narcissists dislike themselves "deep down inside?" *Psychological Science,* 18(3), 227-229.

Cannoni., & and Bombi, A. (2016). *friendship and romantic relationships during early and middle childhood.* Sage. Retrieved March 13, 2017 from http://journals.sagepub.com/doi/abs/10.1177/2158244016659904#articleCitationDownloadContainer

Cohn, D. (2013). Love and marriage. *Pew Research Institute.* February 13, 2013. Retrieved May 2, 2017 from http://www.pewsocialtrends.org/2013/02/13/love-and-marriage/

Cooley, C. (2009). *Human nature and the social order.* Cornell University Library. First published in 1902.

Crandall, C. (1994). Prejudice against fat people: Ideology and self-interest. *Journal of Personality and Social Psychology*, 66(5), 882-894.

Crisp, R. J.; Turner, R. N. (2009). Can imagined interactions produce positive perceptions? Reducing prejudice through simulated social contact. *American Psychologist.* 64(4), 231–240.

Crocker, J., & Luhtanen, R. (1990). Collective self-esteem and ingroup bias. *Journal of Personality and Social Psychology*, 58(1), 60-67.

Crocker, J., & Major, B. (1989). Social stigma and self-esteem: the self-protective properties of stigma. *Psychological Review,* 96(4) 608-630.

Dion, K., Berscheid, E., & Walster, E. (1972). What is beautiful is good. *Journal of Social Psychology,* 24, 285-290.

Dunham, Y., Srinivasan, M., Dotsch, R., & Barner, D. (2013). Religion insulates ingroup evaluations: the development of intergroup attitudes in India. *Developmental Science,* 17(2), 1-9.

Durkehim, E. (1982). *The rules of sociological method. the free press.* Introduction by Steven Lukes. First published 1895.

Eagly, A. & Mladinic, A. (1989). Gender stereotypes and attitudes toward women and men. *Personality and Social Psychology Bulletin*, 15, 543-558.

Eastwick, P., & Finkel, E. (2008). Sex differences in mate preferences revisited: Do people know what they initially desire in a romantic partner? *Journal of Personality and Social Psychology*, 94, 245–264.

Eastwick, P., Eagly, A., Finkel, E., & Johnson, S. (2011). Implicit and explicit preferences for physical attractiveness in a romantic partner: A double dissociation in predictive validity. *Journal of Personality and Social Psychology,* 101(5), 993-1011.

Eisenberger, N., Lieberman, M., & Williams, K. (2003). Does rejection hurt? An FMRI study of social exclusion. *Science,* 302(5643), 290-292.

Erikson, E. H. (1950). *Childhood and society.* New York: Norton.

Faris, E. (1937). The social psychology of G.H. Mead. American *Journal of Sociology,* 43(8), 391-403.

Farley, J. (2000). *Majority-minority relations* (4th Ed.), Upper Saddle River, New Jersey: Prentice Hall.

Feingold, A. & Mazzella, R. (1998). Gender differences in body image are increasing. *Psychological Science,* 9(3), 190-195.

Fenigstein, A., Scheier, M. F., & Buss, A. H. (1975). Public and private self-consciousness: Assessment and theory. *Journal of Consulting and Clinical Psychology,* 43(4), 522-527.

Festinger L (1954). A theory of social comparison processes. *Human relations,* 7(2), 117–140.

Fisher, H. (2014). *The science of love. BBC science: Human body and mind.* Retrieved June 30, 2017 from https://www.bbc.co.uk/science/hottopics/love/
Fiske, S. T., & Taylor, S. E. (1991). *Social cognition (2nd ed.).* New York: McGraw-Hill.

Flament, C. (1963). *Applications of graph theory to group structure.* Prentice-Hall Series in Mathematical Analysis of Social Behavior, Englewood Cliffs, N. J.

Fromm, E. (1981). *On Disobedience and Other Essays.* Seabury Press.

Fugère, M., Cousins, A., & MacLaren, S. (2015). (Mis)matching in physical attractiveness and women's resistance to mate guarding. *Personality and Individual Differences, 87*, 190-195.

Galinsky, A., Fast, N., Gruenfeld, D., & Sivananthan, N. (2009). Illusory control: a generative force behind power's far-reaching effects. *Psychological Science, 20*(4), 502-508.

Giddens, A. (1990). *The Consequence of Modernity.* Stanford University Press.

Gilbert, D. T., & Hixon, J. G. (1991). The trouble of thinking: Activation and application of stereotypic beliefs. *Journal of Personality and Social Psychology, 60*(4), 509-517.

Gillis, J., & Avis, W. (1980). The male-taller norm in mate selection. *Personality and Social Psychology Bulletin, 6*(3), 396-401.

Gitlin, T. (2011). Patriotism. *The Chronicle of Higher Education.* Retrieved January 2017 from https://www.chronicle.com/article/An-Era-in-Ideas-Patriotism/128493

Glick, P. & Fiske, S. (1996). The ambivalent sexism inventory: Differentiating hostile and benevolent sexism. *Journal of Personality and Social Psychology,* 70 (3), 491–512.

Glick, P. & Fiske, S. (2001). An ambivalent alliance: hostile and benevolent sexism as complementary justifications for gender inequality. *The American Psychologist,* 56, 109-18.

Goddard, N. (2012). *Core Psychology* (3rd ed.). Chapter 5: Psychology, 63-82.

Goffman, E. (1956). *The Presentation of Self in Everyday Life.* Anchor Books.

Goffman, E. (1967). *Interaction Ritual: Essays on Face-to-Face Behavior.* Pantheon. Reprinted 1982.

Goffman, Erving (1959). *The Presentation of Self in Everyday Life.* New York: Doubleday.

Goodwin, J., Jasper, J., & Polleta, F. (2009). *Passionate politics: emotions and social movements.* University of Chicago Press.

Grannovetter, M. (1973) The strength of weak ties. *American Journal of Sociology,* 78(6), 1360-1380.

Graziano, W., Brothen, T., & Berscheid, E. (1978). Height and Attraction: Do men and women see eye-to-eye? *Journal of Personality,* 46(1) 128-145.

Green, V., Pituch, K., Itchon, J., & Sigafoos, J. (2006). Internet survey of treatments used by parents of children with autism. *Research in Developmental Disabilities,* 27, 70-84.

Griffin, A. M., & Langlois, J. H. (2006). Stereotype directionality and attractiveness stereotyping: is beauty good or is ugly bad? *Social Cognition,* 24(2), 187–206.

Ha, T., Overbeek, G., & Engels, R. C. M. E. (2010). Effects of attractiveness and social status on dating desire in heterosexual adolescents: an experimental study. *Archives of Sexual Behavior, 39*(5), 1063–1071.

Haddock, G., Zanna, P., & Esses, V. (1993). Assessing the structure of prejudicial attitudes: the case of attitudes toward homosexuals. *Journal of Personality and Social Psychology,* 65, 1105-1118.

Hall, Edward T. (1966). *The Hidden Dimension.* Anchor Books. Pp. 111-129.

Haney, C., Banks, W., & Zimbardo, P. (1973). A study of prisoners and guards in a simulated prison. *Naval Research Review,* 30, 4-17.

Haney, C.; Banks, W. C.; Zimbardo, P. G. (1973). Interpersonal dynamics in a simulated prison. *International Journal of Criminology and Penology,* 1, 69–97.

Harrison, M., & Shortall, J. (2011). Women and men in love: Who really feels it and says it first? *Journal of Social Psychology*, 151(6), 727-736.

Heerdink, M., van Kleef, G., Homan, A., & Fischer, A. (2015). Emotional reactions to deviance in groups: the relation between number of angry reactions, felt rejection, and conformity. *Frontiers in Psychology*, 6(1). Retrieved May 2017 from https://www.frontiersin.org/articles/10.3389/fpsyg.2015.00830/full

Heider, Fritz (1958). *The Psychology of Interpersonal Relations*. John Wiley & Sons.

Hendrick, S. & Hendrick, C. (1993). Lovers as friends. *Journal of Social and Personal Relationships,* 10(3), 459-466.

Hogg, M. (2001). A social identity theory of leadership. *Personality and Social Psychology Review,* 5(3), 184-200.

Hogg, M. & Vaughan, G. (1995). *Social Psychology: An Introduction.* Prentice Hall.

Hogg, N. (2014). From uncertainty to extremism: Social categorization and identity processes. *Current Directions in Psychological Science*, 23(5), 338 – 342.

Homans, G. (1958). Social behavior as exchange. *American Journal of Sociology,* 63(6), 597-606.

Homans, G. (1961). *Social Behavior: Its Elementary Forms.* New York: Harcourt, Brace & World.

Hurrelmann, K. (1988). *Social structure and personality development: The individual as a productive processor of reality.* Cambridge University Press.

Hussein, B. (2012). The Sapir-Whorf Hypothesis today. *Theory and Practice in Language Studies,* 2(3), pp. 642-646.

Jenson, K. (2015). What's social about social media? *Social Media and Society.* May 11, 2015. Retrieved February 17, 2017 from http://journals.sagepub.com/doi/abs/10.1177/2056305115578874 #articleCitationDownloadContainer

Johnson D., Johnson R. (2004). *Assessing students in groups: Promoting group responsibility and individual accountability.* Thousand Oaks: Sage.

Jones, B., Little, A., Burt, D., & Perrett, D. (2004). When facial attractiveness is only skin deep. *Perception*, 33, 569–576.

Joseph, N. & Alex, N. (1972). The uniform: A sociological perspective. *American Journal of Sociology,* 77(4), 719-730.

Keen, C. (2007). Love still dominates pop song lyrics, but with raunchier language. *University of Florida News,* May 31, 2007. Retrieved March 4, 2018 from http://news.ufl.edu/archive/2007/05/love-still-dominates-pop-song-lyrics-but-with-raunchier-language.html

Kelley, H. H., & Thibault, J. W. 1978. *Interpersonal relationships: A theory of interdependence.* New York: John Wiley.

Kennison, M. (2013). *Introduction to language development.* Sage.

Kitching, A., Roos, V., & Ferreira. (2014). Ways of relating and interacting in school communities: lived experiences of learners, educators and parents. *Journal of Psychology in Africa*, 21(2), 245-256.

Kniffin, K. M., & Wilson, D. S. (2004). The effect of nonphysical traits on the perception of physical attractiveness: Three naturalistic studies. *Evolution and Human Behavior, 25(2),* 88-101.

Kropp, P. R., Hart, S. D., Webster, C. W., & Eaves, D. (1994). *Manual for the Spousal Assault Risk Assessment Guide.* Vancouver, BC: British Columbia Institute on Family Violence.

Kuhn, M. (1960). Self-attitudes by age, sex and professional training. *Sociological Quarterly,* 1, 39-56.

Kurzban, R., & Weeden, J. (2005). Hurry date: Mate preferences in action. *Evolution and Human Behavior,* 26, 227-244.

Kuypers, B., Davies, D., & Hazewinkel, A. (1986). Developmental patterns in self-analytic groups. *Human Relations,* 39(9), 793–815.

Langlois, J. (2006). Pretty Faces: Easy on the brain? *Developmental Psychology,* 23(3), 363-369.

LaPiere, R.T. (1934). Attitudes v's actions. *Social Forces,* 13, 230-237.

Leary, M., & Baumeister, R. (2000). The nature and function of self-esteem: Sociometer theory. In M. P. Zanna (Ed.), *Advances in experimental social psychology,* Vol. 32, pp. 1-62). San Diego, CA, US: Academic Press.

Lundblad, R. (2001). Social, religious, and personal contributors to prejudice. *Faculty Publications - Grad School of Clinical Psychology.* Paper 72. Retrieved March 30, 2018 from http://digitalcommons.georgefox.edu/gscp_fac/72

Luo, S., & and Zhang, G. (2009). What leads to romantic attraction: Similarity, reciprocity, security, or beauty? Evidence from a speed-dating study. *Journal of Personality,* 77(4), 933-964.

Martel, L. F., & Biller, H. B. (1987). *Stature and stigma: The biopsychosocial development of short males.* Lexington, MA, England: Lexington Books.

McCloud, S. (2008). Robbers Cave. *Simply Psychology.* Retrieved February 26, 2018 from: https://www.simplypsychology.org/robbers-cave.html

Merton, R. 1957. *Social theory and social structure.* New York: Free Press.

Milgram, S. (1963). Behavioral study of obedience. *Journal of Abnormal and Social Psychology*, 67, 371-378.

Milgram, S. (1963). Behavioral study of obedience. *Journal of Abnormal and Social Psychology*, 67, 371-378.

Milgram, S. (1965). Some conditions of obedience and disobedience to authority. *Human relations,* 18(1), 57-76.

Milgram, S. (1974). *Obedience to authority: An experimental view.* Harpercollins.

Mills, C. (1959). *The Sociological Imagination.* Oxford University Press, London.

Montoya, R., Horton, R., Kirchner, J. (2008). Is actual similarity necessary for attraction? A meta-analysis of actual and perceived similarity. *Journal of Social and Personal Relationships,* 25(6), 889-922.

Mowen, J., & Brown, S. (1981). On explaining and predicting the effectiveness of celebrity endorsements. *Advances in Consumer Research,* 8, 437-441.

National Public Radio. (October 31, 2012). *Is racial prejudice on the rise?* Retrieved April 2018 from https://www.npr.org/2012/10/31/164029897/is-racial-prejudice-on-the-rise

NDTV. (March 10, 2017). *Hatred, prejudice on rise in Donald Trump's America.* Retrieved April 2018 from https://www.ndtv.com/world-news/hatred-prejudice-on-rise-in-donald-trumps-america-poll-1668132

Orth, U. & Robins, R. (2014). The development of self-esteem. *Current Directions in Psychological Science,* 23(5), 381-387.

Paul, S. (2012). *The Truth About Love.* Huffington Post, August 6, 2012.

Retrieved May 2, 2018 from
https://www.huffingtonpost.com/sheryl-paul/love-is-loss-and-other-li_b_1614066.html

Perrin, S., & Spencer, C. (1980). The Asch effect: a child of its time? *Bulletin of the British Psychological Society,* 32, 405-406.

Pettigrew, T. (1958). Personality and sociocultural factors in intergroup attitudes: a cross-national comparison. *Journal of Conflict Resolution,* 2(1), 29 – 42.

Pew Research Center. (2017). *U.S. Muslims Concerned About Their Place in Society but Continue to Believe in the American Dream.* Retrieved March 2018 from http://www.pewforum.org/2017/07/26/findings-from-pew-research-centers-2017-survey-of-us-muslims/

Pinker, S., & Bloom, P. (1990). Natural Language and Natural Selection. *Behavioral and Brain Sciences,* 13(4), 707-784.

Psychology Today. Kurt Lewin. *How our environment shapes our behavior.* Published on March 1, 2001.

Putnam, R. (2000). *The Collapse and Revival of American Community.* Simon & Schuster.

Rauh, S. (2016). Ten Surprising Health Benefits of Love. *WebMD.* Retrieved May 4, 2017 from https://www.webmd.com/sex-relationships/features/health-benefits#1

Rispens, S., & Jehn, K. (2011). Conflict in workgroups: Constructive, destructive, and asymmetric conflict. In D. De Cremer, R. van Dick, & J. K. Murnighan (Eds.), *Social psychology and organizations* (pp. 185–209). New York, NY: Routledge/Taylor & Francis Group.

Ritzer, George. (2008) *Sociological Theory. The Exchange Theory of George Homans.* New York, NY: McGraw-Hill Companies.

Rochat, P. (2003). Five levels of self-awareness as they unfold early in life. *Consciousness and Cognition,* 12, 717-731.

Rosenberg, M., Schooler, C., Schoenbach, C., & Rosenberg, F. (1995). Global self-esteem and specific self-esteem: different concepts, different outcomes. *American Sociological Review*, 60(1), 141-156.

Salmela-Aro, K., Aunola, K., & and Nurmi, J. (2007). Personal goals during emerging adulthood: a 10-year follow up. Journal of *Adolescent Research*, 22(6), 690-715.

Sapir, E. (1929). The status of linguistics as a science. *Language*, 5, 207-19.

Schachter and Singer's Theory of Emotion. Retrieved February 26, 2018 from: https://www.verywellmind.com/the-two-factor-theory-of-emotion-2795718

Schachter, S. (1959) *The Psychology of affiliation*. Stanford: Stanford University Press.

Schachter, S. and Singer, J. E. (1962). Cognitive, social and physiological determinants of emotional states. *Psychological Review,* 69: 379-399.

Shahani-Denning, C. (2003). Physical attractiveness bias in hiring: What is beautiful is good. *Hofstra Horizons*, Spring 2003, 15-18. Retrieved May 17, 2018 from http://www.hofstra.edu/pdf/orsp_shahani-denning_spring03.pdf

Sherif, C., Sherif, M., & Nebergall, R. (1965). *Attitude and attitude change: the social judgement-involvement approach*. Greenwood Press.

Sherif, M. (1936). The *psychology of social norms.* Oxford, England: Harper.

Siegman, A., Anderson, R., & Berger, T. (1990). The angry voice: Its effects on the experience of anger and cardiovascular reactivity. *Psychosomatic Medicine*, 52(6), 631-643.

Simmel, G. (1922). *Conflict and the web of group affiliations.* Translated and edited by Kurt Wolff (1955), Glencoe, IL: Free Press.

Smith, A., & Anderson, M. (2016). Five facts about Oonline dating. *Pew Research Institute.* March 29, 2016. Retrieved April 2, 2017 from http://www.pewresearch.org/fact-tank/2016/02/29/5-facts-about-online-dating/

Spitz, R.A. (1945). Hospitalism: An inquiry into the genesis of psychiatric conditions in early childhood. *Psychoanalytic Study of the Child,* 1, 53-74.

Spitz, R.A. (1946). Hospitalism: A follow-up report on investigation described in volume I, 1945. *The Psychoanalytic Study of the Child*, 2, 113-117.

Sprecher, S. (1989). The importance to males and females of physical attractiveness, earning potential, and expressiveness in initial attraction. *Sex Roles,* 21(9), 591-607.

Steele, C. (1997). A threat in the air: How stereotypes shape intellectual identity and performance. *American Psychologist*, 52(6), 613-629. Retrieved May 2018 from http://psycnet.apa.org/record/1997-04591-001

Steele, C., & Aronson, J. (1995). Contending with group image: the psychology of stereotype and social identity threat, in Zanna, Mark P. *Advances in experimental social psychology*. Amsterdam: Academic Press, 34, 379–440.

Sternberg, R. (1987). Liking versus loving: A comparative evaluation of theories. *Psychological Bulletin,* 102, 331-345.

Sternberg, R. (1998). Styles of thinking and learning. *Canadian Journal of School Psychology,* 13(2), 15-40.

Sternberg, R. J. (1986). A triangular theory of love. *Psychological Review, 93*(2), 119-135.

Stulp, G., Buunk, A., & Pollet, T. (2013). Women want taller men more than men want shorter women. *Personality and Individual Differences,* 54(8), 877-883.

Thibaut, J. W., and Kelley, H. H. (1959). *The social psychology of groups.* New York: John Wiley & Sons.

Tjosvold, M. (1991). *Team Organization: An enduring competitive advantage.* Chichester, UK: John Wiley & Sons.

Toledano, E. (2013, February 14). May the best (looking) man win: The unconscious role of attractiveness in employment decisions. *Cornell HR Review.* Retrieved May 18, 2018 from http://www.cornellhrreview.org/may-the-best-looking-man-win-the-unconscious-role-of-attractiveness-in-employment-decisions/

Treviño, A. Javier. (2006) *George C. Homans: History, Theory, and Method.* Boulder, CO: Paradigm.

Treviño, A. Javier. (2009). George C. Homans, the human group and elementary social behaviour, in the *Encyclopaedia of Informal Education.* www.infed.org/thinkers/george_homans.htm.

Tuckman, B., & Jensen, M. (1977). Stages of small-group development revisited. *Group Organizational Studies*, 2, 419-27

Turner, J., & Tajfel, H. (1986). The social identity theory of intergroup behavior. *Psychology of Intergroup Relations*, 7-24.

Turner, J., Hogg, M., Oakes, P., Reicher, S., & Wetherell, M. (1981). *Rediscovering the social group: a self-categorization theory.* Oxford/New York: Blackwell.

Twenty Statements Test (TST) and Guidelines. Retrieved April 23, 2018 from http://www.angelfire.com/or3/tss2/tst.html

University of Pennsylvania. First impressions of beauty may demonstrate why the pretty prosper. *Science Daily,* 25 January 2006.

Van Kleef, G. A., van den Berg, H., & Heerdink, M. W. (2015). The persuasive power of emotions: Effects of emotional expressions on attitude formation and change. *Journal of Applied Psychology*, 100(4), 1124-1142.

VanDellen, M., Campbell, W., Hoyle, R., & Bradfield, E. (2011). Compensating, resisting, and breaking: A meta-analytic examination of reactions to self-esteem threat. *Personality and Social Psychology Review*, 15, 51-74.

Vanhove, A., & Gordan, R. (2013). Weight discrimination in the workplace: a meta-analytic examination of the relationship between weight and work-related outcomes. *Journal of Applied Psychology*, 44(1), 12-22.

Verniers C, Vala J (2018) Justifying gender discrimination in the workplace: The mediating role of motherhood myths. *PLoS ONE*, 13(1): e0190657. https://doi.org/10.1371/journal.pone.0190657

Wargo, E. (2011). Beauty is in the mind of the beholder. *Association for Psychological Science,* April. Retrieved, May 20, 2018 from https://www.psychologicalscience.org/observer/beauty-is-in-the-mind-of-the-beholder

Watt, S. & Larkin, C. (2010). Prejudiced people perceive more community support for their views: The role of own, media, and peer attitudes in perceived consensus. *Journal of Applied Social Psychology,* 40(3), 710-731.

Weeden, J., & Sabini, J. (2005). Physical attractiveness and health in western societies: A review. *Psychological Bulletin,* 131, 635-653.

White, M. (1975). Interpersonal distance as affected by room size, status, and sex. *The Journal of Social Psychology*, 95(2), 241-249.

Whorf, B. (1956). *Language, thought and reality. Selected writings.* Ed.: J.B. Carroll. MIT, New York: J.Wilky/London: Chapinaon & Hall.

Williams, K. (2007). Ostracism: The kiss of social death. *Social and Personality Psychology Compass*, 1(1), 236-247.

Zarbatany, L., & Marshall, K. (2015) Are first impressions of unknown children and early adolescents affected by the facial attractiveness of their best friend? *Merrill-Palmer Quarterly*, 61(4:2). Retrieved April 10, 2018: https://digitalcommons.wayne.edu/mpq/vol61/iss4/2

Zimbardo, P.G. (2007). *The Lucifer Effect: Understanding How Good People Turn Evil.* New York: Random House.

Index

Made in the USA
Columbia, SC
11 August 2020